Exploring *HyperCard*

Steven Anzovin

COMPUTE! Books
Greensboro, North Carolina
Radnor, Pennsylvania

Edited by Jill Champion

Printed in the United States of America

10 9 8 7 6 5 4 3 2 1

Library of Congress Cataloging-in-Publication Data

Anzovin, Stephen.
Exploring hyperCard / Steve Anzovin.
p. cm.
Includes index.
ISBN 0-87455-152-8 :
1. Macintosh (Computer)—Programming. 2. HyperCard (Computer program) 3. HyperTalk (Computer program language) I. Title.
QA76.8.M3A66 1988 88-20376
005.265—dc19 CIP

The author and publisher have made every effort in the preparation of this book to ensure the accuracy of the programs and information. However, the information in this book is sold without warranty, either express or implied. Neither the author nor COMPUTE! Publications, Inc. will be liable for any damages caused or alleged to be caused directly, indirectly, incidentally, or consequentially by the programs or information in this book.

The opinions expressed in this book are solely those of the author and are not necessarily those of COMPUTE! Publications, Inc.

COMPUTE! Books, Inc., Post Office Box 5406, Greensboro, North Carolina, 27403, (919) 275-9809, is a Capital Cities/ABC, Inc. company and is not associated with any manufacturer of personal computers.

To my family

Contents

Preface

The introduction of the Macintosh in 1984 was a pivotal event in the development of the personal computer. The early Macs were odd-looking, underpowered devices, but they sparked unusually fierce devotion among many Mac users who vowed that the easy-to-use Macintosh made other computers obsolete. Even as the latest generation of the Macintosh has become well integrated into the larger world of personal computing this loyalty persists.

This phenomenon was repeated in mid-1987 with the release of *HyperCard*, a new software package for the Mac that is part database, part programming environment, and part system software. The computer press has been full of amused reports of "HyperMania," the near-religious fervor the program engenders among its disciples. While not everyone experiences an epiphany upon opening *HyperCard* for the first time, there is little doubt that *HyperCard* has stirred more excitement in the Macintosh community than any event since the introduction of the Macintosh itself. This is curious because even people who breathe, eat, and sleep *HyperCard* may not be able to tell you exactly what the program is, or just why it's so appealing.

The aim of *Exploring HyperCard* is to help you understand what *HyperCard* is and why it has caused such a stir. Along the way, you'll learn how to navigate in the *HyperCard* universe and how to use *HyperCard* to create your own applications without having to learn difficult programming techniques. You may even come to a new understanding of what a computer can do for you.

How to Use This Book

If you're a new Macintosh owner, you'll get the most from *Exploring HyperCard* if you're comfortable with the basic operations of your Mac. Take time to study the *Macintosh Owner's Guide* until you know how to handle the computer, work with disks and files, use the Finder, and so on. Take a look, also, at the *HyperCard* manual, which provides an easy-to-follow, if incomplete, guide to the *HyperCard* fundamentals.

More important—and more fun—tour the program itself via its introduction on the *HyperCard* Help disk, and keep this book handy for reference as you navigate through the Help stacks. *Exploring HyperCard* will help you understand just how some of the effects were created. When you're ready to create your own stacks, work through the tutorials in this book first.

The first section of *Exploring HyperCard* introduces *HyperCard* fundamentals. Chapter 1 covers the genealogy and philosophy of the program. Chapters 2, 3, and 4 explore the *HyperCard* universe in detail, including techniques for navigation, object creation, and handling text and graphics. The basics of *HyperCard*'s programming language, *HyperTalk,* are covered in Chapter 5. Even if you've read through the *HyperCard* manual that comes with the program (and if you haven't yet, you should), you're likely to find information in this section that will be new to you.

The second part of *Exploring HyperCard* shows you how to take the principles discussed in the first part and put them into action. Chapters in this section are linked to sample stacks illustrating one or more aspects of stackbuilding. The design principles behind planning and assembling simple stacks is the subject of Chapter 6. Chapter 7 takes you through the creation of a simple database stack. In Chapter 8, the writing of extended scripts to link together several stacks is covered in a sample stack for a small, phone-based retail business. Chapter 9 details the use of graphic and sound effects in an educational stack.

The appendices include an extensive *HyperTalk* glossary, with example scripts for each term and an alphabetical index; both will be invaluable resources as you begin writing your own scripts. Also included in the appendices are tables of keyboard equivalents; a guide to *HyperCard*-related books, newsletters, commercial stacks, and public domain offerings; and a complete subject index. Two special features are also sprinkled throughout the text: *Tips* alert you to advanced techniques and point out bugs in the programs; *1.2 Notes* covers the new aspects of the most recent version of *HyperCard,* released in mid-1988.

Exploring the *HyperCard* Universe

HyperCard is unlike any other program you'll encounter. Although there are plenty of familiar commercial applications that work within the *HyperCard* framework, the program's real usefulness to you can only be realized with your own creative input. This book makes suggestions for how you should approach working with *HyperCard,* but there is no one right way to do this, just as there is no one right way to write, paint, raise children, or do other things. Once you've mastered the basics with the help of *Exploring HyperCard,* use your own judgement and experience to guide you in your further explorations.

Acknowledgments

The author wishes to thank Martha Steffens of Apple Computer, Inc., Bill Novy of American Business Products in Englewood, New Jersey, and Sharon Zardetto Aker for giving generously of their time and comments.

Diane Kopperman Podell of C. W. Post College, Long Island University, provided invaluable research assistance. At COMPUTE!, Stephen Levy supplied support and expert guidance. Bill Atkinson and the *HyperCard* team get kudos for *HyperCard* itself—thanks, Bill.

And thanks again to my wife, Janet, for her patience and understanding of what is important and what isn't, in writing and in life.

Steven Anzovin
May 1988

PART I: *HYPERCARD* BASICS

Chapter 1

Memex, Project Xanadu, the Knowledge Navigator, and *HyperCard*

You're staring at the *HyperCard* screen. You've been through the *HyperCard* introduction, and you've peeked into the manual. You've come to the conclusion that *HyperCard* is one of the most amazing, exciting, intriguing programs you've ever seen—as well as the most mysterious. *HyperCard* is neither fish nor fowl; it doesn't seem to be a database, graphics program, or any other typical application, although, to a degree, it resembles each of those. Nor is it like the typical programming language. There's nothing quite like *HyperCard* for any other computer.

On any expedition into new terrain, it's helpful to have a guide, which is what *Exploring HyperCard* is all about. This chapter will give you a handle on *HyperCard*'s nature, history, and purpose so that later, when you get down to the nitty-gritty of constructing your own *HyperCard* applications, you'll have a wider perspective to keep you moving in the right direction.

Defining *HyperCard*

What is *HyperCard*, and what can you do with it? *HyperCard* has a number of aspects and abilities, so a multifaceted definition is more useful than a concise one.

Think of *HyperCard* as being like a *ziggurat*—a stepped pyramid. At the bottom level, *HyperCard* is an easy-to-use database manager. You can see this from the programs included in the *HyperCard* package, like the address book or the collection of area codes. You can store any text, graphic, or sound information in *HyperCard* and browse through the program to retrieve it in almost the same way you can record images on a videotape and then play them back later. *HyperCard* offers the additional advantages of very fast random text searches and the ability to print out text in a number of report formats. *HyperCard* is thus an ideal vehicle for organizing and distributing simple databases.

At the next level, *HyperCard* is a full-featured graphics program. You can create pictures with the wide selection of painting tools to illustrate your text information or create applications entirely with pictures. Without this graphics capability, *HyperCard* would be interesting still, but dry. Graphics also help extend *HyperCard*'s usefulness into the educational realm, where pictures are often the only way to communicate with your audience.

Go up another level, and you begin to discover *HyperCard*'s creative possibilities. Here, you'll find a new environment for constructing custom applications, only this programming environment is different from all others—it's tailored to nonprogrammers. You can create, arrange, and delete the elements of the program in whatever combination best suits your needs, using the Macintosh editing skills you already possess. And, a variety of readymade program parts are supplied in the *HyperCard* package that "snap together" to give you limitless combinations of features.

At the next highest level, you can take complete control of *HyperCard* and make it sing. *HyperCard* is the home of a new programming language, *HyperTalk* (the subject of Chapter 5 and Appendices A and B). This simple-to-learn language gives you complete power over every aspect of the program and, incidentally, makes *HyperCard* the best classroom ever devised for learning computer programming fundamentals. Here, you can also add sound, voice, and animation, and you can move information between *HyperCard* and other applications.

Finally, at what might be considered the topmost level, *HyperCard* is an alternative Macintosh interface. It can do nearly everything the Finder can do, including opening and running other programs, opening and closing files, and more. You never really have to leave *HyperCard*—and many *HyperCard* addicts never do.

The real key to *HyperCard* is flexibility. It is undoubtedly the most versatile piece of software ever written. *HyperCard* can hold the information you choose, have the structure you choose, and control as much of your Macintosh work as you choose. You can learn just enough about *HyperCard* to use information provided by other people, or you can take full control and captain the program into uncharted waters. You can use it to meet your own information needs or to distribute information to others who need it.

HyperCard Structure

HyperCard is built on a deceptively simple structural foundation. As even the most casual browser through the program knows, *HyperCard* works much like a simple 3 × 5 inch index card file. What you see on the screen is a *HyperCard* "card" containing words and pictures as well as sounds, animation, and various controls. You can write and draw on the card, add new cards and delete old ones whenever you like, and even shuffle them about in a stack, reorganizing them in whatever order you find most useful. *HyperCard* cards can be grouped together like index cards in a file box; this is called a *stack*. (*Stacks* are the equivalent of files or documents of other Mac applications.)

So far, *HyperCard* may seem to work in a very familiar way and, in fact, doesn't appear to offer much of an advantage over the old paper index cards, which are certainly a lot cheaper and more portable. However, stacks of cards are not all there is to *HyperCard*. *HyperCard* has some advanced capabilities that can't be matched by any other information medium. In fact, the historical and theoretical antecedents of *HyperCard* go back more than 40 years, to the very beginning of the computer age. A brief review of these ideas will help you understand some of the deeper implications of the program.

Memex

In July 1945, Vannevar Bush—Franklin Roosevelt's science advisor and the inventor of an analog computer—published an article titled "As We May Think" in *The Atlantic Monthly*. In it, he described a curious problem facing researchers of all kinds: The explosive growth of the research community during World War II had generated a tidal wave of new information, all of which could lead to remarkable new opportunities, but there was a catch—finding just the information needed in the growing record of data was like finding a needle in a haystack, and the problem was getting worse all the time. In a society where information was rapidly becoming the principle medium of exchange, this was a catastrophe in the making. Bush knew that much of the truly important information was being buried under a mountain of inconsequential facts, and, without free access to the right information, society as a whole was poorer.

Bush proposed a technological solution to the problem of information accretion: He described a device called a *memex* (a conflation of the words memory, memo, and index). A memex was, in Bush's words, "a device in which an individual stores all his books, records, and communications, and which is mechanized so that it may be consulted with exceeding speed and flexibility." It was the size of a desk and contained in microfilm form every document and information source that might have a bearing on the owner's work. The memex owner could immediately call up any documents, speeding through them at will and jumping from one subject to another as necessary. The central concept of the memex was to provide quick, easy, and unrestricted access to any part of the information record, by anyone.

The memex was more than just a glorified microfilm reader; it provided, in Bush's words, "an immediate step to associative indexing, the basic idea of which is a provision whereby any item may be caused at will to select immediately and automatically another." In other words, the memex would have the capability to allow the researcher to build an associative, repeatable research trail through any body of information. You could open an investigation into one topic and then immediately jump to a related topic as a new notion occurred to you, all the while photographing the documents you were consulting as you went along, creating a permanent record of your train of thought.

To illustrate how memex worked, Bush offered the example of a researcher looking into the the relative merits of the short Turkish bow over the English longbow during the Crusades. After consulting encyclopedia articles on ancient warfare, the researcher could branch to archaeological studies of bow materials—specifically the construction and composition of the laminated Eastern bow. This could lead, in turn, to engineering studies on elasticity, and to even more distant sources as needed. The research path would be determined not by an imposed pathway, but by association along a route that followed the play of associations in the researcher's mind. The entire research trail could be annotated, stored, reproduced photographically, and distributed to anyone who wanted it. Users of the research trail would incorporate it into their own trails, and it would be instantly accessible whenever required. Bush imagined a new profession of "trail blazers" whose vital task would be to establish links among hitherto-unconnected regions of the information record.

He thought the memex could be implemented with advanced versions of 1940 technologies—vacuum tubes, electrical and mechanical relays, dials and levers, microfilm, dry photography (the forerunner of xerography), and black-and-white television—few of which were really appropriate for the task. Only the invention of low-cost microcomputers, like the Macintosh, and high-speed optical and magnetic mass storage has made the memex concept finally feasible on more than an experimental scale. (In fact, it's hard not to describe the memex with today's computer terminology, since the device is so close in concept to the desktop computer.)

Even if Bush had the technology wrong, he did understand that all the information must be extremely compressed—on the order of at least a million times more compact than the equivalent information in paper form—to make it physically easy to handle and distribute. After all, part of the problem with conventional repositories of information—libraries—is that the information you want is somewhere among thousands or millions of books that must be stored in one location. You must travel to them, rather than have the information in its bulky printed form travel to you. (Bush estimated that with proper compression, the entire human record could be squeezed to fit in a large truck. However, even with optical disk storage and gigabyte hard drives, we are nowhere near attaining that level of information compression yet.)

He also saw the need for, but did not describe in detail, a method of organizing and coding all the information so that it could be found quickly, easily modified, and automatically rerecorded. Those aspects—the information compression, organization, coding, modification, and storage—might be seen as the "software" part of the memex. While the development of information hardware, or computers, has proceeded rapidly to the point that a memex-like machine could have been built only a decade or so after Bush described it, the software part has lagged well behind.

The Xanadu Project

Enter Theodore Nelson, a brilliant and unorthodox graduate student at Harvard in 1960. Nelson learned about Bush's article and the existence of computers around the same time and immediately put 2 and 2 together. Spurred by his personal need for a memex-like device to organize and provide access to his own disorganized notes, Nelson set out to write a computer program that would supply the software part of the memex, with a digital computer acting as the hardware part. Nelson's goal was to store, retrieve, and print his notes, plus edit and add to them at will, with the computer keeping a complete and easily accessible record of every version of every note. The computer would even be able to show what was different about each version. Further, Nelson wanted to be able to create links from one piece of information to any other, so that he could jump from one note to the related one at any time. As in Bush's memex, the computer would keep track of every access and trail so they could be reproduced later.

As Nelson developed his ideas, he realized he was defining a new kind of document. He gave it a name: *hypertext*—text and pictures linked to related information in associative patterns. All hypertext documents would be part of a vast interconnected structure held together by references, links, and trails. The hypertext universe would eventually include the entire sum of human knowledge.

One might imagine that such a vast structure would be beyond organization, but Nelson maintained that people would impose various forms of order on the hypertext universe, just as they have on the print universe. In fact, those who found new and useful ways to order information would be among the most highly valued of creative individuals, like Bush's trail blazers. Nelson and those who agreed with him believed that the nonlinear, multidimensional, associative, and intuitional hypertext universe was better suited to the way the mind works. Others coined the term *hypermedia* to indicate that the hypertext concept could be extended to encompass sounds, music, voice, video, film, animation, and any other digitally encodable information.

The actual programming task of creating hypertext proved more complicated then Nelson had imagined. By the mid-1970s, Nelson and his followers had come up with a rough first draft that included a new kind of file format and indexing system that could, in principle, revolutionize the world information economy. Nelson saw his effort in romantic terms and gave it an exotic name, Project Xanadu, after the poem by Samuel Taylor Coleridge:

> In Xanadu did Kublai Khan
> A stately pleasure dome decree. . . .

As of yet, however, Nelson has not successfully marketed a hypertext product. "What is really lacking," says Nelson, "are the visionary artists, writers, publishers, and investors who can see the possibilities and help carry such ideas into reality."

The Knowledge Navigator

Nelson may have found his supportive visionaries (at least, the ones with money) at Apple Computer. John Sculley, CEO of Apple, is sold on a variant of the hypertext idea he calls the *knowledge navigator*. As Sculley describes it in his recent book, *Odyssey: From Pepsi to Apple* (Harper & Row, 1987), the knowledge navigator is much like a portable memex with graphics, voice, and sound. Its task will be to guide you through the maze of twenty-first century information. As with hypertext, via information "highways," you can jump effortlessly from any area of information to another.

A crucial part of the navigator would be a software-based ally with artificial intelligence that would help convert mere information to useful knowledge tailored to your exact requirements. You wouldn't even need to decide what was important and what was trivial—the ally would learn all about your interests through your interaction with the navigator and present to you only the information you wanted to know. Sculley envisions that such a mass personalized knowledge-based system is the next major goal for personal computing, and he has pledged Apple to develop it. Moreover, he sees the knowledge navigator as the key to a new renaissance in American education, creativity, and entrepreneurship.

What is Apple's first step toward the knowledge navigator? It is *HyperCard*. Apple programming genius Bill Atkinson, developer of *MacPaint* and the Mac's QuickDraw graphics routine, describes his latest work, *HyperCard*, as "an erector set that allows programs to be written by people who aren't programmers." It's certainly a novice programmer's delight, but *HyperCard* is also a major step toward Bush's memex and Nelson's hypertext. It provides the high information compression Bush described and makes possible the richly interconnected information structures envisioned by Nelson.

For example, *HyperCard*'s cards can contain not only words and pictures, but also sounds, music, animation, and special devices called *buttons* for doing work. You can search for information in *HyperCard* by specifying the exact information you need and then letting *HyperCard* find the right card for you. Information in *HyperCard* can be organized in more than one way at the same time—alphabetically within the stack and also by associative reference to related ideas in other stacks. Cards and stacks can be linked together, letting you jump from one body of information to another by just clicking on a button. *HyperCard* even keeps a trail of where you've been in the program so that you can backtrack to any recently viewed card. There is no theoretical limit to the amount of information you can store and access in *HyperCard* format, and any number of copies of your *HyperCard* information can be made and shared with your family, friends, and colleagues.

While *HyperCard* is not the first application to use these concepts, it has attracted the most attention and, given Apple's marketing clout, is likely to set the standard for future developments. In fact, Apple plans to release a version of *HyperCard* for the Apple II series, and it's likely that other *HyperCard*-like programs will soon appear for other computers. Right now, however, HyperCard is unique to the Mac.

***HyperCard* Power**

HyperCard offers a powerful new way to manage information. You can apply that power immediately to problems you need to solve now in the personal, business, educational, and creative realms.

The number of possible applications for *HyperCard* is enormous; the stacks supplied with *HyperCard* should give you some ideas of your own. Several of these, such as the date and address books, are mainly personal information organizers and are meant to take the place of the popular daytimer-type executive notebooks. This area has also been an early focus for programmers developing commercial *HyperCard* stacks; these third-party *HyperCard* applications (several are listed in Appendix D) can organize everything in your life from phone lists to travel plans to checkbooks. This kind of application is one easy place to start when you begin designing your own applications.

HyperCard is also excellent for business use, especially in those areas not addressed by available applications such as databases and spreadsheets. The key, again, is flexibility. Every business is different and has different information needs, but while commercial applications are hard to customize, *HyperCard* is easy. Once you've transferred your information to *HyperCard* format, you can link it together in the way that's most useful to you.

For example, now you may keep personnel, pension, and insurance records in different filing systems, in different file cabinets, and maybe in different rooms. Suppose an employee calls your office with a question involving both pension and insurance information. To get the required information, you might have to promise to call back, search through the personnel file cabinet, pull the employee's file, go to another office, search through the pension information file cabinet, pull a second file, go to a third office, search through the insurance information file cabinet, pull a third file, return to your office, and call back. Then, if you're neat and orderly, you'll want to replace all those files. The *HyperCard* way is much easier. While the employee is on the phone, you call up the employee's personnel file on your Mac by doing a fast text search. Buttons on the card take you immediately to cards containing pension and insurance information, and then back again. You can print a copy of any information and send it on to the employee, all without leaving your desk. If you have to call back, *HyperCard* remembers the employee's number and dials it for you. This kind of easy information access is a particular boon to small businesses, which often are hard put to handle the overhead of providing information to investors, employees, suppliers, and customers. And, a *HyperCard* application like the one just described would take only a few hours to create.

Among the many other possible business uses for *HyperCard* are hypermedia reports, newsletters and publications, desktop presentations, custom forms, online corporate directories, online catalogues and telephone ordering systems, and point-of-sale and public access information systems.

HyperCard has even greater potential in education. Until now, the Macintosh hasn't spawned a wide variety of educational programs, even though the Mac's highly visual interface and its point-and-click simplicity make it ideal for training and educating. One of the greatest barriers has been that the Mac is notoriously hard to program, so educators have shied away from creating their own software.

HyperCard should go far toward changing that. You can create the entire range of educational programming with *HyperCard*, from simple drill programs and computerized slideshows (*HyperCard* has slick video-style transitions built in) to sophisticated simulations and interactive training. The program itself can monitor student responses and tailor the lesson to suit student strengths and weaknesses. For example, you can program the lesson so that a student who enters a wrong answer is immediately shown a new screen that discusses the problem in more depth, and then asks the question again.

HyperCard's graphics and sound capabilities make it easy to design programming for preschoolers. The computer bulletin boards and information services are already full of flash-card programs, alphabet drills, math tutors, *HyperCard* storybooks, and more. Any of these can be modified for your own students. Surprisingly, some of the same visual techniques can be applied successfully to remedial programs and entry-level employee training. Students themselves can learn to program with *HyperCard* to create hypermedia reports, demonstrations, stories, and experiments.

Perhaps the most exciting possibilities for *HyperCard* aren't the practical ones at all. The revolutionary possibilities of *HyperCard* art, literature, and entertainment have barely been tapped.

HyperCard Pro and Con

You'll read a lot of positive things about *HyperCard*—in this book and other places as well. The program has a large, enthusiastic following and is well on its way to becoming a standard method for distributing information to the Macintosh community.

Commercial developers have jumped on the bandwagon and are already offering programs that use the *HyperCard* interface or that offer ways to transfer data to and from *HyperCard*. Hundreds of public domain stacks have been posted to computer bulletin boards and information exchanges. If you have a base of information you want to share or a commercial product to offer, the *HyperCard* format is a logical vehicle—Apple is bundling *HyperCard* with all new Macintoshes and is making it readily available to everyone else, so most Mac owners will have the program and will be familiar with its operation.

However, not everyone believes *HyperCard* represents the wave of the future. A common criticism directed at the program and at "hypermedia" applications in general is that they encourage aimless rambling rather than concise thinking. Why bother to bring your work to a satisfying conclusion when there's always another exciting trail to explore?

There's some justice to this claim, especially when directed toward people who might normally have trouble keeping to a straight and narrow workpath—students, for example. It's important to keep in mind that hypermedia needs structure to avoid complete anarchy. For example, educational *HyperCard* applications shouldn't be designed as completely open environments, but should be carefully structured to allow the student free access to important information in the usual hypermedia manner without straying too far afield. Every trail should lead back to the main path.

Nor is *HyperCard* appropriate to every task. For example, works with a strong one-way narrative, such as symphonies and mystery stories, don't profit much by the hypermedia approach (although it's possible to design new, nonlinear musical and text forms that do). And no matter what you do with *HyperCard,* it will never match the power of a fully relational database, a sophisticated spreadsheet, a high-end word processor, or an advanced graphics program.

Nonetheless, *HyperCard* offers something that makes up for its other shortcomings: independence. For the first time, you'll find that you can approach your computer as a craftsperson—not as a passive user, but as someone with the tools to build whatever you wish with the Macintosh and *HyperCard* as your partners. Even if you don't become a "HyperManiac," you'll discover a groundbreaking program that will give you the power to do things with your Macintosh you never thought possible. This book will help you by providing hands-on experience with *HyperCard*'s tools. Keep in mind, however, that nuts and bolts alone don't make a useful machine; you must have your own vision of what *HyperCard* can do for you and for others and then be willing to devote the necessary time and sweat to realizing it.

Chapter 2

Getting Started with *HyperCard*

This chapter will briefly review the basics of setting up *HyperCard* and browsing through the program. If you've been running your Macintosh and *HyperCard* for a while, you may wish to skim through to the next chapter. *HyperCard* novices, however, should read this chapter carefully because it contains basic setup information not covered in the *HyperCard* manual.

HyperCard Hardware

HyperCard runs on every Apple Macintosh computer in current production—the Mac Plus, the Mac SE, and the Mac II, as well as the new Mac clones—with two 800K disk drives or a hard disk. It will not run on Macintosh 128K or 512K computers that have not been upgraded to 1 megabyte RAM, 800K floppy drives, and 128K ROM.

The *optimum* hardware configuration for serious *HyperCard* users is a Mac II or accelerated Mac Plus or SE, at least 2 megabytes of memory, and a 40-plus megabyte hard disk drive. You'll use all that power and storage and will probably want more, especially if you make *HyperCard* the hub of your Macintosh activities. *HyperCard* comes on four 800K disks, requires 250K of memory, and wants to control about 750K. The program's online help system uses 700K more, and once you begin collecting stacks, you'll be able to fill up a meager 20-megabyte hard disk in no time. In short, although you can run *HyperCard* on a two-floppy-drive Mac Plus, you'll find the confines of your memory and storage space rather tight.

HyperCard is not copy-protected and can easily be installed on a hard disk; in fact, a hard disk is highly recommended. It works with all large-screen displays and video cards for the various Macs, with one caveat: Since *HyperCard* runs in a window of fixed size (512 × 340 pixels at 72 dots per inch—the size of the original 9-inch diagonal Macintosh screen), you can't expand the *Hyper-*

Card working area to fill a larger screen. You'll find more on using *HyperCard* with larger screens later in this book.

Like all Macintosh applications, *HyperCard* will print out on Apple's ImageWriter, ImageWriter II, and ImageWriter LQ dot-matrix printers, and the LaserWriter, LaserWriter II, LaserWriter IISC, LaserWriter IINT, and LaserWriter IINTX laser printers. Follow the directions in your owner's manual for hooking up and testing your printer.

TIP: *HyperCard* and the Mac II. A few additional things you should know when running *HyperCard* on a Macintosh II:

- Use the Control Panel DA to set your Mac II's display to two-color mode (two bits, or one bitplane) to see *HyperCard*'s visual effects. Set Characteristics to Black & White/Grays and Grays to 2.
- If you're using two or more monitors, make sure the *HyperCard* window and the menu bar are on the same monitor. Otherwise, visual effects don't work. (This also applies to any Mac with more than one monitor.)
- Current versions of *HyperCard* do not support color.
- There will be an unused border around the active *HyperCard* window on your display. You won't be able to open other *HyperCard* windows, but you can position other applications in the unused screen space (assuming you're running *MultiFinder*).

System Software

System software is like a computer's traffic manager. The Mac's System file takes care of disk operations, peripherals, and other basic matters while the Finder provides a consistent method of displaying and working with files. The System and Finder programs are located in the System Folder on any startup disk.

Experienced Mac users know there have been many upgrades of the System and Finder, the Mac's operating system software. Unfortunately, early versions of the System and Finder don't work with many types of hardware and software. Your best bet is to use the latest version, System Update 5.0, which includes System version 4.2, Finder version 6.0, and *MultiFinder*. If you've just purchased your Mac, 5.0 is the version you received with your computer. System Update 5.0 can also be purchased from your Apple dealer or from many Macintosh user groups.

Any system software with version numbers higher than those in System Update 5.0 can be used with *HyperCard*. It's also possible, but not recommended, to run *HyperCard* with

- System 3.2 and Finder 5.3 or later versions on the Mac Plus.
- System 4.0 and Finder 5.4 or later versions on the Mac SE.
- System 4.1 and Finder 5.5 or later versions on the Mac II.

Do not use the System file that comes on the HyperCard *Startup disk with the Mac II.*

System Upgrade 5.0 includes *MultiFinder,* Apple's first multitasking operating system. With *MultiFinder,* you can run more than one application at a time in separate windows, moving among them at will without having to return to the Finder to close one application and start another. This power and flexibility has a cost; you'll need at least two megabytes of memory to run *HyperCard* with another sizable program, such as *Excel* or *Microsoft Word.* To run several programs concurrently with *HyperCard,* you should have four megabytes of memory.

> **TIP: *HyperCard* Application Memory Size.** Under *MultiFinder,* you must set *HyperCard*'s Application Memory Size in the program's Get Info box to 750K or more. Setting it lower will yield unpleasant consequences, especially if you're working with graphics.

Setting Up

HyperCard has three versions in current circulation: version 1.0.1, the first version, released in September 1987; version 1.1, released in spring 1988, which contains some bug fixes and other minor enhancements; and version 1.2, released in summer 1988, with a number of new features and terms. All versions come on four 800K disks, as follows:

***HyperCard* Startup** contains a custom System folder, the *HyperCard* program, and the *HyperCard* Stacks folder. The Stacks folder includes the Address, Area Codes, Datebook, File Index,

Home, Phone, Quotations, and HyperCalc stacks. You can start *HyperCard* directly from this disk.

***HyperCard* & Stacks** contains duplicates of the *HyperCard* program and the *HyperCard* Stacks folder, and the More Stacks folder, which contains the Book Shelf, Documents, Periodic Table, Plots, and Slide Show stacks. (Version 1.2 does not contain the Book Shelf and Periodic Table stacks.)

***HyperCard* Help** contains the Help Stacks folder with the Help, Help Index, and Help Samples stacks. These stacks provide assistance and basic information about how *HyperCard* works.

***HyperCard* Ideas** contains the Idea Stacks folder with the Art Ideas, Button Ideas, Card Ideas, Clip Art, and Stack Ideas stacks. Use readymade parts from this disk in your own *HyperCard* applications.

When you begin work on the Macintosh, you must insert a startup disk into the internal drive (or configure your hard disk to start up automatically). All startup disks, including hard disks, must contain a System file. The *HyperCard* Startup disk includes a System folder with a special version of the System file in it, but no Finder. The Finder isn't strictly necessary on disks that will only be used for *HyperCard*—as you'll discover, *HyperCard* can perform many of the functions of the Finder, and in any case, you won't be able to fit the System, Finder, and *HyperCard* on one 800K floppy disk.

For safety reasons, you should make backup copies of the four *HyperCard* disks, using four blank disks, before you begin using *HyperCard*. Always use the copies for your work, not the originals. To do this, boot up your Mac with your System Tools disk or any startup disk (including a hard disk) with the latest version of the System and Finder on it, and then copy the *HyperCard* disks in the usual way. (Making copies of disks is described in the owner's guide.) Don't boot with the *HyperCard* Startup disk, as that will launch you directly into the program, bypassing the Finder, and you won't be able to copy disks with *HyperCard*. If you have a hard disk, you can transfer all the *HyperCard* files to the disk, except for the duplicate copies of *HyperCard* and the *HyperCard* Stacks folder on the *HyperCard* and Stacks disk. Even so, it's still a good idea to make floppy disk copies of your originals.

Once you've gained some experience with *HyperCard*, you can create a customized startup disk that contains only the System files, fonts (typefaces), and desk accessories (DAs) that you need. The System file on the *HyperCard* Startup disk contains no desk accessories, but it does offer a range of fonts:

- Chicago 12
- Courier 10 and 12
- Geneva 9, 10, 12, 14, and 18
- Helvetica 10 and 12
- Monaco 9
- New York 9, 10, 12, 14, and 18
- Times 10, 12, and 18

If you wish to install desk accessories or change the fonts on your *HyperCard* Startup disk, use the Font/DA Mover on the System Tools disk that came with your computer. (See the *Macintosh Owner's Guide* for a discussion of how to use the Font/DA Mover.) Note that there's very little room on the *HyperCard* Startup disk to add anything without removing something else.

With the unenhanced System, you are limited to 15 desk accessories, but some commercial utilities make it possible to add up to 256 DAs. There is no definite limit to the number of fonts you can install, although it is a good idea to keep the number down to 25 or less for convenience and to avoid possible corruption of your System file. Again, some commercial utility programs let you add as many fonts to your System as you wish. For more on fonts, see Chapters 4 and 6.

You'll want to have *MacInTalk,* a speech synthesis program, for talking stacks—just move the icon into your Startup disk's System folder. (You may have to make room by deleting an unnecessary stack.) *MacInTalk* is available from your Apple dealer or local user group.

Advanced users can install special resources on their Startup disks or any other disks with ResEdit, a public-domain utility program also available from dealers and user groups. Among many other things, ResEdit lets you add new sounds to your *HyperCard* stacks; this is covered in more detail in Chapter 9.

You can make room on your disk and save a little loading time if you discard files in your System folder that aren't necessary—for example, a printer driver for a printer you don't own. For example, you should customize your *HyperCard* Startup disk if you own a LaserWriter printer. The System folder on the *Hyper-*

Card Startup disk contains only an ImageWriter II printer driver file. Install a LaserWriter printer driver on the Startup disk by moving it over from the System Tools disk that came with your Mac or LaserWriter, and then discard the ImageWriter printer driver file. (Be sure to keep copies of both drivers on a backup disk.) If your Startup disk is full, you may have to delete a file to make room for the LaserWriter driver.

LaserWriter owners should note that *HyperCard* should be used with LaserWriter file version 4.0 or higher. (Use the Get Info . . . option in the File menu of the Finder to see the version number of your LaserWriter driver.)

MultiFinder includes a Background Printing spooler that lets you use the LaserWriter for printing while you work on another application. With *HyperCard,* you'll need a lot of free disk space for big jobs like background printing all the cards in a large stack. A hard disk with free megabytes takes care of the spooling file Background Printing creates.

There's more on printing at the end of this chapter.

Starting *HyperCard*

Once you've copied your disks and completed any customizing of your Startup disk, you can start *HyperCard* by inserting the *HyperCard* Startup disk into the first drive and then turning on your Mac. *HyperCard* will load directly and you can begin work with the program without having to open it from the desktop. If you load *HyperCard* Startup into a second drive, or if you've transferred *HyperCard* to your hard disk, simply open the program by clicking on its icon, just as you would any other Macintosh application. If you're using *Hypercard* versions 1.0.1 or 1.1, make sure the disk is unlocked (isn't write-protected) because *HyperCard* will reject any locked disk.

TIP: Making *HyperCard* the "Startup Application." If you want to boot directly to *HyperCard* from a disk other than the *HyperCard* Startup disk, use this technique:

- Go to the Finder.
- Select the *HyperCard* icon.
- Choose Set Startup from the Special menu.
- When you reboot, *HyperCard* will load automatically.

If you've installed *HyperCard* on a startup disk other than the *HyperCard* Startup disk, pull down the Apple menu at the extreme left and select the Control Panel DA. Set the time and date if you haven't already. At the bottom you'll see a set of controls for setting the Mac's RAM cache, an area set aside in memory for storing instructions and data specified by the current application. The default setting is 32K. Unlike many programs, *HyperCard* likes to set its own RAM cache. Click on the RAM cache OFF button so *HyperCard* can implement its own cacheing scheme more effectively.

Exploring *HyperCard*

Now let's take a quick tour through *HyperCard*. We'll look at all the basic elements of the program and cover the techniques for getting around from part to part. Figure 2-1 lays out the basic *HyperCard* terrain of objects, tools, windows, and menus.

Figure 2-1. The *HyperCard* Terrain

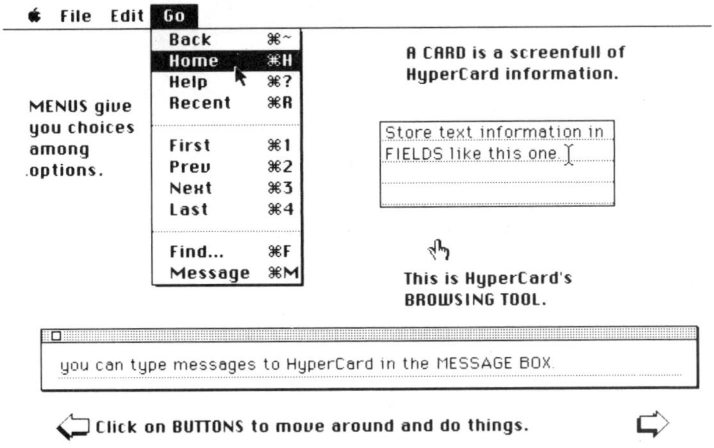

Tools, menus, and windows will be familiar to you from your other Mac experiences, but you may be wondering what objects are. In the *HyperCard* context, an *object* is one of several classes of special items that form the structure of the program. The objects we'll be concerned with in this chapter are cards, stacks, backgrounds, buttons, and fields. Chapter 3 discusses the nature of objects and their characteristics in more detail.

Cards

Upon opening *HyperCard,* you'll see the screen shown in Figure 2-2. This is a *card*—the fundamental *HyperCard* unit for carrying and displaying information. As noted in Chapter 1, *HyperCard* cards are analogous to ordinary index cards—you can put text or pictures on them (up to 32K worth of information), shuffle and sort them in any way, and add or delete cards as required. Unlike paper cards, *HyperCard* cards can be "linked" so that you can zip from one card to any other almost instantly.

Figure 2-2. The Home Card

In current versions of *HyperCard,* cards come in only one size—512 × 340 pixels at 72 dots per inch—and only one card can be viewed at a time. That isn't as much of a limitation as it might seem, given the rapidity with which you can zoom from one card to another.

The card in Figure 2-2 is special—it's the *Home* card. Anytime you open *HyperCard* directly, you'll see this card. It's designed to be a logical beginning and ending place for your *HyperCard* explorations—almost like the Finder is for other Macintosh programs. (Of course you can open any *HyperCard* stack from the Finder or an Open File dialog box in the usual way without going Home first.) The pictures on the Home card are actually gateways to other stacks—just click on the pictures and you'll go right to the first card in that stack. Go to the Home card by choosing Home from the Go menu (see below) or by typing Command-H. (A complete list of *HyperCard* keyboard commands is included in Appendix C.)

Stacks

The Home card is actually the first card in the Home *stack*. A stack—the *HyperCard* equivalent of a file or document—is a bundle of cards "stacked" like file cards in a roll file. *HyperCard* will always take you to the first card of a requested stack unless you tell it to do otherwise.

Cards in a stack are usually devoted to a theme; for example, they might contain the addresses and phone numbers of your business contacts, or they might contain pictures of boats. The number of cards in a stack (in other words, the *maximum file size* of a stack) is limited only by the amount of storage space you have available—you can easily design one stack to use up all the space on a 20-megabyte hard disk. Like the typical Mac file, stacks can be created, copied, and deleted at any time with options in the File menu (see below). *Stackware* is Apple's term for public domain or commercial stacks.

One stack you cannot do without is the Home stack. It contains special instructions that *HyperCard* automatically reads when the program is opened or closed. The Home stack must be on the same disk as *HyperCard* itself for the program to work, and there should be only one Home stack per disk.

> **TIP: A Home Stack Problem.** Some stacks created with pre-release versions of *HyperCard* won't work properly with released versions of the Home stack. You may see an error message telling you *Old File Format*, especially when you try to run *HyperCard* from a hard disk. To run those troublesome stacks, you'll need to obtain a pre-release copy of the Home stack. (Try Apple dealers or user groups.) In all other cases, however, you should use the latest released version of *HyperCard* and the Home stack.

Backgrounds

Often, all cards in a stack share the same *background*—the same general appearance and built-in functions. Backgrounds, in fact, are objects in their own right, intermediate between cards and stacks. It's the background that in most cases establishes the basic look and feel of a stack, providing features that otherwise would have to be duplicated on each card. Cards, in turn, carry features and information unique to each card. Figure 2-3 diagrams the relationship between stacks, backgrounds, and cards. To get a look at the background of the Home card, press Command-B; then press Command-B again to see the card.

Figure 2-3. Stacks, Backgrounds, and Cards

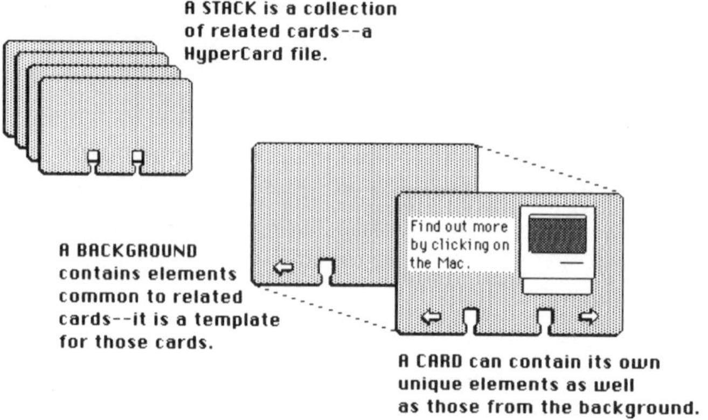

A STACK is a collection
of related cards--a
HyperCard file.
Find out more
by clicking on
the Mac.
A BACKGROUND
contains elements
common to related
cards--it is a template
for those cards.
A CARD can contain its own
unique elements as well
as those from the background.

Stacks, of course, can have more than one background, and many do. A stack with just one background, such as an address stack, is a *homogeneous stack*. A stack with many backgrounds, each tailored to a specific function, is a *heterogeneous stack*.

Buttons

Take a look at the left and right arrows at the bottom of the Home card. These arrows are typical examples of *buttons,* areas you click on to initiate an action, such as going to another card. You can use buttons as a kind of rapid transit system, speeding you from one part of *HyperCard* to the next. Try the right-pointing arrow now by placing the hand pointer over it and clicking—you'll move to the next card in the Home stack. (You only need to click once to operate a button.) Clicking the left-arrow button on the card you're at now will take you back to the Home card. The pictures on the Home card are another type of button—test each one and then click on the Home button (always a picture of a house) to return to the Home card. Press Command-Option to see the outlines of all the buttons on a card—useful if you can't find the right place to click in an indifferently designed stack.

Buttons are also smart switches that can initiate any *HyperCard* action. Part II of this book will provide many examples of how to make buttons do just about anything that's possible in the *HyperCard* world.

Fields

The last objects we'll discuss here are *fields*, areas where you can type in text just as you can in any Macintosh word processor. For example, the heading and copyright notice on the Home card are text contained in fields.

When you pass over an area where you can add or edit text, the hand pointer turns into an I-beam cursor, just as it does in the Finder when you want to change the name of a file, folder, or disk. Try modifying any of the fields you find on the Home card by typing your name into them. You can edit the text, using the standard Macintosh editing techniques of selecting text by dragging over it and then cutting, copying, or pasting with options in the Edit menu (see the discussion of *HyperCard*'s menus below). Backspace over text to erase it permanently. To move from field to field on a card, press Tab or click in the next field. Shift-Tab takes you to the previous field.

TIP: Typing into Fields. Fields, you'll discover, come in different sizes and shapes and text capacities. One peculiarity of fields is that if you keep typing after you've apparently filled the field, text will be added to the field anyway, but that text won't be visible. This can easily happen if you accidentally hit Return (rather than Tab) to move to the next field, and then keep typing for a while. It isn't a good idea to leave the hidden text there, especially when the text is being used by the stack to do something else—there could be unforeseen consequences.

One way to retrieve it is to select all the text that shows in the field and then cut and paste it into a second field. The hidden text (or at least as much of it as will fit) will now show in the first field. Cut and paste that text, retrieve the original (first) text from the second field, and put it back into the first field.

If you've typed only a small amount of hidden text, it may be easier to use Backspace to delete it. Another method involves making the field large enough to show all the text and then manipulating the text as necessary. The next chapter describes techniques for altering the characteristics of fields.

Menus

Even if you're a Macintosh novice, you know many tasks can be performed in any Mac program by making selections from pull-

Figure 2-4. File and Edit Menus

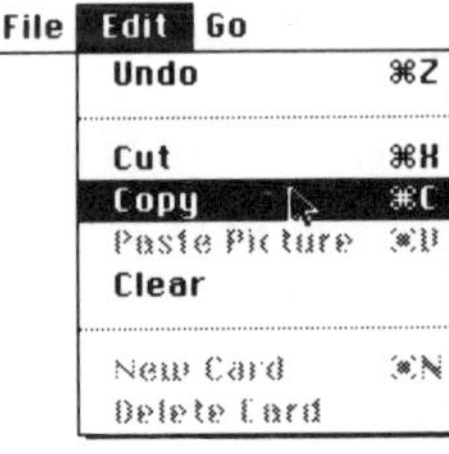

down menus. Figures 2-4 and 2-5 show the *HyperCard* menus available to you now.

Figure 2-5. Go menu

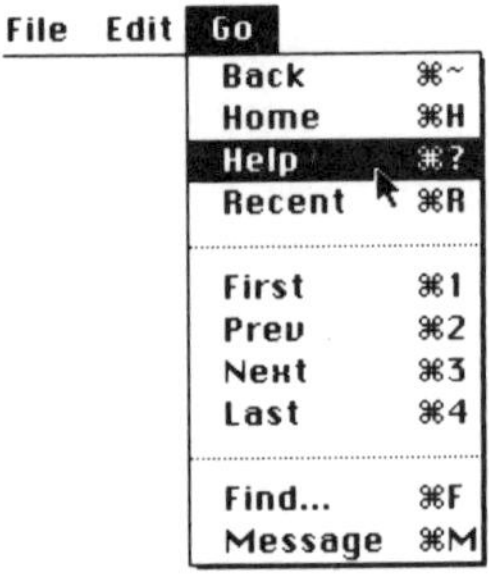

All Mac programs share a similar menu structure, which is part of the Mac's consistent interface. The File menu manages stack (file) and printing operations, and the Edit menu allows you to edit any selected item—object, text, or graphic. Note the Undo (Command-Z) option in the Edit menu. Choosing Undo lets you recover instantly from your last action (a real boon for error-prone mortals).

The third menu, Go (Figure 2-5), will be new to you, but it's the most important one to understand for navigating *HyperCard*. Let's now try each option in the Go menu and put together what we've covered so far by touring around the Home stack. If you're not at the Home card, go there now.

Back (˜ [tilde], Esc, or [down arrow]) takes you to the last card you visited, not necessarily the same card as the card before this one in the stack. Try it; you'll go to whatever card you last saw before the current (the Home card in this case) card. Return to the Home card by choosing Back again. There's a standard button for Back as well—the hooked, left-pointing arrow.

Home (Command-H) always takes you to the Home card; buttons that take you Home are always represented by little houses.

Help (Command-?) takes you to the Help stack, *HyperCard*'s online source of information about the program. If the *HyperCard* Help disk is not in the second drive, or if the Help stacks aren't on your hard disk, when you choose Help, *HyperCard* will prompt you to insert the Help disk. A button that provides Help is usually a question mark.

Recent (Command-R) calls up a special card that contains miniature pictures of the 42 cards you've visited most recently. Recent is shown in Figure 2-6. You can go to any of these cards, no matter which stack it's in, by clicking on its miniature picture (which is really a button). The card picture with the box around it is the card you looked at last. Use Recent when you need to find a particular card but can't remember how to get there. If you call up Recent now, the Home card will be boxed.

Figure 2-6. Recent

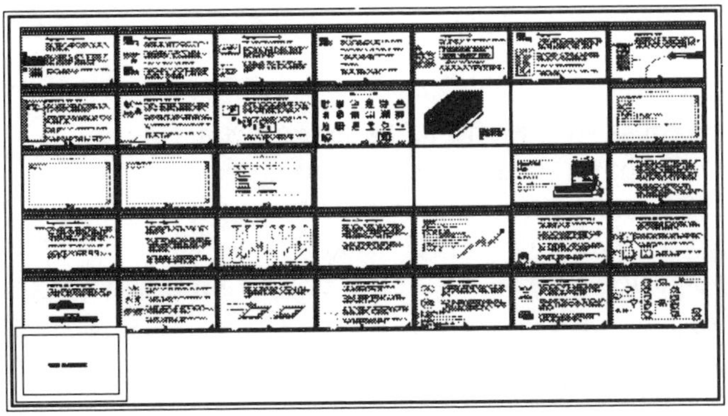

First (Command-1 or Command- [left arrow]) takes you to the first card in the stack. In the Home stack, the Home card is the first card. A First button is a left arrow or pointer against a vertical "stop" line.

Prev, or "previous" (Command-2 or [left arrow]) takes you to the card just before the current card in the stack. From the Home card, this is a card called *User Preferences.* User Preferences is not only the card previous to the Home card; it's also the last card in the Home stack. Because of the way cards are ordered in a stack, the card *previous to the first card* in a stack *is the last card* in the stack. A Prev button is a left arrow or pointer.

Next (Command-3 or FD [right arrow]) goes to the next card in the stack. From the Home card, the next card is titled *Look for Stacks In*. The next card after that is *Look for Applications In*. If the current card is the last card of a stack, the next card will be the first card of a stack. A Next button is a right arrow (FD) or pointer.

Last (Command-4 or Command-FD [right arrow]) takes you to the last card in the stack. A Last button is a right arrow (FD) or pointer against a vertical "stop" line.

> **TIP: Arrow Keys.** The arrow keys are handy for moving you forward, backward, and sideways through a stack, but they only work if the arrow buttons (or other buttons with the same functions) are present on the card.

Find and Message gives you the ability to search for text and send messages to *HyperCard*. Both use the message box, a special *HyperCard* window. We'll look at the message box in more detail next.

The Message Box

Choose Message or press Command-M to see the *message box*—a long, narrow window that appears at the bottom of the screen (Figure 2-7). Use the message box to issue messages to *HyperCard* in *HyperCard*'s scripting language, HyperTalk (the subject of Chapter 5 and Appendices A and B). You'll find the message box to be a flexible and useful tool.

Figure 2-7. The Message Box

The message box provides another way to navigate in *HyperCard*. To go in any direction or to any available stack, just type *go* and the direction or stack name. Try these navigation commands from the Home card, hitting Return or Enter after each command:

- go next
- go back

- go to stack Phone
- go home

You can also use the message box to get information from *HyperCard*, such as the time or date. Type these into the message box:

- the date
- the time
- the name of this stack

When you hit Return or Enter, the information you've requested appears in the message box. To clear the message box or any word in it, select the text and hit the Backspace key.

The message box can handle algebraic computations, too. Try these, pressing Return to do each calculation:

- 150 + 576
- 2 / (3 * (4 − 5)) / 6
- 3 * pi (* means *multiplied by*)
- 12 <cir> 2 (<cir> is the exponent symbol, so this is 12 to the second power)
- sqrt(2) (the square root of 2)

Move the message box by dragging it with the drag bar along the top, and close it with the close box at the upper left—or type *close message box* into the message box.

Find

You can look for any string of characters using Find in the message box. *HyperCard* will find each occurrence of the string in every field and put a box around it. For example, a text search is the quickest way to find the name of a business contact on a card in a large address stack.

Choose the Find command now (or press Command-F); the message box reappears, this time containing the command *Find* followed by open and close quotation marks (Figure 2-8). *Any text you're trying to find must be enclosed by quotation marks.*

Figure 2-8. Find

find "thesaurus"

Let's try a quick search in the Home stack:

- First, go to the User Preferences card and type your name into the field *User Name* (we'll be returning to User Preferences later).
- Now return to the Home card. Choose Find, type your first name between the quotation marks, and hit Return.
- You'll see, briefly, a spinning beachball, which lets you know *HyperCard* is performing the search. In an instant, *HyperCard* will find the User Preferences card and put your first name in a box.

In a large stack, especially address book–type stacks, you'll often find more than one occurrence of the word for which you're looking. For example, searching an address stack for the name *Jim* is likely to turn up several *Jims.* Just keep hitting the Return key after each search to get to the *Jim* you're looking for. You can also select any text from a field and paste it between the quotation marks. End a search by hitting Command-. (period).

TIP: Efficient Searching. You can specify as few as three characters in the string of text you're searching for, but obviously the more characters you specify, the more focused your search will be. Asking *HyperCard* to find the string *the* when you want to find *thesaurus* is an inefficient way to go about it. Using a space or a dash for any of the three characters will result in a slower search.

Search for more than one word by listing all the words separated by a space, as in:

find "thesaurus dictionary"

HyperCard will find every word *thesaurus* that exists on a card containing the word *dictionary,* but only *thesaurus* will be boxed since it's the primary search word. You can specify any number of words up to the length of the message box. For even more efficient searches, limit the search to a particular background field. If you know the field's name, number, or id (all field characteristics discussed in the next chapter), you can use this search format:

find "thesaurus" in background field "Books"

You cannot search through *card* fields in this way. The following *will not* work:

find "thesaurus" in card field "Books"

Version 1.2 Note: New Find Capabilities
Find chars, find word, find whole, and *find string* are new variations of the find feature. You can type these new options into the message box and try them out.

Find chars finds the searched-for characters anywhere inside a word or words. For example,

find chars "the"

will find matches in the words *the, thesaurus,* and *anthem;*

find chars "on the"

will find matches to *on* and *the* in any order on the card (for example, in the phrases "national anthem" and "theoretical nonsense").

Find word finds whole words only (strings of characters set off by spaces at either end). For example,

find word "the"

will find the word *the* anywhere on the card, but not the letters *t-h-e* in *anthem.* If there's a space in the searched-for string, as in

find "the flag"

HyperCard will find each occurrence of the words *the* and *flag,* even if they're in a different order.

Find whole (Shift–Command-F) finds only the exact searched-for word or phrase. For example,

find whole "the"

will find all occurences of the word *the,* but not the string of letters *t-h-e* in *anthem.* It works by looking for characters at the beginning of a word, and will only match whole words. Typing

find whole "the flag"

will match only the phrase "the flag."

Find string finds the exact string you're looking for within any word or phrase, including spaces. For example,

find string "the"

will find the string *the* anywhere within another word.

find string "the flag"

will find the phrases "the flag" and "absinthe flagon," but not "the American flag."

As you might guess, searched-for strings have to be on the same card, but not necessarily in the same field.

User Preferences

Go to the User Preferences card if you're not there now (Figure 2-9). You'll see a choice of five radio buttons labeled *Browsing, Typing, Painting, Authoring,* and *Scripting.* These refer to *HyperCard*'s five *user levels,* or grades of sophistication. Each user level includes the capabilities of the one above it and adds new capabilities as well. Type your name into the field at top and click on any of the buttons to set the desired user level, described below.

Figure 2-9. User Preferences

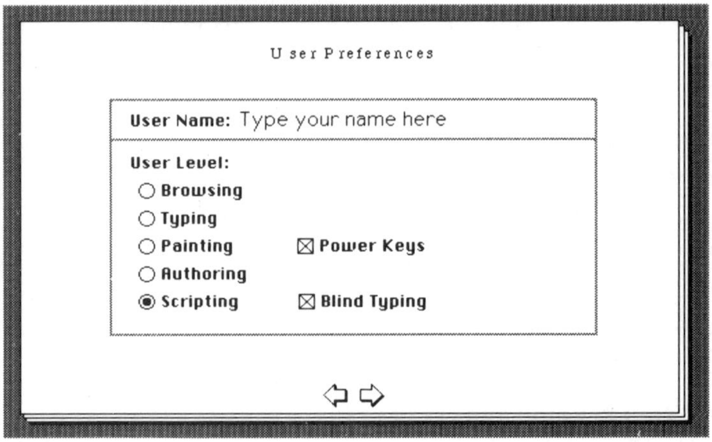

Browsing limits you to moving about and finding information. The hand pointer you've been using is the *HyperCard browse tool* and appears whenever you enter the program.

Typing, the level you're in now, adds the capability of typing in fields and issuing commands to *HyperCard* in the message box.

Painting gives you access to *HyperCard*'s *MacPaint*-like painting tools.

Authoring adds object-designing tools; it's also the general term for creating new *HyperCard* stacks.

Scripting allows you to write *HyperCard* scripts in HyperTalk, *HyperCard*'s scripting language.

The reasons for supplying multiple user levels are:

- *HyperCard* users may want to learn about the program slowly, beginning at a low level and progressing to the next, with its additional powers and choices, only when they're ready.
- Many *HyperCard* stacks may be designed for people unfamiliar

with *HyperCard*, and setting the user level to the least complicated setting makes it less intimidating for them to approach the program.

However, this book assumes that you fall into neither of these categories and that you want to learn all you can about *HyperCard* as soon as you can. If that's the case, set your user level to scripting and leave it there. Click the scripting button or type *set user level to scripting* in the message box.

To the right, you'll see two check-box-style buttons—Power Keys and Blind Typing. Checking the Power Keys button allows you to use special key commands with *HyperCard*'s graphics tools; Blind Typing makes it possible to type commands into the message box even if it isn't showing. Check both.

> **TIP: Text Arrows.** When you set your user level higher than browsing, *HyperCard* version 1.1 and later offer an additional option—Text Arrows—on the User Preferences card. Checking Text Arrows lets you use the arrow keys to move around in field or message box text instead of going from card to card. The left and right arrows move you back and forth along the line of text; the up and down arrows move you up and down, one field line at a time. You can still use the arrow keys to go from card to card by pressing Option and the desired arrow.

The Expanded Menus

Once you've set the user level to scripting, two new menus (Tools and Objects) will be added to the menu bar, and new commands will be added to the File and Edit menus. Figure 2-10 shows how File and Edit look now.

Figure 2-10. The Expanded File and Edit Menus

File
New Stack...
Open Stack... ⌘O
Save a Copy...
Compact Stack
Protect Stack...
Delete Stack...
Page Setup...
Print Card ⌘P
Print Stack...
Print Report...
Quit HyperCard ⌘Q

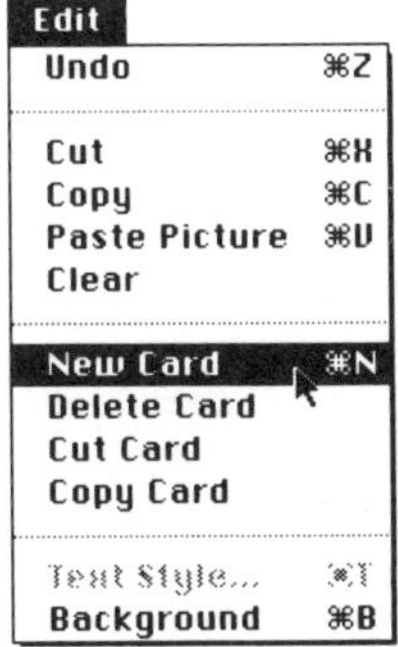

Figure 2-11. The Tools Menu

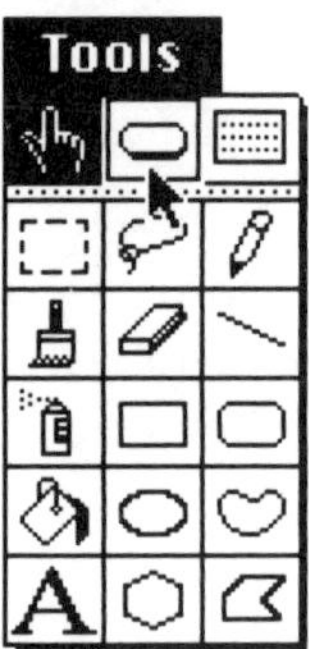

The Tools menu (Figure 2-11) gives you access to *HyperCard*'s selection of general and painting tools. *General tools* let you set a working mode (browsing with the browse tool, working with buttons or fields with the button or field tools); only one general tool can be active at a time. *Painting tools* let you create *HyperCard* graphics, a subject covered in Chapter 4.

The Tools menu doesn't function like the typical Mac menu. It can be "torn off" the menu bar by pulling it down and dragging it by a bottom corner. Try this for yourself. Note that you can move the Tools menu anywhere on the screen using the drag bar at its top, and that you can close the menu with the close box at its upper left. Even after you've torn off a Tools menu, it's still available from the menu bar, but you can't tear off two Tools menus at the same time—try doing so and see what happens.

The Objects menu provides detailed information on all the *HyperCard* objects. Figure 2-12 illustrates the Objects menu.

Figure 2-12. Objects Menu

Saving, Printing, and Quitting

Now you've seen *HyperCard*'s basic elements. There are three other aspects of the program that should be covered in an introductory overview; these are *saving, printing,* and *quitting* the program.

Saving Your Work

The experienced computer user quickly gets into the habit of saving work to disk, early and often. If you forget to do this, you risk losing the results of your current work session should something unexpected happen, such as a loss of power to the computer. With *HyperCard,* however, you needn't worry about saving your work—the program does it for you automatically every few minutes, and also whenever you leave a stack or the program. This guarantees that you'll never lose more than a few minutes of work. (By the way, this is the reason you can't run *HyperCard* from a locked disk; the program must be able to write to every disk in the system at any time. The one exception to this rule is if the stack you're in is meant to be locked; see Chapter 6.)

Printing Your Work

HyperCard offers many ways to print your work. If you've used other Macintosh applications, most of these printing options will be familiar to you, but some will not. Pull down the File menu and select each of the following menu options.

Page Setup. Before you try to print anything in *HyperCard,* make choices from the Page Setup dialog box to set the basic parameters for printing (page orientation and size, special effects, and so on). The ImageWriter and LaserWriter Page Setup boxes are shown in Figures 2-13 and 2-14.

Figure 2-13. ImageWriter Page Setup

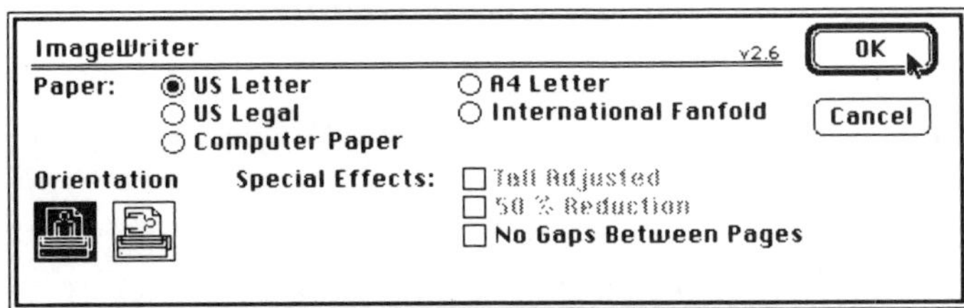

Figure 2-14. LaserWriter Page Setup

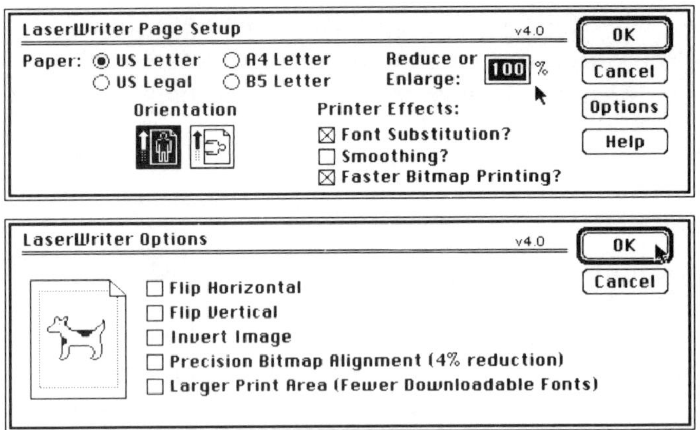

There's much more printing flexibility with a LaserWriter, and the LaserWriter Page Setup box reflects this. Generally, settings you use with other Macintosh programs—especially graphics programs—will work well for *HyperCard* in most cases.

TIP: *HyperCard* and the LaserWriter. The most important thing for LaserWriter owners to know is that *HyperCard* doesn't output *PostScript* files. To print *HyperCard* text at LaserWriter resolution (300 dpi), you must choose Font Substitution from the LaserWriter Page Setup box. Unfortunately, *HyperCard* version 1.0.1 won't always print text in LaserWriter fonts, even when you've chosen Font Substitution. Trial and error is the only way to find out if the fonts installed in your LaserWriter will work with Font Substitution. If you don't choose Font Substitution, all fonts wil be bitmapped. (There is a utility stack that adds *PostScript* capabilities to *HyperCard*—see Appendix D.)

HyperCard graphics print at the Mac's standard resolution of 72 dpi (dots per inch), not 300 dpi. The Smoothing option smooths out the jagged edges of Macintosh graphics to some degree, but slows printing considerably, as do the Flipping and Invert options. To lessen the slight distortion caused by the difference in resolution between the Mac's 72-dpi resolution and the LaserWriter's 300-dpi resolution, use Precision Bitmap Alignment.

Printing Cards and Stacks

Use Print Card in the File menu (or press Command-P) to print an image of the current card. To print images of all the cards in a

Figure 2-15. Print Stack Dialog Box

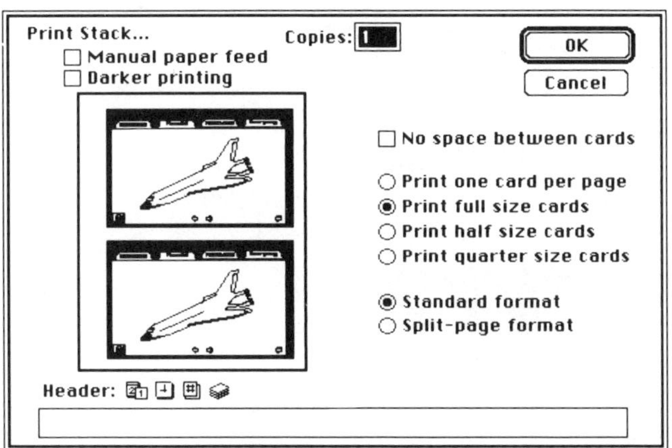

stack, choose Print Stack . . . You'll see the Print Stack dialog box (Figure 2-15).

You have the choice of printing 1, 2 (full-size), 8 (half-size), or 32 (quarter-size) cards per page. You may want to try a sample printout of each size now to see how they look. Half-size cards are just legible with an ImageWriter, but the quarter-size format should only be used with a LaserWriter.

Standard format and Split-Page format offer two different printing layouts, so you can bind your printed stack in an ordinary binder or folded over in a minibinder. Add a header to each page by typing into the header box at the bottom.

Printing Reports

With *HyperCard*'s Print Report feature, you can print only the textual information in the stack if you want, and you can even choose which cards and fields to print. Choose Print Report . . . to see the Print Report dialog box.

There are three ways to arrange report data on the page: by labels, by rows, and by columns. Choose *Labels* to print any field in blocks that fit standard adhesive labels. Use the dimension boxes at the bottom of the Labels dialog box to match the exact size of the adhesive labels you plan to use. Choose *Columns* to print each selected field in its own column. You must also check the *With the current background* button. Choose *Rows* to print all the selected fields on a card together in a row, as for an address list. Rows and columns can be adjusted by dragging the vertical

Figure 2-16. Labels Print Report Dialog Box

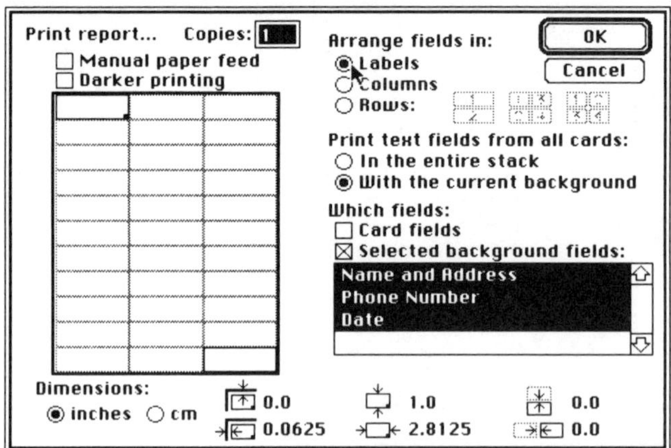

and horizontal dotted lines in the page layout window. Figures 2-16, 2-17, and 2-18 show the ImageWriter versions of the Print Report dialog boxes.

You must also choose which fields you want to print from the scrollable directory box. In most cases, you'll be printing selected background fields from cards with the current background. (See Chapter 3 for more on background and card fields.) You can select or deselect more than one field or all of the fields by clicking on them while pressing the Shift key.

There are commercial and public domain stacks that enhance *HyperCard*'s report-generating powers; see Appendix D for more information.

Figure 2-17. Columns Print Report Dialog Box

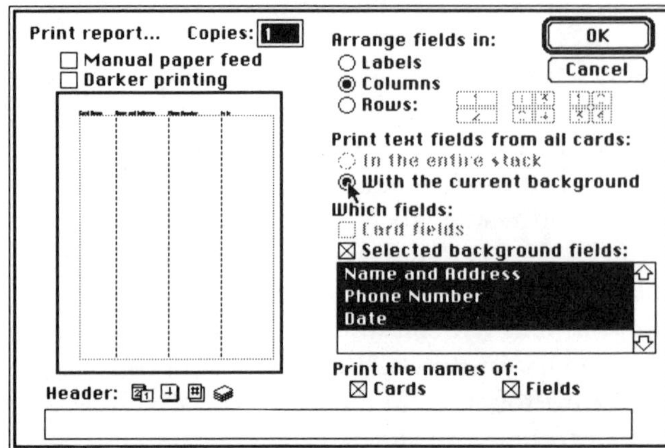

Figure 2-18. Rows Print Report Dialog Box

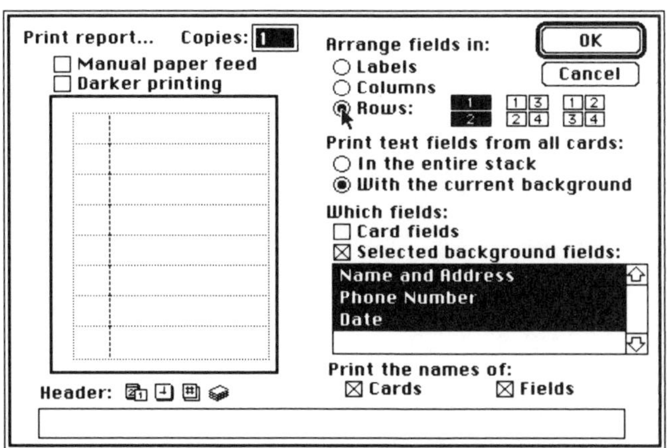

Quitting *HyperCard*

To quit the program, choose *Quit* from the File menu or press Command-Q. If *HyperCard* Startup is your startup disk, your Mac will shut down and eject any disks. With any other startup disk, you'll return to the Finder. If you're running under *MultiFinder,* you can go directly to another application by choosing it from the Apple menu.

Now that you've acquired all the skills you need to browse through *HyperCard,* this is a good time to explore the *HyperCard* Introduction and the Help stacks on the *HyperCard* Help disk, as well as some of the stacks on the other disks. There's a lot of fascinating material to see.

In the next chapter, you'll look at *HyperCard* from another vantage—that of a naturalist exploring the anatomy, taxonomy, and behavior of *HyperCard*'s objects.

Chapter 3

HyperCard Objects

In Chapter 2, you were introduced to the concept of *HyperCard* objects. An object, you'll recall, is one of several classes of special items that form the structure of *HyperCard*. Creating your own *HyperCard* stacks is mainly a matter of creating and tailoring objects to suit your needs. So, to go further as a *HyperCard* author, you need a firm grasp of the characteristics of objects and their interrelationships.

The Object Hierarchy

You know there are five major types or classes of *HyperCard* objects: *stacks, backgrounds, cards, fields,* and *buttons.* All objects have certain general characteristics—for example, they can be modified, created, and deleted (the main activities of a *HyperCard* author)—as well as unique properties you can set.

Each type of object does not exist in a vacuum—it has a definite relationship with the others and that relationship is hierarchical. This hierarchy is like a ladder of *HyperCard* objects, as shown in Figure 3-1. The hierarchy begins at the bottom rung with buttons and fields, and progresses to the card, the background, the stack, the Home stack, and finally, at the top rung, to *HyperCard* itself. This arrangement of levels should already feel natural to you if you've spent much time working with *HyperCard*.

As you can see, each rung includes the one below—cards contain fields and buttons; stacks contain fields, buttons, cards, and backgrounds; and everything is contained within *HyperCard* itself. Cards can't contain stacks, however, and fields can't contain other fields. Changes you make at higher levels—to the stack or Home stack—encompass every object below.

At this stage, the notion of an object hierarchy may seem rather theoretical to you. In fact, it's of crucial importance when you begin to design stacks yourself, and especially when you begin writing scripts. Chapter 5, which is about scriptwriting, and Chapter 6, which is about planning stack designs, will have more to say on the subject. For now, keep in mind that good stack designers generally start at the top rung—the stack level, or perhaps the Home stack level—and design down to the field/button rung.

Figure 3-1. The Object Hierarchy

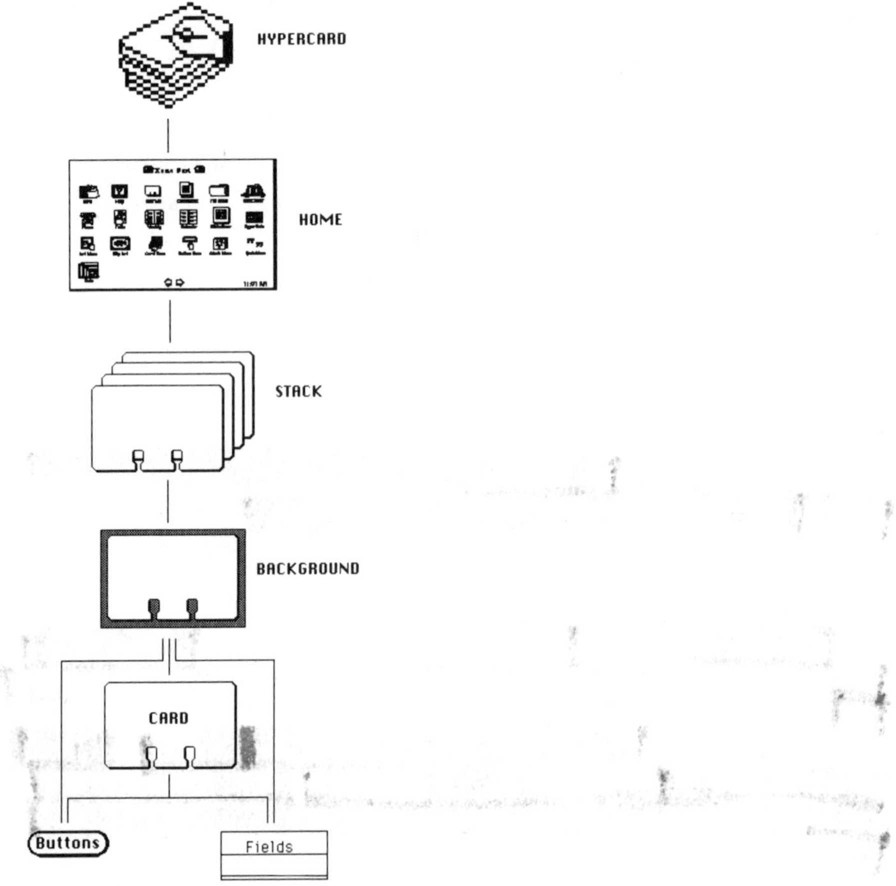

Objects in Layers

The object hierarchy can be thought of as the macroscopic structure of *HyperCard*—the "Big Picture." You can also look at *HyperCard* from another angle—that of the anatomy of what you see on the screen.

HyperCard screens are composed of two domains: the card domain and the background domain. The background domain contains the objects and graphics common to all cards sharing the same background. For example, the arrow buttons that move you around a stack usually reside in the background domain; all cards in the stack need those buttons, so the stack designer naturally assigns them to the background. Those buttons and any other objects in the background domain are *background objects*. The card domain contains objects and graphics belonging to only one card. A button that takes an action pertaining only to the current card will be in the card domain; it, and other objects in the card domain, are called *card objects*.

Figure 3-2. Layers

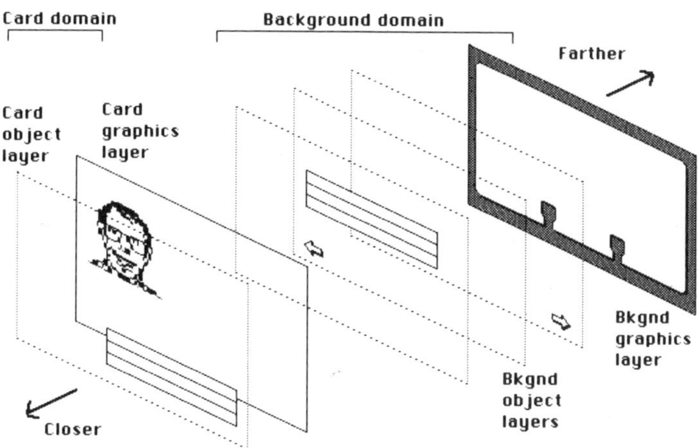

Figure 3-2 shows an "exploded" view of a typical *HyperCard* screen. As you can see, when you look at a *HyperCard* screen, you're actually looking at a sandwich of *layers*. Think of each button, field, card, and background as being on its own sheet of transparent plastic. The sheets of plastic are laid one on top of the next in a very definite order to create the screen. The structure of layers is invisible when you look at the screen, but the layers must be carefully arranged to produce the right effect.

Every time a new object is added, a new layer is created, and every time an object is deleted, its layer is deleted as well. New layers are always laid on top of existing layers within the same domain; for example, a new background field is laid on top of all the other background objects, but under every card object. (In *HyperCard* parlance, these layers aren't referred to as being *above or below*, but as *closer or farther*, with farther meaning *farther from the viewer*. From now on, we'll use this terminology.)

It's possible (and sometimes desirable) to layer objects so that closer ones obscure farther ones; therefore, thoughtful positioning and layering of objects is important when authoring a stack. The *Bring Closer* (Command-+ [plus]) and *Send Farther* (Command-– [minus]) options in the Objects menu provide the tools to rear-

Figure 3-3. Moving Objects Closer and Farther

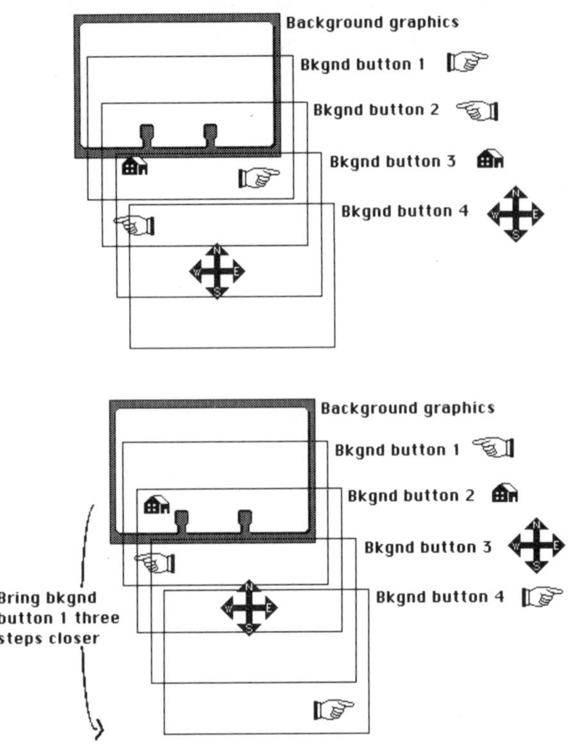

range the order of objects at any time. Figure 3-3 illustrates how this works.

Graphics have their own layers, just like objects. A graphic can be in the background or card domain, but will always be behind fields and buttons in its domain. Graphics can never be moved in front of objects in the same domain. See Chapter 4 for more on *HyperCard* graphics.

Chapters 6 and 7 provide some practical lessons in arranging object layers.

Modes

Another fundamental fact of life for *HyperCard* authors is that the program operates in *modes*. A mode is a restricted state of the program; an example is a state in which you can only work with buttons. There are six *HyperCard* modes—*background mode, card mode, browse mode, field mode, button mode, painting mode,* and *script-editing mode.*

Background mode. (Choose *Background* from the Edit menu, or press Command-B to toggle in and out.) You can create, delete, and manipulate background objects and graphics. You know you're in background mode when the menu bar acquires a *striped* border. Figure 3-4 shows the background mode.

Figure 3-4. Background Mode

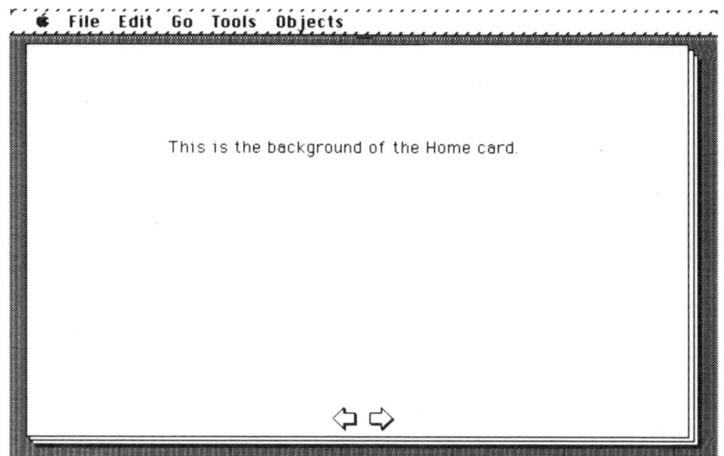

Card mode (the default mode). You can create, delete, and manipulate card objects and graphics.

Browse mode. (Choose the *browse general tool* in the Tools menu, shown in Figure 3-5.) You can operate buttons, enter text into fields, and move about at will. The pointer is a browsing hand whenever you're in browse mode.

Button mode. (Choose the *button general tool* in the Tools menu.) You can manipulate buttons but not operate them. Boxes will appear around all buttons to signal that you're in button mode.

Field mode. (Choose the *field general tool* in the Tools menu.) You can manipulate fields but not type into them. Boxes will appear around all fields to signal that you're in field mode.

Painting mode. (Choose any *painting tool* from the Tools menu.) You can paint and design but not work with or use buttons and fields.

Script-editing mode. You can only edit scripts in the script window (a custom dialog box). Even the menu bar is disabled in this mode. (Find more on scripting in Chapter 5.)

Figure 3-5. The General Tools and Painting Tools

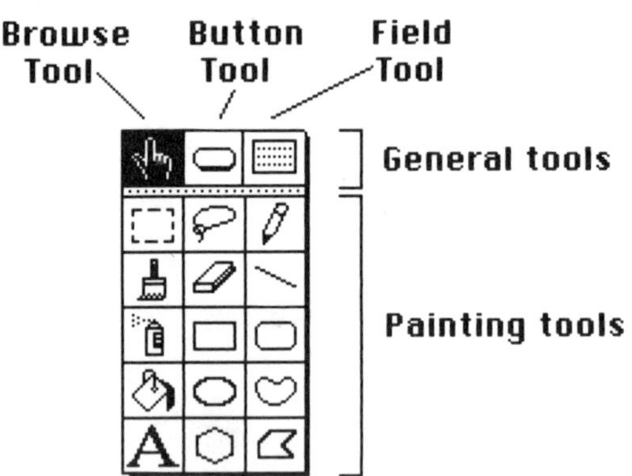

Background and card modes are mutually exclusive—you can't work in the background and card domain at the same time, but you can work with other objects, such as fields and buttons, in either mode. The browsing, field, button, and graphics modes are also mutually exclusive, as you might guess from the fact that only one general or painting tool can be active at one time. In other words, you can't manipulate buttons, fields, and graphics at the same time.

Take the time now to try switching in and out of these modes with the Home card, always a convenient choice. Tear off the Tools menu and move it to a corner of the screen.

- Hit Command-B to enter background mode. All the card objects and graphics vanish, leaving the background graphics (the "stack of cards" border) and the arrow buttons. Text in background fields is also invisible and the menu bar gains a striped border. Sometimes, although not on the Home card, background details may appear that you can't see in card mode because they were obscured by opaque graphics or objects in card layers. Hitting Command-B again will take you out of background mode. Card objects and graphics will reappear.
- The browse tool is the default general tool and is the one that's currently active.
- Select the button tool. The outlines of all the buttons on the Home card will appear, showing you their actual sizes and proportions (buttons are always rectangular). Try clicking on one; the button won't perform its usual function, but its box will turn into what's called a *marquee*, in Mac jargon, meaning the

button is selected for further work. Switch to background mode with the button tool selected to see what happens.

- Select the field tool. The button boxes vanish and the field outlines now appear, whether they're background or card fields. Click on a field; you won't be able to type into it, but you'll select it for further work (its outline will turn into a marquee). While you're in field mode, try clicking on a button—nothing happens.
- Select any painting tool. Buttons and fields are deactivated, and three new menus appear—*Painting, Options,* and *Patterns.* These are discussed in Chapter 4.

TIP: Mode Switching. From the viewpoint of *HyperCard,* exclusive modes are a necessity. The compartmentalization keeps the program from complete functional chaos, but to the serious stack maker, modes are a nuisance. On a Mac Plus or SE, switching from one mode to the next is just slow enough to be annoying. You'll be switching modes dozens of times in the course of stack making, going from button mode to field mode to background mode to painting mode, as the whims of creation steer you.

Two things can help alleviate the problem. One is thorough preplanning. The clearer you are about how to proceed in building your stack, the less often you'll have to switch back and forth between modes to do something you should have done to start with. The other is a 68020 or 68030 accelerator board. An accelerator board will speed up *HyperCard* to the point that you won't be waiting on mode switching any more.

Object Properties

Every class of *HyperCard* objects has well-defined *properties.* A property is any characteristic of an object, such as its name, location, or style. Properties can be *global* (they can belong to all objects in the program) or as *specific* as the text height of a field. Figure 3-6 lists the major *HyperCard* objects and their properties.

As you can see, there are many properties for every object, and most properties offer choices; for example, there are seven possible button styles and more than a hundred possible button icons (plus any you create and install yourself). Much *HyperCard* authoring work involves setting the properties of objects you've created.

In addition to properties for the objects you're already familiar with, there are two other classes of properties belonging to

Figure 3-6. Object Properties

GLOBAL	STACK	BUTTON	FIELD
blindtyping	cantModify (1.2)	autoHilite	autoTab (1.2)
cursor	cantDelete (1.2)	hilite	id
dragspeed	freeSize	icon	loc(ation)
editbkgnd	name	id	lockText
language	script	loc(ation)	name
lockMessages	size	name	rect(angle)
lockRecent	**BKGND**	rect(angle)	script
lockScreen	cantDelete (1.2)	script	scroll
numberFormat	id	showName	showLines
powerKeys	name	style	style
userLevel	script	textAlign	textAlign
userModify (1.2)	showPict (1.2)	textFont	textFont
	CARD	textHeight	textHeight
	cantDelete (1.2)	textSize	textStyle
	id	textStyle	visible
	name	visible	
	number		
	script		
	showPict (1.2)		

HyperCard's windows (the tear-off menus and the message box) and the painting mode. These are listed in Figure 3-7.

We'll look at a number of these properties that involve using text and graphics, now and in Chapter 4. For information on properties not mentioned in this section, refer to Appendix A, "*HyperTalk* Glossary," where each property is described and its use demonstrated.

Figure 3-7. Window and Painting Properties

WINDOW
loc(ation)
rect(angle)
visible

PAINTING
brush
centered
filled
grid
lineSize
multiple
multiSpace
pattern
polySides
textAlign
textFont
textHeight
textSize
textStyle

Object Names and Numbers

Before going further, you should be familiar with *HyperCard*'s conventions for naming objects. All *HyperCard* objects (except for the Home stack, the windows, and *HyperCard* itself) can have names assigned to them. It's a good idea to name any important object you create. For example, in a card catalogue stack, you might name one background field *Call Number* and another *Author.* Although names are not especially important for backgrounds, cards, or buttons, they're important for stacks and fields. You must name stacks—that's the only way to refer to them; it's also important to get into the habit of naming every field you create.

Backgrounds, cards, fields, and buttons are also automatically stamped at the time of their creation with unique and permanent identification numbers—for example, *card id 2345.* In addition, cards, fields, and buttons have *order numbers*. A card's order number tells you the card's position in its stack relative to the first card in the stack; field and button order numbers tell you, in effect, what layer the object is on, with Field or Button 1 being the farthest away. You can use given name, id number, or order number to specify an object. Just keep in mind that order numbers can change anytime you rearrange the objects, but id numbers are forever.

Getting Object Information

You can find out anything you want to know about any *HyperCard* object from its Info dialog box, available from the Objects menu. Pull it down now. You'll see options for Button Info . . . , Field Info . . . , Card Info . . . , Bkgnd Info . . . , and Stack Info. . . . These Info boxes not only provide basic information on objects but also let you modify their properties and gain access to their scripts—the HyperTalk programs that tell the objects what to do. (See Chapter 5 and Appendices A and B for more on scripts.) The Button Info and Field Info boxes are available only when the button or field tools are selected, but the other boxes are always available.

Let's look at each box. Again, return to the Home card and tear off the Tools menu.

Stack Info. Information about the number of backgrounds in a stack, as well as a stack's other vital specifications, can be found in the Stack Info dialog box (see Figure 3-8).

Figure 3-8. Stack Info Dialog Box

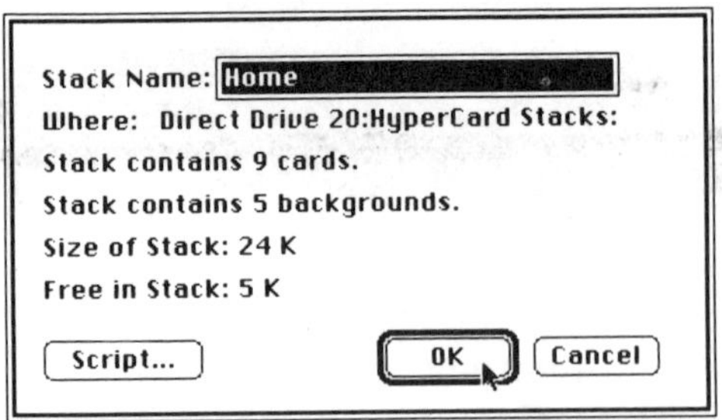

There are three ways to change a stack's name:

- From the Finder, as with any other Mac file or document.
- By changing the name in the Stack Info dialog box.
- By typing *Set the name of this stack to "[whatever name you want]"*

Note: If you change the name of the stack, any links (connections) to the stack from other stacks will be broken, since the links will be looking for the stack under the old name. You'll have to reforge any links you wish to keep. Linking is discussed at the end of this chapter.

> **TIP: Stack Size and Stack Compacting.** The Stack Info box tells you both the size of the stack in bytes and the *free space* of the stack (that is, how many unused bytes there are trapped in the stack). Think of free bytes as empty cardboard boxes stored in the attic—they take up space, but they don't hold anything. The free space of the stack can be useful information if your storage space is tight or if you want to get the maximum speed from the program. Frequently used or modified stacks tend to get bigger and bigger, accumulating free space, eating disk storage, and slowing access to information.

Use *Compact Stack* in the File menu to eliminate free space in the stack; the stack will take up less room while retaining all its information. This is especially valuable for a hard disk user reaching the limit of his or her disk's capacity.

To eliminate free space:

- Go to the stack you want to compact.
- Choose *Compact Stack* from the File menu.
- The stack will compact. Check the Stack Info box before and after to see the amount of free space that has been reclaimed.

> **Version 1.2 note: Compacting old stacks.** The first thing to do when using version 1.2 to open an old stack created with an earlier version is to compact the stack. Otherwise, 1.2 may not be able to recognize objects in the stack.

Background Info. Basic information on the current background can be obtained from the Background Info dialog box, available through the Objects menu (Figure 3-9). You don't have to be in background mode to see it.

Figure 3-9. Background Info Dialog Box

Background Name:
Background ID: 2282
Background shared by 2 cards.
Contains 1 background fields.
Contains 2 background buttons.
☐ Can't delete background.
Script... OK Cancel

You can prevent a user from unintentionally deleting the background by clicking on the *Can't Delete Background* check box.

Card Info. Choose Card Info . . . to see the dialog box in Figure 3-10.

Figure 3-10. Card Info Dialog Box

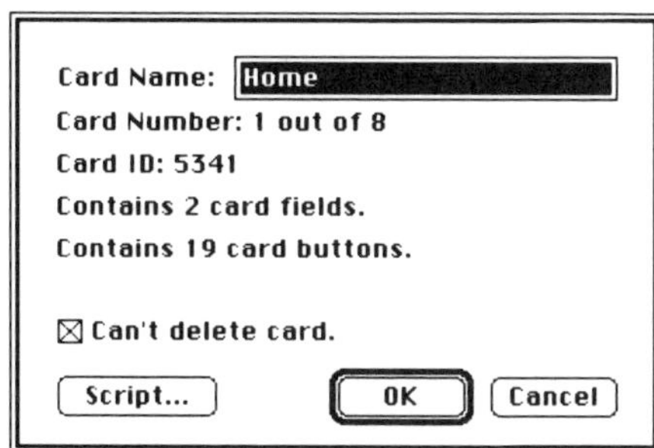

The card number tells you the position of the card in the stack; it can change any time you add, delete, or move cards in the stack, so don't treat the card number as an absolute. You can prevent a user from unintentionally deleting the card by clicking on the *Can't delete card* check box.

Fields. To see the Field Info box, choose the field tool, select the field at top center on the Home card, and then choose Field Info . . . . You can also double-click on the field. Even if you're not in field mode, you can still see the Field Info box by moving the *I*-beam text cursor to the field and choosing Field Info . . . .

Fields have many more properties than stacks, backgrounds, or cards, as you'll see in Figure 3-11.

Figure 3-11. Field Info Dialog Box

Field Name:
Bkgnd field number: 1
Bkgnd field ID: 6
Lock Text
Show Lines
Wide Margins
Font...
Script...
Style:
transparent
opaque
rectangle
shadow
scrolling
OK
Cancel

By clicking on the desired button, you can choose among five styles and three formats of fields. Try each of these with the selected field, toggling between the browse and field tool to see the effect each option has. Transparent fields allow any object or graphics behind the field to show through, even if there's text in the field. Opaque fields hide anything underneath, as do all other field styles. A scrolling field lets you put more text into a field than fits on the screen—in fact, you can nearly fit 16 pages into a scrolling field. Use the scroll bar to read to the bottom of the field.

Click on the Font . . . button in the Field Info box to see the Text Style dialog box (Figure 3-12). Text Style lets you change the

Figure 3-12. Text Style Dialog Box

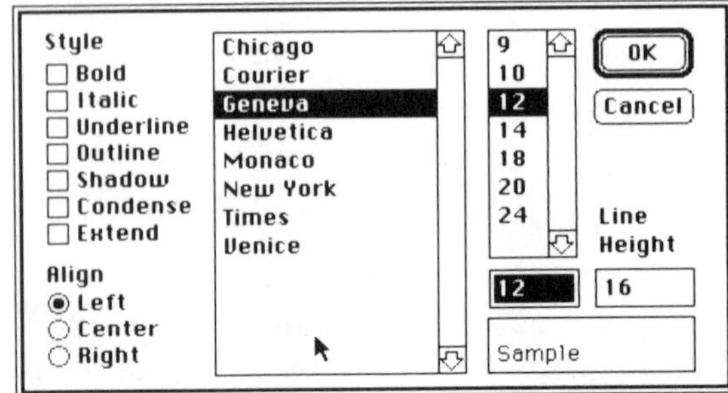

typeface, font, style, alignment, and line height of the text in the field. Try several different fonts, styles, and line heights to get a feel for the possibilities—keep in mind that the fonts you see are the ones installed in the System file on your *HyperCard* disk. You can double-click on a typeface or font to select it and close the Text Style dialog box at the same time. The Text Style dialog box is also available through the Edit menu; select a field and then choose Text Style. . . .

TIP: Maximum Number of Fields Bug. *HyperCard* version 1.0.1 contains a bug concerning the number of fields and the Compact Stack feature. If your stack has a background with more than 126 background fields, or a card with more than 126 card fields, using Compact Stack won't work. This bug won't affect most people, and it's fixed in subsequent versions of the program.

Version 1.2 Note: Autotabbing Field Info boxes in *HyperCard* 1.2 contain a *check boxes* that allow you to set new properties of nonscrolling fields called *autotab*. With autotab on, press the Return key when the I-beam cursor is in the last line of the current field to go to the next field, just as if you had pressed the Tab key. This addresses the widespread problem of users habitually hitting Return rather than Tab to go to the next field.

Button Info. Like fields, buttons have a wide range of properties and can be manipulated with great flexibility.

To see the Button Info box, choose the button tool, select the Intro button at upper left, and then choose Button Info . . . (Figure 3-13). You can also double-click on the button.

Figure 3-13. Button Info Dialog Box

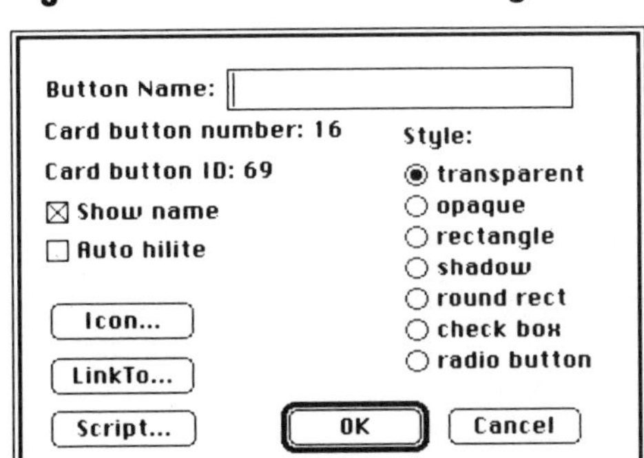

If the button has a name, *showName* lets you toggle the name on and off. The Intro button does not have a name—the word *Intro* is actually a card graphic—so let's name it. Click on showName, type *Test* into the name box, and then click on OK or hit Return or Enter. Now you can see *Test* superimposed over the button picture. Return to the Info box, click showName again, click on OK or press Return or Enter, and the name will disappear. When you click the button, autoHilite makes the button show reverse black-and-white; try that option with the button, too.

There are seven button styles; try each with the Intro button. Transparent buttons show any graphics or objects behind them; opaque buttons hide anything behind them, as do the other button styles. Choose the check box and radio button styles when an option can be toggled on and off, or when you're presenting a list of choices and you want to provide feedback to the user about what choice has been made.

The Icon . . . button takes you to the Icon Selection dialog box shown in Figure 3-14. A button icon is a picture attached to a button—it's a property of the button and goes with it wherever the button goes. Most of the buttons on the Home card (with the exception of the arrow buttons) don't have icons—those pictures are card graphics laid behind transparent buttons and have no real connection to the buttons other than being in the same area of the screen. You can, however, give any of the buttons an icon, or you can change an icon by choosing one from the Icon Selection Box and clicking OK. The icon will be superimposed over the

Figure 3-14. Button Icons

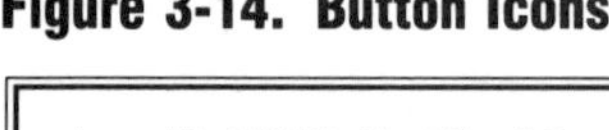

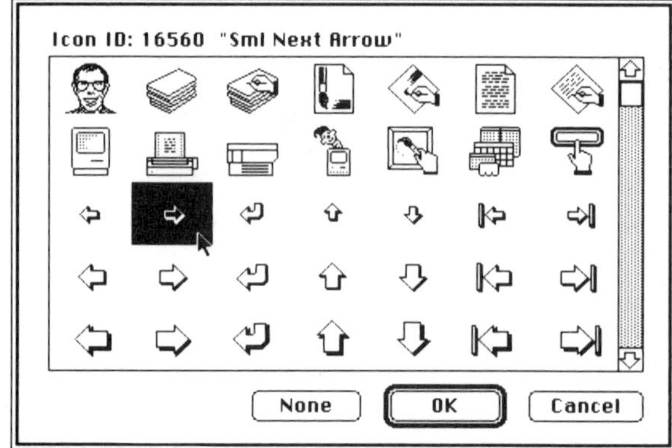

original button picture. Remove an icon from a button by clicking on None.

With the various styles and icons available, you have nearly unlimited ways to vary the appearance of buttons. Try a few choices on the New button for yourself.

TIP: Custom Button Icons. *HyperCard* provides more than a hundred button icons, but you may want to design others. Icons aren't like other Mac pictures; they're special Mac *resources*, and you can't just cut, paste, and edit them without some advanced techniques. For those who must have custom icons, a number of public domain utilities allow you to add to *HyperCard*'s icon resources. Here's what you need:

- An icon creation and modification utility program, such as one of the following:
  - *Icon Extractor* by James L. Paul, 513 West A Street, Tehachapi, California, 93561 (shareware)
  - *Iconstructor* by Lawrence W. Walker, 549 Cassidy Avenue, Lexington, Kentucky, 40502 (shareware)
  - *Icon Manager* by Walter J. Biess, 8 Rue des Cultures, 78110 Le Vesinet, France (shareware)
- These and other icon utilities are available on bulletin boards and through dealers and user groups.
- *ResEdit,* the public domain resource moving program, available everywhere.

The process, in brief, is to use an icon utility to create new icons or grab existing ones, such as those in the resource files of other applications. If necessary, you must convert them from ICN# icons to ICON icons—a process Icon Extractor does particularly well—so that *HyperCard* can use them. (The icon program will show you how.) Then, use ResEdit or an equivalent program to move the icons to *HyperCard*'s ICON file. Once you've done this, the new icons will appear in the Icon Selection window, available for any button.

You don't need a separate icon creation program if all you want to do is edit one of the icons already in *HyperCard.* Launch ResEdit with *HyperCard* in one of the disk drives and find the *HyperCard* window that appears. Choose ICON from the list that appears in the *HyperCard* window; another window will open showing *HyperCard*'s button icons. Double-click on the one you want to change, and redraw it with the arrow pointer in the icon edit window that appears. When you're through, close the edit window and save your changes.

Before you try this, practice with the utilities you're using to get a feel for them and for handling resource files. Always work with a *copy* of *HyperCard*, not the original.

Creating Objects

The Edit and Objects menus give you the tools to create any of the five common *HyperCard* objects. Try each variety of creation for yourself.

To create a stack:

- Bring up the stack and card you want to use as the model.
- Select New Stack . . . from the File menu. A dialog box (Figure 3-15) will ask you to name the new stack (be sure to give it a name different from that of the stack you're using as a model) and will query whether you want to copy the current background. The default option is to copy the current background.

Figure 3-15. New Stack Dialog Box

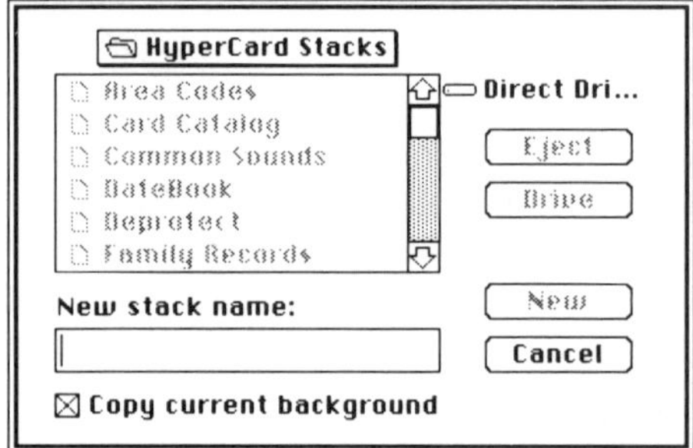

- *HyperCard* will create a file for the new stack on the current disk in the folder containing the Home stack. If you've chosen to model the stack on the current background, the new stack will consist of one card with a background copied from the Find background (card objects and text in fields will not be copied). Otherwise, the stack will have a blank background.

To create a background:

- Choose *New Background* from the Objects menu.
- *HyperCard* creates a blank background on a blank card.

To create a new card modeled on an existing card:

- Go to the card from which you want to model the new card.
- Choose *New Card* from the Edit menu, or press Command-N.

- *HyperCard* will create a new card, insert it behind the current card, and then take you to the new card. The new card will be an exact copy of the model card except for text fields, which will not be transferred.

To create a field:

- Choose the field tool.
- Decide if you want a card or background field. If you want a background field, enter background mode by choosing Background from the Edit menu or pressing Command-B.
- Choose *New Field* from the Objects menu. A new, empty field will appear in the center of the screen. It will already be selected, ready for modification.
- Double-click on the new field to make style and format choices in the Field Info and Fonts dialog boxes.
- Size and position the field (see below).

To create a button:

- Choose the button tool.
- Decide if you want a card or background button. If you want a background button, enter background mode by choosing Background from the Edit menu or pressing Command-B.
- Choose *New Button* from the Objects menu. A new, round, rectangle-style button named *New Button* will appear in the center of the screen. It will already be selected, ready for modification.
- Double-click on the new button to make style and format choices via the Button Info and Icon dialog boxes.
- Size and position the button (see below).

Copying Objects

Cut and *Paste* options in the File and Edit menus let you create as many copies of objects as you wish. Note that the menus change to match the currently selected object. For example, in field mode with a field selected, the Edit menu reads *Cut Field, Copy Field,* and so on.

For standard cutting and pasting of objects, it's usually easier to use the keyboard editing shortcuts: Command-X for cut, Command-C for copy, Command-V for paste.

TIP: Before You Copy. Many Mac programs allow you to select more than one file, object, or other item by Shift-clicking on them, and then let you manipulate the selected items as though they were one item. In drawing programs such as *MacDraw,* this is called *grouping.* Current versions of *HyperCard* don't offer this feature. *You can only work on one HyperCard object at a time.* Keep this in mind if you're planning to make many similar objects by copying one object many times. Set all the properties of the original object *before* you make the copies, or later you'll have to set the properties of each copy separately.

To copy a stack:

- Go to the stack.
- Choose *Save a Copy . . .* from the File menu.
- A standard Save File dialog box will ask you to give the stack copy a new name. Be sure to give it a name different from the original stack you're copying.

To copy a background:

- Go to a card with that background.
- Copy a card with that background.
- Paste the card in its new location.
- If necessary, delete any card objects.

To copy a card:

- Go to the card you want to copy.
- Choose *Copy Card* from the Edit menu.
- Go to the card *before* the place you want to put the copy. This can be in the current stack or in any other stack.
- Choose *Paste Card.* The card will be pasted behind the current card in the stack (it will receive a card number one higher than the current card), and then *HyperCard* will show you the pasted card.

Note: The card numbers of all the cards after the pasted card will change as well. If the card is pasted into another stack, that stack will also gain a new background.

To copy a field onto the same card:

- Choose the field tool.
- Select the field you want to copy.
- Press the *Option key* and drag. A duplicate of the field will peel off and follow the pointer to the new location. This duplicates only the field, no text. If you're copying a background field, the new field will be a background field also and will appear on all cards with the same background.
- Set any new properties of the copy with the Field Info and Text Style boxes.

To copy a field to another card:

- Choose the field tool.
- Select the field you want to copy.
- Choose *Copy Field* from the Edit menu. This copies the field only, no text in it.
- Go to the stack and card where you want to paste the field.
- Choose *Paste Field.* The field will appear on the screen at the same location as the original; move and size it as required (see below). If it's a background field, it will appear on all cards that share the same background.

To copy a button on the same card:

- Choose the button tool.
- Select the button you want to copy.
- Press the *Option key* and drag. A duplicate of the button will peel off and follow the pointer to the new location. If you're copying a background button, the new button will be a background button also and will appear on all cards with the same background.
- Set any new properties of the copy with the Button Info and Icon Selection boxes.

To copy a button to another card:

- Choose the button tool.
- Select the button you want to copy.
- Choose *Copy Button* from the Edit menu.

- Go to the stack and card where you want to paste the button.
- Choose *Paste Button.* The button will appear on the screen at the same location as the original; move and size it as required (see below). If it's a background button, it will appear on all cards with the same background.

Deleting Objects

Deleting objects is even easier than creating them. *Undo* in the Edit menu (or Command-Z) will reverse a mistaken deletion as long as the deletion was the last action taken.

To delete a stack:

- Go to the stack you want to delete. If you try this with one of the stacks that come with *HyperCard,* make sure you have a backup copy.
- Choose *Delete Stack* from the File menu.
- Click on *Delete* in the dialog box that appears. The stack will be erased from your disk.
- *HyperCard* then returns you to the Home card. DO NOT delete the Home stack on your *HyperCard* disks.

To delete a background:

- Delete every card with that background by going to each card and choosing *Delete Card* from the Edit menu. If there is only one card in the stack, delete the stack.

To delete a card:

- Go to the card you want to cut.
- Choose *Delete* from the Edit menu. This deletes the card and takes you to the next card.

To delete a field:

- Choose the field tool.
- Select the field you want to delete.
- Choose *Clear Field* to completely delete the field.
- If the field is a background field, you'll delete it from all cards with the same background.

To delete a button:

- Choose the button tool.
- Select the button you want to delete.
- Choose *Clear Button* to completely delete the button.
- If the button is a background button, you'll delete it from all cards with the same background.

Moving Cards, Fields, and Buttons

To move a card to another position in the same stack:

- Go to the card you want to move.
- Cut the card with *Cut Card* in the Edit menu.
- Go to the card before the place you want to paste the new card.
- Paste the card with *Paste Card.*

Note: The card numbers of all the cards after the pasted card will change.

To move a field:

- Choose the field tool.
- Select the field you want to move.
- Position the pointer over the center of the field.
- Drag the field to a new location anywhere on the card. If the field is a background field, every card with the same background will be affected.

To move a field back and forth from the card to the background domain:

- Choose the field tool.
- Select the field you want to move.
- Enter background mode (Command-B) to see if the field is still there. If it is, it's a background field.
- To move a background field to the card domain, enter background mode, cut the field with *Cut Field* in the Edit menu, exit background mode, and paste the field into the card domain. It will stay in the same position on the screen.
- To move a card field to the background domain, cut the field,

enter background mode, and paste the field to the background. It will stay in the same position on the screen.
- Check background and card modes to confirm the move.

To move a button:

- Choose the button tool.
- Select the button you want to move.
- Position the pointer over the center of the button.
- Drag the button to a new location anywhere on the card. If the button is a background button, every card with the same background will be affected.

To move a button back and forth between the card domain and the background domain:

- Choose the button tool.
- Select the button you want to move.
- Enter background mode (Command-B) to see if the button is still there. If it is, it's a background button.
- To move a background button to the card domain, enter background mode, cut the button with *Cut Button* in the Edit menu, exit background mode, and paste the button into the card domain. It will stay in the same position on the screen.
- To move a card button to the background domain, cut the button, enter background mode, and paste the button to the background. It will stay in the same position on the screen.
- Check background and card modes to confirm the move.

Sizing Fields and Buttons

You can stretch and shrink fields and buttons as necessary with the techniques that follow.

To change the size of a field:

- Choose the field tool.
- Select the field you want to resize.
- Position the pointer over one of the field's corners. The end of the pointer should be exactly over the field corner.
- Drag the corner to resize the field, either smaller or larger. The opposite corner remains stationary.

- Text in the field will wrap to fit the new field dimensions. If any part of the text is cut off, it remains part of the field and will reappear if you make the field larger again.

To change the size of a button:

- Choose the button tool.
- Select the button you want to resize.
- Position the pointer over one of the button's corners. The end of the pointer should be exactly over the button corner.
- Drag the corner to resize the button. The opposite corner remains stationary.
- If the button name is showing, it will try to wrap to fit the new button dimensions. If you make the button too small to display the entire name, some part of the name will be cut off, but it remains part of the button and will reappear if you make the button larger again.

Linking

One button option not discussed earlier is the Link To . . . feature, in the Button Info dialog box. This enables you to create a simple link or path to any card or stack without writing a script for the button, the presumption being that navigation is what most *HyperCard* users create buttons for.

To create a link between a new Home card button and a new stack:

- Make a new stack based on the background of the Home card (as described above). Call it *Test Stack.*
- Return to the Home card.
- Choose the button tool.
- Create a new button with *New Button* in the Objects menu. Double-click on the button to see the Button Info dialog box. Call the button *Link Test.* Set the other properties however you like.
- Click on the *Link* . . . button. You'll see the Link To dialog box (Figure 3-16).

Figure 3-16. Link To Dialog Box

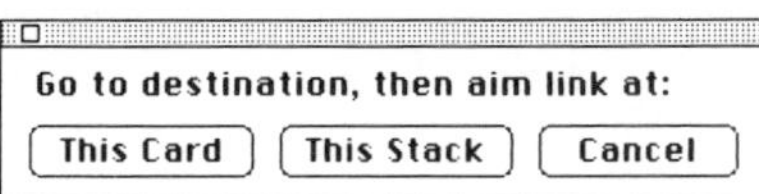

- Using the Open Stack dialog box, go to the Test Stack stack. The Link To . . . dialog box remains on the screen. In a large stack, you could link to any card, but since this stack has only one card, click on *This Stack.*
- *HyperCard* will forge the link and return you to your starting point, the Home card.
- Try the new link to see if it works by clicking on the Link Test button.

Far more elaborate links are possible by writing special linking scripts for a button (or other objects, for that matter). Script links are discussed in most of the chapters of Part II.

Embedded in *HyperCard* is a complete paint program. In the next chapter, you'll encounter *HyperCard*'s artistic side and get some tips on how to integrate text and graphics.

Chapter 4

Text and Graphics Tools

Pictures convey information more efficiently than words or numbers—this is the philosophy behind the Macintosh's iconic interface. Understanding this, *HyperCard*'s creator Bill Atkinson—who wrote the seminal Mac paint program, *MacPaint*—has given *HyperCard* a complete set of painting tools built right into the program. With these tools, you can customize the look of your cards and stacks, adding graphics to augment the text and numeric information. You can go even further, creating new kinds of applications that contain nothing but pictures. In this chapter, you'll review *HyperCard*'s painting tools in preparation for creating some very visual stacks in Part II.

If you're an experienced Macintosh user, you undoubtedly got up to speed on the Mac with *MacPaint* or a similar paint program, such as *SuperPaint*. *HyperCard*'s graphics tools are based closely on *MacPaint* concepts, so you can wade right in. Create a blank card, tear off the Tools menu, and start to play. You'll find many small but welcome improvements over *MacPaint*. Refer to this chapter for more information and tips.

Some Graphics Fundamentals

The most fundamental fact of computer graphics is that you paint with *pixels*. A pixel *(picture element)* is one of the tiny black or white (or color if you have a Mac II) screen dots that make up the Mac's display. Text, graphics, and anything else you see on the screen are made up of pixels (as in Figure 4-1). A paint program

Figure 4-1. Pixels

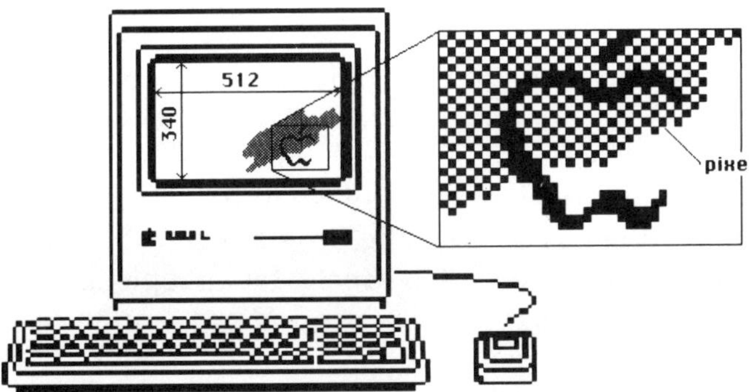

allows you to change each pixel's value (black or white) at will to create a picture, using analogs to the traditional artist's tools such as a pencil, eraser, paintbrush, page or canvas, and so on.

You can use the entire *HyperCard* window (which is 512 pixels wide × 340 pixels high, even on a large-screen display) or any part of it as your canvas. With *HyperCard*, unlike dedicated paint programs, you cannot create pictures bigger than the screen nor can you work in more than one window at a time. Also, present versions of *HyperCard* do not support color graphics. (Appendix D lists public domain and shareware stacks that let you add color and full-page printing capabilities to *HyperCard*.)

Graphics, like objects, occupy their own layers in the background and card domains. Background graphics appear on every card that shares the background, while card graphics are unique to one card. You can achieve some interesting effects by overlaying card graphics on background graphics or other background objects. For example, card graphics overlaid on a background field obscure text entered into the field, but background buttons can work right through card graphics, even if the button is covered.

TIP: Graphics and Stack Size. *HyperCard* graphics eat storage space and memory. Stacks with lots of graphics (for instance, background and card graphics on every card) take up more room than stacks with few graphics. A rather small 30-card graphics stack could easily take up 150K and more, and *HyperCard*'s Compact Stack feature is no help—it doesn't compress graphics. If keeping the size of your stack to the minimum is important, you'll want to limit your use of graphics. File-compression utility programs (*PackIt, StuffIt,* and so on) can be of some help when trying to fit a stack onto one floppy disk, but don't try to compress a stack that's over 770K onto a floppy—a user without a hard disk won't be able to expand it again.

Painting

Now we'll take a quick tour through the painting tools and menu options. A catalogue of every graphics effect possible with *HyperCard* is beyond the scope of this chapter, but we will cover those graphics that you're most likely to use—borders, data graphics, and the clip art supplied with the program.

In all likelihood, you're not a skilled artist—few people are—but this chapter does assume that you'll often find occasion to use graphics in your own stacks, either to create a visual environment for fields and buttons or as an integral part of the information you want to convey. Chapter 9 discusses more sophisticated visual effects.

Create a new stack with a new background. Tear off the Tools menu and position it at the left side of the screen (in *HyperCard* parlance, it now becomes a *palette*). Below the general tools in the Tools menu are the paint tools for drawing, erasing, creating shapes, and creating graphic text (see Figure 4-2).

Figure 4-2. Labeled Tools Menu

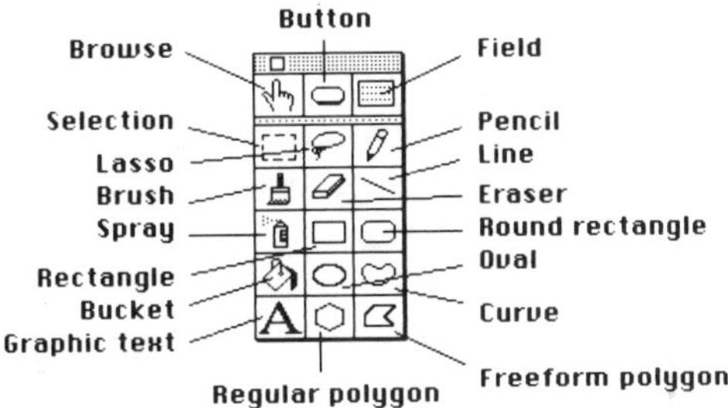

Select any paint tool by clicking on it. Immediately you'll see three new menus—*Paint, Options,* and *Patterns.* (Choose a general tool to restore the Objects menu.) Figures 4-3, 4-4, and 4-5 show the new menus.

The *Paint* menu provides commands for changing selected parts of your picture. The *Options* menu contains tools that aid in

Figure 4-3. Paint Menu

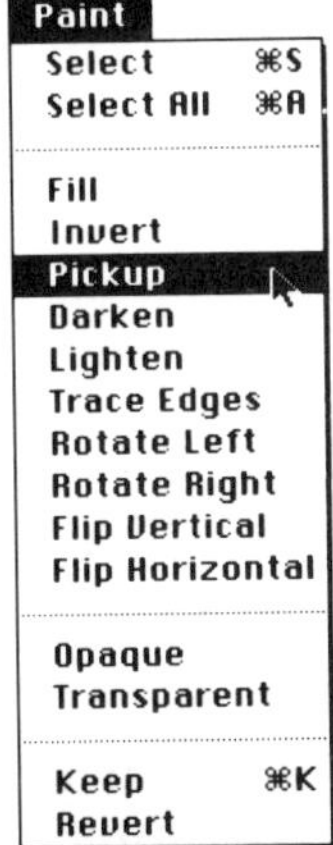

Figure 4-4. Options Menu

Figure 4-5. Patterns Menu

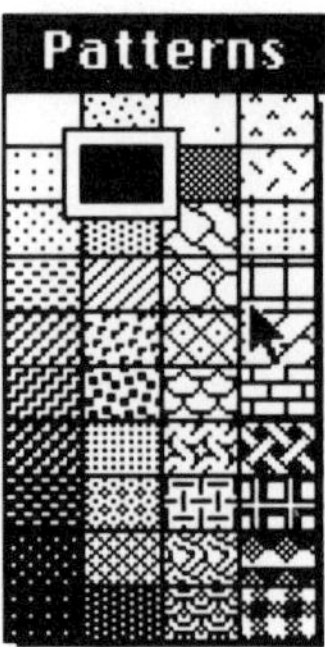

any painting operation or that modify the action of certain tools. The *Patterns* menu contains patterns that you can paint with and use to fill shape. Patterns is a tear-off menu and operates the same way. Select any pattern by clicking on it. Each of these menus is discussed in more detail in the following paragraphs.

Many paint tools can be switched on or off with *power keys*—command keyboard equivalents. A complete list of all graphics keyboard shortcuts can be found in Appendix C.

Now try out each tool. You needn't try to create a finished painting; just doodle with each tool until you feel comfortable with the way it works. When you select a paint tool and move out to the drawing area, the pointer turns into a cursor that lets you know which tool you're using (a pencil cursor for the Pencil tool, for example).

- Dragging the *Pencil* lays down a one-pixel-wide line in black (when you begin drawing on a white area) or white (when you begin drawing on a black area).
- Dragging the *Eraser* over your painting erases it completely. Clear the entire screen, erasing everything you've drawn by double-clicking on the Erase tool. Selecting Undo in the Edit menu (or pressing ˜ [tilde]) will undo your last paint action, as well as let you recover from erasing that goes too far.
- Use the *Selection* (power key S) and *Lasso* tools to manipulate parts of the painting without affecting other parts. *Selection* lets you draw a rectangular selection box around any part of the picture; the *Lasso* lets you draw a freehand loop around the area you want to select—handy for irregular shapes or tight spots. Once you've defined the selection, you can drag it to any other

part of the screen; cut, copy, paste, and clear it with the Edit functions; or modify it with the Paint menu. The most recently selected area stays selected until you choose another tool or select a new area.

> **TIP: Working with Selections.** Quickly copy a selection by pressing the Option key as you start to drag it (just like copying buttons and fields). A copy you can work with just like the original will peel off. Constrain the movement of the selected area to the horizontal or vertical axis only by pressing the Shift key as you begin to drag. Change the size of the selection by placing the tip of the pointer on an edge or corner of the selection and pressing the Command key as you drag. This resizing takes a little time, so drag slowly to maintain some control over the size. Selections can be made larger or smaller by moving away from or toward the center of the selection. To select everything on the screen, double-click on the Select tool.

- The *Brush tool* lets you draw with different brush shapes (32 in all). Call up the *Brush Shape* dialog box (Figure 4-6) by double-clicking on the Brush tool; then click on any brush shape to begin painting. All brushes paint in the current pattern.

Figure 4-6. Brush Shape Dialog Box

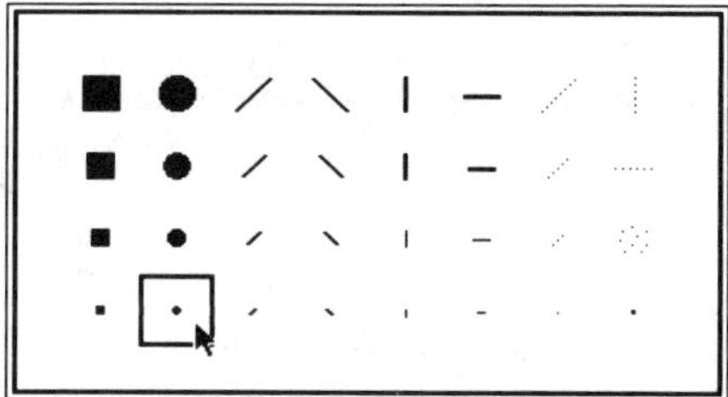

- *Spray* is the tool for stippling or shading in the current pattern.
- Use the *Bucket* to fill any bounded area with the current pattern. Place the tip of the Bucket's drip within the area you want to fill, and then click. The area must be completely enclosed; any gaps will allow the pattern to spill out and fill the open connecting areas in the rest of the painting. If that happens, use Undo and then close any gaps you find using the Pencil or the Brush.
- The *Line tool* draws straight lines. Click where you want the line to begin, then drag to the endpoint. Double-click on the Line

Figure 4-7. Line Size Dialog Box

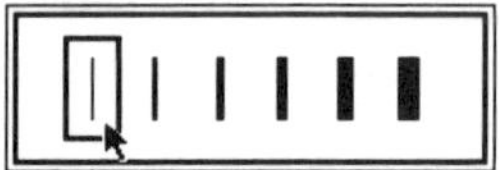

tool to bring up the *Line Size* dialog box (Figure 4-7). Click on one of the six line weights to choose it, or use the power keys 1–8, with 1 being the thinnest and 8 the thickest.

- The *Shape tools*—rectangle, rounded rectangle, curve, oval, regular polygon, and freeform polygon—enable you to make instant shapes in any proportions in the current line size. Draw rectangles and rounded rectangles just like selection boxes, dragging from one corner to its opposite. The oval tool makes ellipses that you can size along the horizontal or vertical dimensions (you can't tilt ovals at an oblique angle). Draw irregular curves with the Curve tool.

  There are two varieties of polygons (multisided figures): *regular* and *freeform*. With the Regular Polygon tool you can draw any of six equilateral shapes chosen from the *Polygon Sides* dialog box (Figure 4-8), accessible by double-clicking on the Regular Polygon tool. *Regular polygons* are created from the center out—drag until you reach the right diameter, and rotate the polygon around its center by dragging the pointer in a circle.

  To create *freeform polygons,* point to the irregular polygon tool (next to the regular polygon tool) and click on it. Outline the shape, clicking at every corner. When you're done, double-click on your last corner. If you want *HyperCard* to automatically connect the last corner to the point where your first line begins, use the same method with one variation: When choosing the freeform polygon tool before drawing your shape, *double-click* instead of just clicking. The double-click will activate *auto-connect* mode. (You can tell when you're in auto-connect mode because the shape tools in the tools menu palette will be shaded.) This auto-connect mode can be more accurately described as *auto-fill* mode because what *HyperCard* is really doing is filling your shape with the currently selected pattern.

Figure 4-8. Polygon Sides Dialog Box

> **TIP: Working with Shape Tools.** These techniques allow you to modify the actions of the shape tools as you draw. To draw a shape outlined in the current pattern, press the Option key as you drag. The patterned outline will be the same width as the current line size. To draw a shape bordered in black and filled with the current pattern, double-click on the tool icon—it will turn into a "filled" icon. Double-click again to return to drawing outlines only. To draw a filled shape with no border (actually, it has a border in the current pattern, so the border is indistinguishable from the rest of the shape), press the Option key as you drag. To make squares with the rectangle tools and circles with the oval tool, press the Shift key as you drag.

The Graphic Text Tool

The *graphic text* (also called *paint text*) tool is the last painting tool and deserves some additional discussion. As you may have guessed, graphic text works similarly to the word processing functions that allow you to add text to fields in the current typeface, font, and style. Graphic text, however, can be typed in anywhere on the painting area, not just within a field, by positioning the *I*-beam cursor and then typing. However, that's not the only difference. All the special things you can do with field text—for example, search for words or manipulate words with scripts (as you'll learn how to do in Chapter 5)—cannot be done with graphic text. Graphic text cannot be edited like field text; it can only be created, altered, or removed with the graphics tools (for example, by painting over it, erasing it, or using the selection tools to move it around). You cannot set a right margin for graphic text (the left margin is aligned with the point where you began typing), so graphic text won't "wrap" automatically to the next line at a specified margin; nor can you insert new text between already-typed words.

It's important to know when to use graphic text and when to use field text. Create a field and put text into it when you want the option of quickly changing the text later, if you want to be able to search for the text, or if you plan to write a script that will use the text in some way. Use graphic text when you won't be changing or searching the text (or when you don't want a stack user to) or when you want to do things like showing text in mirror image or tipped up on its side. One obvious and appropriate use for graphic text is to create labels for charts, graphs, pictures, and cards.

The graphic text tool has access to all available fonts and styles. Double-click on the tool to bring up the *Text Style* dialog box (Figure 3.12). Remember that graphic text cannot be edited like field text once you choose a new tool or exit painting mode—you can only paint over it to make changes. Also, the power keys are temporarily disabled when you select the graphic text tool.

Figure 4-9 illustrates the use of the painting tools in an actual painting.

Figure 4-9. Using the Painting Tools

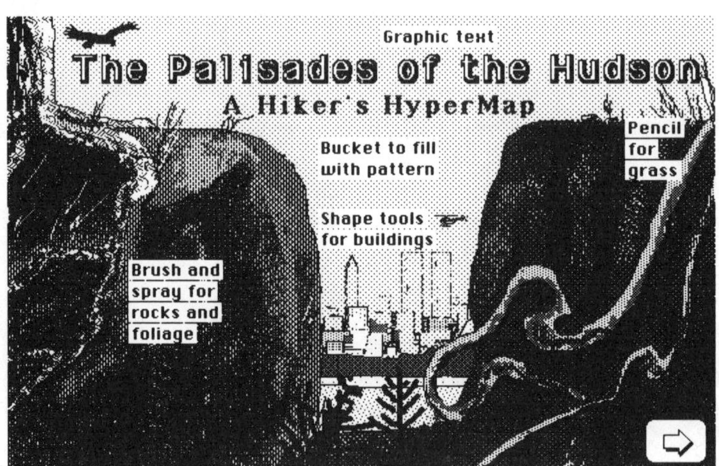

The Paint Menu

The Paint menu provides all kinds of special effects for manipulating selected areas.

Select (power key S) selects the last object drawn.

Select All (power key A) selects the whole screen.

Fill (power key F) works like the Bucket tool to fill the last-drawn of a selected shape with the current pattern.

Invert (power key I) creates a "negative image" of the selection.

Pickup (power key P) lets you select an image *within the outline* of a shape tool. Cover the image (an oval, for example) you wish to pick up with a filled borderless shape; then choose Pickup. The area within the shape will be selected.

Darken (power key D) randomly turns pixels in the selection to black, darkening the value of the whole selected area.

Lighten (power key L) randomly turns pixels in the selection white, lightening the value of the selected area. Darken and Lighten can be invoked repeatedly until you achieve a solid black or white area.

Trace Edges (power key E) outlines the selection by adding a one-pixel border completely surrounding any shape within the selection, while turning the shape itself white. Trace Edges can be done repeatedly by just holding down the E key.

Rotate Left (power key [ ) and Rotate Right (power key]) rotate the selection in 90-degree increments, clockwise (right) or counterclockwise (left), around it's center.

Flip Vertical (power key V) and **Flip Horizontal** (power key H) create mirror images of the selection along a vertical or horizontal line drawn through the center of the selection.

Opaque (power key O) and **Transparent** (power key T) render the white parts of the selection opaque or transparent, respectively. Typing Option-O will show you which areas on the screen are opaque by making them black while the keys are depressed.

TIP: Special Text Effects with the Paint Menu. Normally, graphic text is laid down as black letters on an opaque white background block. This block is automatically selected and remains selected as long as you don't begin typing in a different place or choose another tool, so it's available for manipulations with the Paint menu. Try these effects:

- Choose *Invert* from the Paint menu after typing to turn the text into white letters on a black background.
- Choose *Transparent* from the Paint menu after typing to let a pattern show through around the letters
- Choose *Invert* and *Transparent* and then drag the text over a patterned shape to create patterned letters. Note that these won't be too readable unless you use large-size type.
- Copy the text with *Copy,* or drag the text while pressing the *Option key* to peel off a copy. Make both copies transparent; lighten one copy with *Lighten,* and place the other over it, offset. This creates text with a drop shadow.
- Copy the text with *Copy,* or drag the text while pressing the *Option key* to peel off a copy. Flip it vertically, make it lighter with *Lighten,* and place it directly under the original text. This yields a "reflection."
- Rotate the text sideways to label graphics when there isn't enough horizontal space.
- Use *Trace Edges* to create "op art" letters.

These techniques are illustrated in Figure 4-10.

Figure 4-10. Graphic Text Techniques

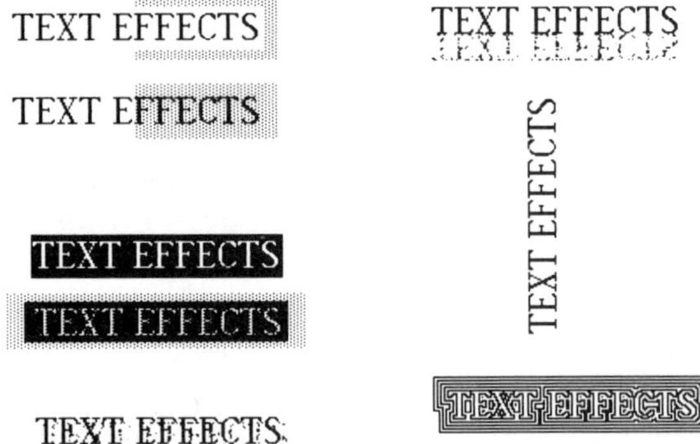

Saving Graphics

HyperCard does not save your work automatically when you're in the graphics mode (when a graphics tool is selected). Instead, you use the *Keep* and *Revert* options in the Paint menu (or press the K or R power key).

Keep saves the current picture.

Revert kills the current work and returns you to the last saved version. Revert is especially useful when used with the selection tool. If you select or lasso an area of your picture and then choose Revert, it will only revert to the earlier version within the selected area. That way, you can keep some new parts of the picture and revert to the earlier version only in the parts you don't like.

It isn't necessary to use Keep to save your graphic work if you're just making a minor change. *HyperCard* will save what you've done when you exit the painting mode or when you leave the stack or program. For extended painting, however, regular Keeping is important.

Suppose you don't like the way your painting looks but you've gone too far to simply Undo the problem. You can return to the last saved version of your painting with the Revert command.

The Options Menu

The Options menu gives you access to additional options that affect all painting operations. These options help you paint more precisely, or automatically perform tasks—such as drawing multiple lines—that would take a lot of time to do manually.

Grid (power key G) imposes an invisible 8 × 8 pixel matrix on the screen. With the grid on, the selection, line, rectangle, rounded rectangle, oval, and polygon tools operate only along the grid lines or center on its vertices, making precise spacing and alignment of lines and shapes easy to achieve.

FatBits (Option-F) is *HyperCard*'s magnifying glass for doing detail work with any painting tool. It shows a section of your painting (64 × 43 pixels, or about 1.5 percent of the screen) in high magnification, over 60×. Enter FatBits by choosing it from the Options menu; by double-clicking on the Pencil; by pressing Option-F; or by positioning the Pencil on the screen, pressing the Command key, and clicking. A small window opens that shows you the magnified area in normal scale. Scroll around the screen while in FatBits by pressing the Option key and dragging the grabbing hand cursor. Exit FatBits by choosing it again from the Options menu; by double-clicking on the Pencil again; by pressing Option-F again; by pressing Command and clicking with the Pencil; or by clicking in the small window.

Power Keys toggles on and off the ability to use the power keys.

Line Size . . . , Brush Shape . . . , and **Poly Sides . . .** call up the dialog boxes shown earlier in this chapter.

Edit Pattern . . . summons the dialog box in Figure 4-11, which is used to edit existing patterns and to create new ones.

Figure 4-11. Edit Pattern Dialog Box

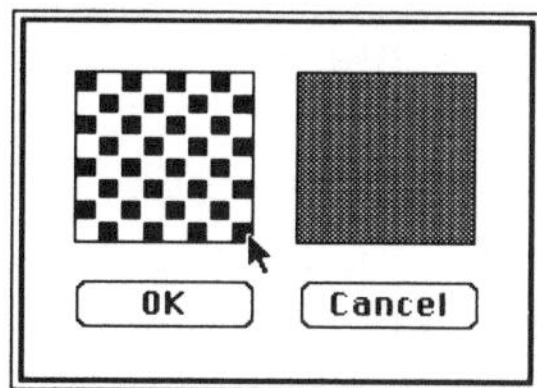

The left-hand box is an 8 × 8 pixel FatBits representation of the current pattern; the right-hand box shows how the pattern looks in normal scale. Click on any black pixel in the FatBits section to turn it white and on any white pixel to turn it black. To save your new pattern, click on OK. The edited/new pattern appears in the position of the original pattern and will be saved there when you choose Keep or exit painting mode. There's no way to add more than the 40 patterns supplied with *HyperCard*,

Figure 4-12. New Patterns

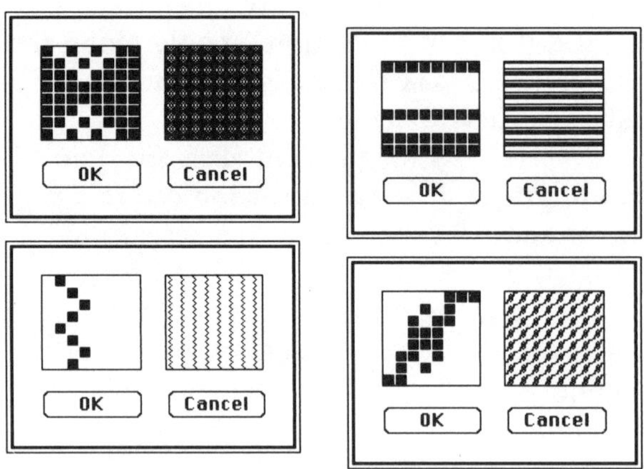

so be sure you really want to eliminate one of the supplied patterns before you do this. (You can always recreate a supplied pattern later, if you want.) Another way to create a new pattern is to call up the Edit Pattern box and then click on any area of the current painting. *HyperCard* will read an 8 × 8 pixel area around the point on which you clicked and make it a pattern. Figure 4-12 shows some new patterns created with Edit Pattern.

Draw Filled causes the shape tools to draw, filled with the current pattern.

Draw Centered (power key C) and **Draw Multiple** (power key M) affect the way the line and shape tools operate, and can be used in tandem for interesting effects. Draw Centered lets you draw a shape from the center out, rather than from the corner. Draw Multiple leaves "traces" as you create a shape. Draw Centered and Draw Multiple have no effect on the Pencil, Brush, Spray, Curve, Bucket, or Freeform Polygon tools. Figure 4-13 shows some shapes drawn with Draw Centered and Draw Multiple.

Patterns Menu

The Patterns menu contains readymade patterns you can use to fill any shape. Every pattern is constructed on an 8 × 8 pixel matrix. Choose any pattern by clicking on it; the current pattern is boxed so you can identify it. Double-clicking on a pattern brings up the Edit Pattern dialog box, shown above.

Figure 4-13. Shapes Drawn with Draw Centered and Draw Multiple

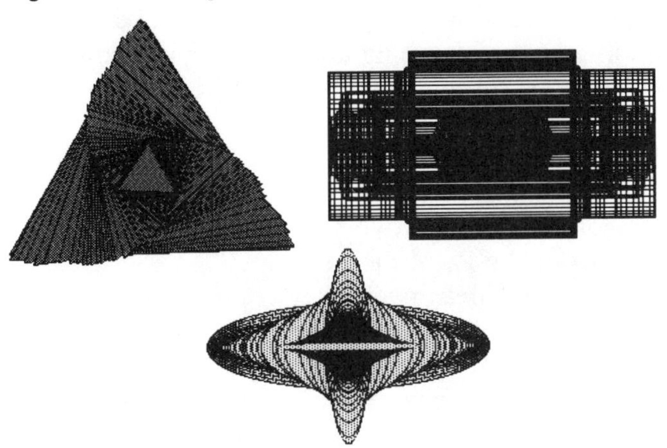

Making a Card Border

Let's practice using the painting tools to create a simple "file cards" border similar to ones used in many *HyperCard* stacks.

- This will be a background graphic, so enter background mode.
- Tear off the Tools menu, select the rectangle shape tool, and tear off the Patterns menu.
- Draw an opaque white rectangle as shown in Figure 4-14. Use the narrowest line size for the outline of the rectangle.
- The rectangle will be ruled with lines 20 pixels apart. To do this, enter FatBits and scroll to the bottom of the rectangle.
- Use the line tool to draw a vertical line 20 pixels high (you can count pixels in FatBits).

Figure 4-14. Card Border 1

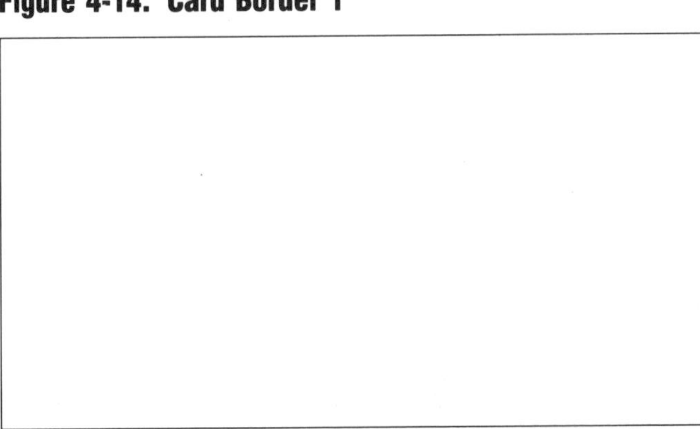

- Draw a horizontal line parallel to the bottom line of the rectangle at the top of the vertical line—there should be 20 pixels between the bottom line of the rectangle and the new horizontal line, not including the 1-pixel thicknesses of the horizontal lines themselves.
- Use the eraser to erase the vertical line.
- Now exit FatBits.
- Use the Selection tool to select the two parallel lines, and choose Transparent from the Paint menu.
- Press Option and Shift, and then peel away copies of the two lines and place them one on top of the other to create the rules for the index card. To maintain proper spacing between the copies, overlay the bottom line of each new copy over the top line of the previous copy. (You'll need to choose Transparent for each new copy.)
- Leave extra space at the top of the index card, and use the line tool to add a narrow double rule as in Figure 4-15.

Figure 4-15. Card Border 2

- Now create a "stack" of index cards. Pick up the whole rectangle with the selection tool, choose Opaque from the Paint menu (most of the card will still be transparent), and press Option to peel off a copy.
- Position the second copy offset slightly to the upper left of the first.
- Repeat the process twice more. The result is shown in Figure 4-16.

Figure 4-16. Card Border 3

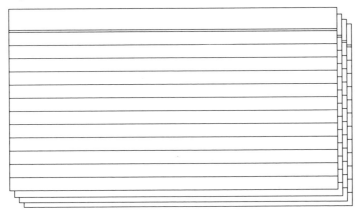

- Finally, add a gray tone around the index cards. Choose the solid gray from the patterns menu, choose the Bucket, and click outside of the index cards. Figure 4-17 illustrates the finished border.

It will be easy to position a background field to fit over the ruled area. Create a new field, open the Field Info box, and click on Font. Set the text line height to 20; then you can position and resize the new field to exactly match the size and ruling of the top index card. A separate background title field can be placed along the top.

Figure 4-17. Card Border 4

Mixing Text and Graphics

Your *HyperCard* graphics will nearly always be used in conjunction with text. The following figures offer some ideas on how to integrate text and graphics effectively. Included are samples of a diagram, a chart, and a map.

Figure 4-18. Diagram

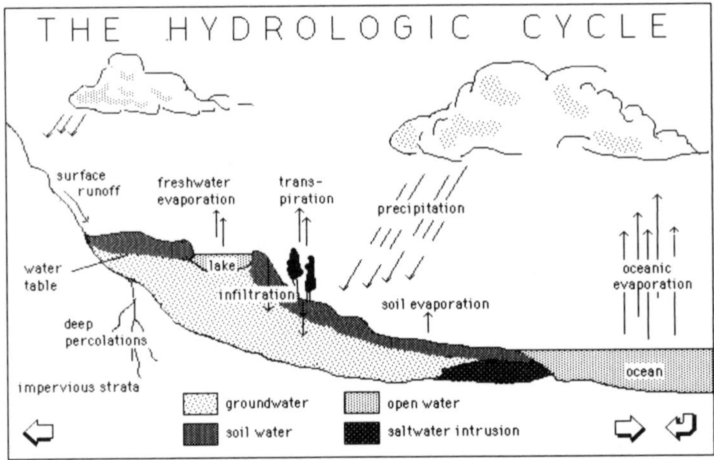

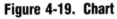

Figure 4-19. Chart

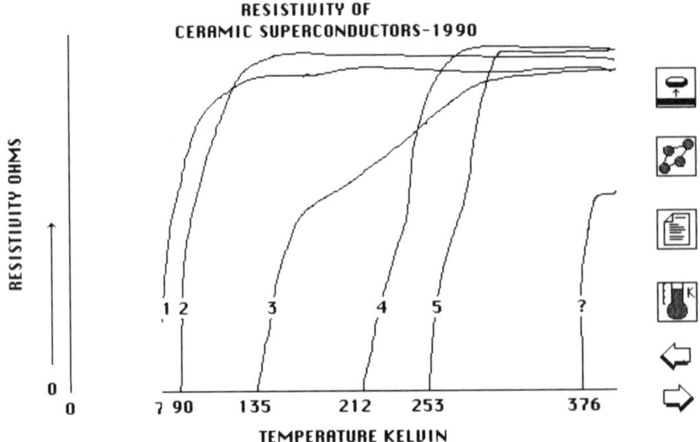

Figure 4-20. Map

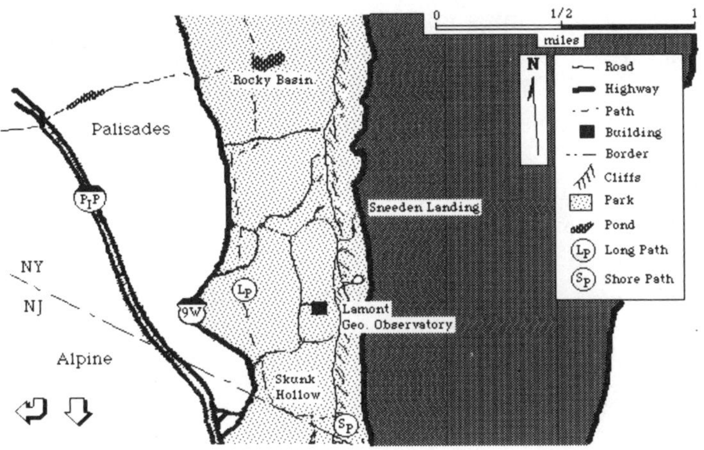

TIP: Effective Data Graphics. Your *HyperCard* stacks may call for maps, charts, graphs, and other kinds of *data graphics* for presenting numeric, geographic, or structural information. (In fact, a map or diagram of a complex stack, with buttons linked to the represented parts, is a required aid for the user navigating the stack.) Data graphics can make the complex relationships among data easier to understand—but only if the graphic itself is easy to understand. There are a few guidelines to follow when designing data graphics:

- Get the data right, and make sure you understand the relationship between data sets. If you don't, neither will the stack user.
- Make sure data always takes precedence over design. Let the data guide your choice of design.
- Avoid cluttering your graphic with extraneous patterns (especially patterns that vibrate), lines, and dingbats. The fewer marks to distract from the message of the data, the clearer that message will be.
- Use labels whenever necessary; spell out words and place them near what they describe.
- Once you've designed your data graphic, look at it critically to see what should be removed and what should be added for clarity.

Far and away, the best book on designing data graphics is *The Visual Display of Quantitative Information* by Edward R. Tufte (Graphics Press, Box 430, Cheshire, Connecticut, 06410). No designer should be without it.

Clip Art

The *HyperCard* package comes with a healthy selection of *clip art* (readymade pictures you can use freely in your own stacks). Tour through the Art Ideas, Card Ideas, and Stack Ideas stacks on the *HyperCard* Ideas disk to see graphics you can modify as your own. You can paste whole cards of art into your stacks using the techniques discussed in the previous chapter, or use the Selection tool or Lasso to copy art to the Clipboard.

There are also scores of disks full of clip art available from commercial developers—everything from dinosaurs to nineteenth-century scenes to a thousand different varieties of flowchart arrows. Any clip art can be incorporated into your *HyperCard* stacks using the techniques outlined below.

Importing and Exporting Graphics

HyperCard can import, create, and export graphics that conform to the standard *MacPaint* file format. Popular paint programs such as *MacPaint*, *FullPaint*, and *SuperPaint* all create and save *MacPaint* documents, although that may not be the only document format they create. Most structured drawing programs, such as *MacDraw*, *MacDraft*, and *Cricket Draw*, offer the option of saving *MacPaint* documents, too. Other Mac picture file formats, including PICT, TIFF (Tag Image File Format), and EPSF (Encapsulated *PostScript* File) are not compatible with current versions of *HyperCard*, although there are public domain utilities and DAs to help you translate images from any format to the *MacPaint* format, and there is at least one stack (see Appendix D) that enables you to import PICT documents directly into *HyperCard*.

Making sure you're still in painting mode, pull down the File menu. The usual options are not available; instead, the only available choices are Import Paint and Export Paint.

To import pictures:

- Make sure your graphics program creates *MacPaint* files.
- Align the upper left corner of your picture with the upper left corner of the screen (leaving room for the menu bar). If you don't, you may lose the lower right part of your picture. Also, keep in mind that if your picture is bigger than the *HyperCard* screen size, you'll have to trim it, shrink it, or break it up into screen-size panels and load each onto a separate card.

- Open *HyperCard* and go to the stack you'll be working with.
- Select a painting tool from the Tools menu and New Card from the Edit menu.
- Enter card or background mode, depending on where you want to load the graphic; then choose Import Paint from the File menu.
- Select the picture you want to import from the Open File dialog box that appears. The picture will then load into *HyperCard* as an opaque graphics layer.
- Another way to import graphics to *HyperCard* is through the Clipboard or Scrapbook.

  Copy the image into the Clipboard or Scrapbook from your application.

  Load *HyperCard*.

  Then paste the image onto a card.

To export pictures:

- Go to the card that contains the picture you want to export. Keep in mind that *HyperCard* will export the whole screen as a standard *MacPaint* file.
- Choose a paint tool; then Export Paint from the File menu.
- *HyperCard* will display a standard Save File dialog box asking you to name the picture and designate the disk and folder you want to save it in.
- Graphics can also be exported via the Clipboard or Scrapbook in the usual way.

> **TIP: Screen Shooting.** You can capture any Mac screen to disk, including *HyperCard* screens, by pressing Command-Shift-3. This will create a picture file named *Screen 0,* which you can then load into a paint program. You can save up to ten screens in this way (Screen 0–Screen 9) before you have to delete or rename some of them. Command-Shift-4 sends the screen to your printer instead of to a picture file. Note that this screenshot feature doesn't work if you're pulling down a menu or viewing a dialog box. To include menus and dialog boxes in your picture, you should use a screenshot DA called *Camera,* by Keith A. Esau. It's widely available on bulletin boards and from user groups.

With object and graphics manipulation under your belt, you're ready to tackle the last frontier of *HyperCard* authoring—writing scripts. That's the subject of the next chapter.

Chapter 5
Scripting with HyperTalk

As you've seen in earlier chapters, there's much you can do with *HyperCard* using the tools and techniques you've already encountered. But to gain real control over the power of *HyperCard*, to realize the full potential of the program to do the kind of work you need it to do, you'll have to take one more step and learn to program in *HyperCard*'s scripting language, HyperTalk.

If you've never programmed a computer before, the prospect may seem daunting. The typical vision of a computer programmer is of a bleary-eyed nerd working all night on code made of solid blocks of numbers containing only 0s and 1s. That picture may not fit your self-image, or you may feel you don't have the time to learn any programming languages, most of which seem to be composed mainly of backslashes, asterisks, periods, and arcane abbreviations.

HyperTalk programming isn't like that. There are no 0s and 1s, no unusual punctuation marks. HyperTalk is very much like English; using it is similar to talking to a two-year-old child. Parents know that the best way to talk to a toddler is with direct commands and clear questions, using words the child understands. If you use words or sentence structures the child doesn't know, you'll get a blank look and no reaction. (Of course, sometimes you get no reaction even if the child does understand what you're saying.) It's the same with HyperTalk. Once you've mastered HyperTalk's English-like vocabulary and simple sentence structure, you can make *HyperCard* do anything within its power—and *HyperCard*, unlike children, will always obey.

This chapter will ease you into familiarity with HyperTalk. The first section gives you some background on the theory behind HyperTalk; the second one describes the use of the script editing window, where you enter scripts; and the last section analyzes several sample scripts, so you'll be ready to tackle the longer scripts in Part II of this book.

What Are Scripts?

Scripts are sets of instructions in HyperTalk that define the actions and responses of *HyperCard* objects. It's a script, for example, that tells a Home button to take you Home, or tells a stack to hide or show the message box. Scripts are also properties of objects, like the text height of a field or the style of a button.

Just to get a sense of what a script looks like, here's a short button script:

```
on mouseUp
  go to the first card in this stack
end mouseUp
```

Without knowing anything much about HyperTalk, you can get a good idea of what this script is all about. An event connected with the mouse is triggering the button to take the user to the first card in the current stack. When that's done, the script ends. Believe it or not, many button scripts are just this simple and comprehensible. By the end of this chapter, you'll be able to write scripts much longer and more involved than this one.

Although we'll be working primarily with button scripts in this chapter, you should know that all objects have scripts. However, not all scripts contain instructions. The typical field, for example, has a blank script; no special instructions are needed for the field to accomplish its basic function of acting as a container for text information. Most buttons, on the other hand, require unique scripts to tell them what to do. From now on, when this book refers to scripts, it means scripts containing instructions. Just remember that many objects you'll create need no scripting on your part to perform their jobs.

Nor is it always necessary to write a script just to send a command to an object or to *HyperCard*. The message box provides a perfect way to issue short communiqués to the program without having to go through the trouble of creating an object and writing a script for it. The message box does have its limitations, though. You can only type in one line at a time, and the message box doesn't recognize many of the more advanced aspects of HyperTalk, such as control structures (see below). If you have a complex set of tasks you want performed, a script is the only way to go. However, the message box is perfect for displaying the results of many scripts, as you see when you work through the scripts in Appendix A (the HyperTalk glossary).

Separate objects are separate entities, and so are their scripts. Modifying one script won't necessarily affect any other script—writing scripts is a very modular process. This modularity makes it easy to test and fix scripts, which doesn't mean that scripts can't be interdependent—you'll often write scripts that use the result of an action determined by the script of another object, or scripts that direct another script to start executing its instructions.

Messages and Message Handlers

The communication between scripts mentioned above is a form of *message passing*. A *message* is any kind of internal *HyperCard* communication. For example, you've used the message box to send HyperTalk messages to *HyperCard*, such as *go last*. Messages can be passed among objects, between *HyperCard* and any object, and from external programs (such as the Finder) to *HyperCard*. In fact, the main activity of *HyperCard* is the passing of messages, which happens many times a second. *HyperCard* even sends "idle" messages to the current card when nothing else is happening (you can use these idle messages to do various kinds of useful work). Think of *HyperCard* as a complex communications network like the phone network, with messages constantly passing back and forth among all the objects in the program, including *HyperCard* itself. How does an object recognize messages meant for it? The object's script must contain a component called a *message handler*, which can trigger the action of the script when it receives the proper message. In the case of a button, for example, it works like this:

- You move the browse hand over the area of the button.
- As the browse hand moves across the perimeter of the button, *HyperCard* sends a *mouseEnter* message to the button. While the pointer is inside the boundary of the button, *HyperCard* sends *mouseWithin* messages to the button. The button doesn't have message handlers for these messages, so they're ignored.
- You click on the button.
- *HyperCard* detects the mouse click on the area of the button and sends a *mouseUp* message (which means, in HyperTalk, that the mouse button has been released at the end of a click) to the button.
- The button intercepts the *mouseUp* message. At the beginning of the button's script is a message handler that begins *on mouseUp*. Since the message received by the button matches the first line of the message handler, the button "knows" to take the actions specified by the script.

- The button follows the instructions in its script (this invariably involves sending more messages via the HyperTalk statements in the script) until it encounters the end of the message handler—in this case, the script line *end mouseUp*.
- Since the message has been received and acted upon, it goes no further.

Messages and the Object Hierarchy

Suppose there's more than one button with a message handler beginning *on mouseUp*? How does *HyperCard* know exactly which button to send the mouseUp message to? It's actually quite simple: Messages are routed through *HyperCard* along the object hierarchy. (See Chapter 3, Figure 3-1.) Message routing works like this:

- When *HyperCard* first detects an event, such as a mouse click, it passes a message to the object—referred to as the *target*—under the browse tool. Messages are generally routed immediately to their most obvious level. For example, an *openCard* message goes directly to the card level.
- If the *target*—a button—has the proper message handler (a script that begins *on mouseUp*), the message is received and acted upon. (The object with the currently executing handler is called *Me*, logically enough).
- If the target can't receive the message, the message is bounced back to *HyperCard*. *HyperCard* then sends the message to the next rung up the ladder. If the next object up—the card—also doesn't have the proper message handler, the message continues on up the hierarchy until it meets an object that does have the proper message handler.
- Eventually, the message may reach the top rung—*HyperCard* itself. If *HyperCard* can't do anything with the message, the message is ignored and *HyperCard* begins waiting for the next event. If *HyperCard* doesn't recognize the message (if, for example, you use a word in a script that isn't allowed in HyperTalk), the program displays an error dialog box. The entire process is diagrammed in Figure 5-1.

One thing you should note about this system of message passing is that only one message can be passed and acted upon at any one time. You've seen a practical example of this if you've

Figure 5-1. Message Passing

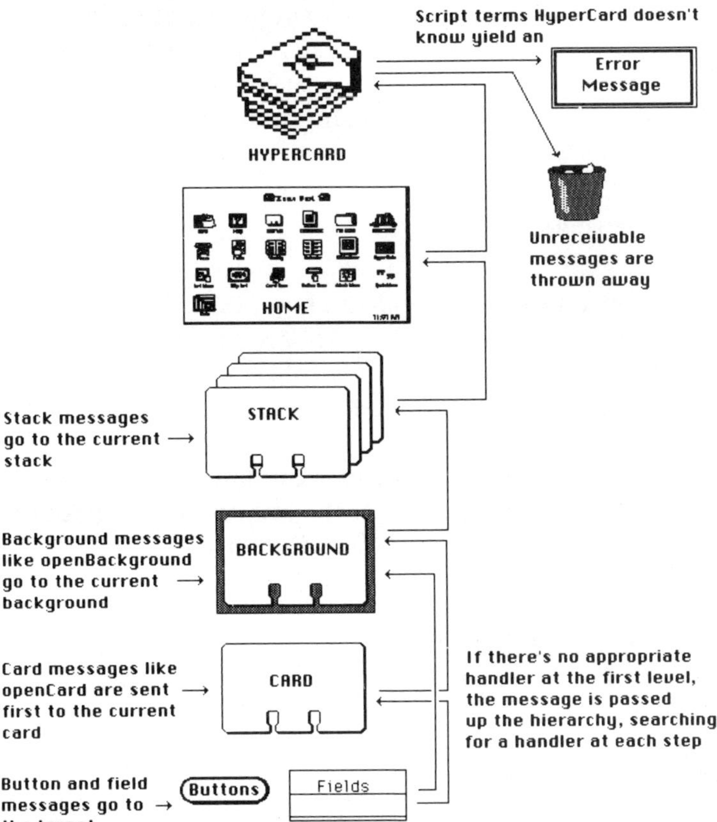

tried to activate two buttons at once—only one works. In general, *HyperCard* works so fast that this restriction is not noticeable, but occasionally you'll be forced to wait as a long message works its way through before you can go on to the next task. Things in general go much faster on a Mac II or an accelerated Mac Plus or SE, so consider improving your hardware if you hate to wait for your Mac.

It's important to understand the principles of messages and message passing for two reasons: One, you'll often want to use scripts to fire off messages to other objects (with one mouse click, for example, you can trigger the scripts of ten different objects); two, you'll need to decide which rung of the hierarchy to assign your scripts. Chapter 6 deals with this in more detail.

HyperTalk Basics

Now that you understand how HyperTalk communicates, let's look more closely at HyperTalk as a language. As noted, HyperTalk has been designed to be as close as possible to English in structure and syntax. You can use English grammar to guide you in writing a HyperTalk sentence. For example,

```
go to the first card of the "Help" stack
```

is a legitimate sentence in English and in HyperTalk. However, HyperTalk also understands statements that are more compressed than standard English allows—statements that have a pidgin-English flavor. For example, "Go card 1" is poor English but efficient HyperTalk.

HyperTalk is forgiving about improper capitalization and the number of spaces between words, but it is very unforgiving about spelling—terms and names in messages and scripts must be

Table 5-1. Abbreviations and Synonyms

Versions 1.0.1, 1.1, and 1.2	Version 1.2 only
abbr, abbrev, abbreviated	
bkgnd, background	bg
bkgnds, backgrounds	bgs
btn, button	
buttons	btns
card	cd
cards	cds
char, character	
chars, characters	
field	fld
fields	flds
gray	grey
loc, location	
mid, middle	
msg, message	
picture	pict
poly, polygon	
prev, previous	
rect, rectangle	
reg, regular	
secs, seconds	sec, second (time increment, not ordinal)
ticks	tick

spelled correctly or you'll get an error message when you try to run the script. In compound words like *mouseUp,* the first letter of the second part of the word is capitalized, but this is only a convention. Some abbreviations are allowed; the most common are *msg* for the message box, *bkgnd* for background, *loc* for location, and *rect* for rectangle. Table 5-1 lists allowed abbreviations and synonyms for common HyperTalk terms.

A limited number of connecting words and prepositions are also available to help make writing HyperTalk scripts more like writing English. *Is, to, before, into, after, of, by, this, contains,* and so on can be used in HyperTalk. However, you must use the right preposition in the right circumstances. For example, you can write "click *at* field 1" in HyperTalk, but writing "click *on* field 1" will only earn you an error message. The words *of* and *in* are interchangeable.

Statements

Most statements in HyperTalk follow a simple imperative structure—verb-adverb-object-indirect object, or, in HyperTalk, *command-parameters.* Here are four *HyperCard* statements broken down into their functional parts:

Command	Parameter(s)
go	back
doMenu	"New Card"
get	word 1 of card field 3
visual	dissolve very fast to black

You'll find 11 kinds of terms in HyperTalk statements. The main categories are *commands, constants, control structures, functions, operators, properties,* and *system messages*. The terms in each of these categories have been chosen and defined by HyperTalk's developers. In addition, there are four kinds of terms that change with each use: *object names, literals, chunks,* and *containers.* Each category of terms is defined briefly in the following paragraphs.

Command. One of the action words such as *go, find, get, put, sort, open, play,* and so on. Almost all commands can be easily tested from the message box.

> **TIP: HyperTalk Command Bug.** After steady use, you may find that *HyperCard* no longer recognizes certain HyperTalk commands, like *get* and *put*. This is a bug in version 1.0.1. You can have temporary relief from this problem by replacing the corrupted copy of *HyperCard* with fresh copies made directly from your original disks. *Never use your original disks as your working disks.* The best solution is to upgrade to later versions of the program.

Constant. A word which substitutes for a predefined value that never changes. The value returned by pressing the Tab key, for example, is a constant. Examples are *up, down, quote, return, true,* and *false.*

Control structures. (Also known as *conditional structures.*) Terms that allow a script to make a decision or repeat an action with variations. Control structures include *if. . .then, if. . .then. . .else,* and *repeat.* For example:

```
on mouseUp
  if "janet" is in field 1 then
    put field 1 into the msg box
  end if
end mouseUp
```

Like system messages (see below), control structures have to be given an explicit ending—in the example above, *end if.*

Function. Returns the current state of a *HyperCard* or Macintosh activity. A function always returns a result in text or numbers, such as the current time and date, or the number of characters in a text field. Typical functions are the date, the time, and the location.

Operator. A mathematical function, such as + (plus), / (divide), and ^ (exponent). Like functions, operators return a value, such as a sum or quotient.

Property. Any characteristic of a *HyperCard* object, such as its location, style, or name. There is a HyperTalk term for every object property and for every painting property. You can set any object property from a script.

System messages. Scripts are triggered by *system messages*—messages sent by *HyperCard* about the condition of the mouse, keyboard, and other system activities. *MouseUp,* the message that the mouse button has been released, is already familiar to you, but there are several other mouse-related messages, including *mouseDown, mouseStillDown, mouseEnter, mouseWithin,* and *mouseLeave,* as well as system message connected with other objects, the keyboard, and *HyperCard* itself. Any script that begins with a trap for a system message—*on mouseUp*—has to end with the closing of that message trap—*end mouseUp.*

System messages are not the only kinds of messages that can trigger scripts: You can trigger a script with any message as long as you send the message at a lower level in the hierarchy and intercept it with the appropriate handler at a higher level, or send the message to an object at the same level of the hierarchy with the Send command.

For example, a button script could read:

```
on mouseUp
  sourPickle
end mouseUp
```

The message sourPickle is obviously not a term from HyperTalk; however, if the current card has a script with the right handler, such as the following:

```
on sourPickle
  show the msg box
  put "What about my pastrami on rye?" in the msg box
end sourPickle
```

SourPickle can be intercepted like any other message and used to initiate a script; thus you can name and define your own messages at any time. Each of these HyperTalk term categories is discussed in more depth in Appendix A, "HyperTalk Glossary." There, you'll also find a definition of every individual HyperTalk term with a sample script showing how it is used. Take the time at the end of this chapter to browse through Appendix A to get a feel for HyperTalk's large vocabulary. Appendix B, "HyperTalk Quick-Reference Index," is an alphabetical index that will help you to quickly find any term in the HyperTalk Glossary.

Object Names and Numbers

Object names and numbers are really properties of the objects, as you saw in Chapter 3, but deserve additional mention here because you'll use them constantly in scripts. You can specify an object in a script by its given name *(background field "Lincoln")*, order number *(bkgnd field 4)*, id number *(bkgnd field id 2345)*, or—in the case of a card—position in the stack *(next card)*. The id number or given name are the safest ways to refer to an object because object number or card position in a stack may change if objects are added to or deleted from the immediate environment. Even a given name can be changed; id number is the only absolute reference. Also, don't start an object's given name with a number (field "99 bottles of beer")—that will confuse *HyperCard* to no end. If you're specifying an object that isn't in the current stack, use the full path name *(card field "FDR" of card "20th-C" of stack "Presidents")*.

Literals

Literals are text strings of any length, either of letters or of numbers, whose contents do not evaluate to another number. "My name is Miriam" and "12345" are examples of literals. "12 * 2" is not a literal, since it evaluates to 24. Literals are always enclosed in open and close quotation marks and cannot include a carriage return. Proper names, menu options ("Stack Info . . . "), or text you want HyperTalk to treat just as text are all literals and should be in quotation marks.

Containers, Chunks, and Variables

In *HyperCard*, literals and other numeric or text information are held in *containers*. A container holds information until that information is asked for by a script or message. Examples of containers are fields with text in them, the current selection, the message box, and special entities known as *variables*, which are containers created by and purely for the use of messages and scripts. Any of these can hold information for use in a script. *HyperCard* treats the name of the container as standing for the contents of the container.

Most containers are temporary holders, lasting only for the duration of the current message handler and emptying when you quit the program. Only the text in fields is saved to disk.

You can ask for information in a container by item—a piece of text set off by commas, such as part of an address—or by characters, words, and in the case of fields, lines. To put only the street name of the address *150 Goff Rd., Newington, CT* held in container field 1 into container field 2, a script would say:

```
put word 2 of item 1 of field 1 into line 1 of field 2
```

Note: You can add text to any line of a field as long you give the line number in your script and as long as there is enough room in the line to accept the text you want to insert. Other types of containers don't have this ability.

If you want to retrieve text from a container in a different order or arrangement, use the *concatenate* symbol—an *ampersand* (&). Here's an example from the address above:

```
put char 2 of word 3 of item 1 of field 1 & char 2 of word 2 of field 1 & char 1 of word 2 of
field 1 into line 2 of field 2
```

This puts *dog* into field 2. You can concatenate as many items as you like; use a *double ampersand* (&&) to put a space between the concatenated items.

Chunks are just that—pieces of the contents of a container that have been sliced out by a script and used in some way. Use this format to specify any chunk—"char 2 to 8," "item 3 to 5," "word 1 to 7." Specify a chunk by the smallest unit to the largest:

```
char 1 of word 2 of item 3 of line 4 of background field 5 of card id 7
```

You cannot specify a stack in the chunk; you must go to the proper stack first.

Variables are especially flexible and useful containers. There are two kinds: *local* (active only for the duration of the current message handler), and *global* (active until you specifically eliminate them). Variables can have any name you like; the one exception to this is that you cannot name a variable with a HyperTalk term. For example:

```
put field 1 into knockwurst        --HyperCard will put the contents of field
                                   --1 into a local variable named knockwurst

put knockwurst into boiledCabbage       --variable knockwurst is put into a new
                                        --variable, boiledCabbage

put boiledCabbage into field 2     --the contents of boiledCabbage (which are
                                   --the same as the contents of knockwurst)
                                   --are put into field 2
```

The knockwurst and boiledCabbage variables exist only for the duration of the current handler. If you end the script and then try to access knockwurst from another script, *HyperCard* won't remember what you're talking about.

It is used as the name for a local variable that is called for automatically by certain commands, such as *get, ask,* and *convert.* For example, the command

```
get location of button "ClickMe"
```

automatically puts the location of the button into the special local variable, *It.* You can then type "put it into the msg box" to display the button location coordinates in the message box. Once you've used it, *It* is emptied automatically.

Global variables have a longer life. In fact, a global will last as long as you need it to, but you must specifically create it with the global command:

```
on mouseUp
  global pepperoni              --creates a global variable and names it pepperoni
  put field 1 into pepperoni
end mouseUp
```

The global variable *pepperoni,* which now contains the contents of field 1, is still available for use by any other message handler. Simply declare the global at the beginning of the script:

```
on mouseUp
 global pepperoni               --declares the global variable pepperoni,
                                --which still has the same contents
 put pepperoni into field 2
end mouseUp
```

The Structure of Scripts

From the sample scripts above, you should already be getting a sense of how scripts are structured. The basic characteristics of scripts are listed below.

- A script handler must have a definite beginning and end, signaled by *on* and *end* message traps. The standard handler structure is:

  on <messageName>
  <statement>
  end <messageName>

with <messageName> the name of the message that starts the handler—***mouseUp*, for example**

- The body of the script contains statements composed of commands and control structures. Each command and component of a control structure has its own line, followed by a Return keypress.
- The body of the script is automatically indented by *HyperCard*. There may be more than one level of indention if the script contains control structures, especially control structures nested inside other control structures.
- Every level of indention must be "closed" so that the script always ends flush left.
- A script can contain any number of message handlers. Each handler has to conform to the structural charateristics just listed. Message handlers within one script should be separated by a line space.
- Comments on the operation of the script by its author are preceded by a double dash (--); HyperTalk *ignores any text after a double dash.*

The Script Window

All script editing is accomplished in the script editing window (actually, it's a kind of dialog box). The script window is accessible from the object dialog boxes—click on the Script button to see the current object's script. (You don't have to be in background mode to see the scripts of background objects.) Figure 5-2 shows a script in its native environment.

Figure 5-2. Script Window and Sample Script

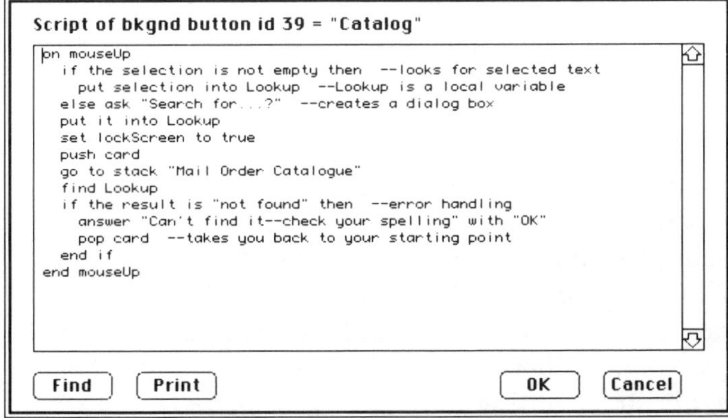

Script of bkgnd button id 39 = "Catalog"

```
on mouseUp
  if the selection is not empty then  --looks for selected text
    put selection into Lookup  --Lookup is a local variable
  else ask "Search for...?"  --creates a dialog box
  put it into Lookup
  set lockScreen to true
  push card
  go to stack "Mail Order Catalogue"
  find Lookup
  if the result is "not found" then  --error handling
    answer "Can't find it--check your spelling" with "OK"
    pop card  --takes you back to your starting point
  end if
end mouseUp
```

Find Print OK Cancel

TIP: Quick Script Access. To bypass the Info dialog box and see the script of an object directly, click on the object's info option in the Objects menu while holding down the Shift key. If the object is a button or field, you'll first have to choose the proper tool and then select the field or button. With buttons or fields, you can also click on the proper tool and then double-click on the desired button or field while holding down the Shift key.

Version 1.2 Note: More Quick Script Access Added script access keyboard shortcuts in Version 1.2 are:

- To see the script of any button or field when in browsing mode, press Shift-Command-Option and click on the field or button.
- To see the script of any field in field mode, press Command-Option and click on the field.
- To see script of any button in button mode, press Command-Option and click on the button.
- To see the script of the current card in any mode, press Command–Option-C.
- To see the script of the current background, press Command–Option-B.
- To see the script of the current stack, press Command–Option-S.
- To exit the script window without saving any changes, press Command-Option and click or press any key.

As with other Mac dialog boxes, the menus don't work while the script window is visible. (This means, for instance, that you cannot change the typeface of the script window without recourse to a resource editor like ResEdit.) You must edit scripts with the keyboard equivalents to the menu editing tools. Table 5-2 lists the keyboard script formatting and editing commands.

The Find and Print functions are available in button form along the bottom of the script window. Click on OK or press Enter to save your script.

You can paste text into a script from any other script or text source via the Clipboard, but you'll probably have to fix the indention. Generally, you'll have to get all the lines of a script flush left by deleting any spaces between the left margin and the beginning of the line, and then hitting the Tab key to invoke *Hyper-*

Table 5-2. Script Editing Keys

Command	Key
Copy	Command-C
Cut	Command-X
Delete selection	Backspace
End command line	Return
Find	Command-F
Find again	Command-G
Find selection	Command-H
Paste	Command-V
Print	Command-P
Save script	Enter'
Select	Command-S
Select all	Command-A
Set indention	Tab
Soft return	Option-Return
Stop action of script	Command-. (period)
Stop printing of script	Command-. (period)
Undo	Command-Z

Card's automatic indention feature. Remember that indentions must balance so that the script ends flush left.

Use a *soft return* (Option-Return) if a line of the script takes more than one line. The soft-return symbol is ^. If you were to use a standard Return, *HyperCard* would interpret everything after the Return as a new command line.

Immediately test a script before you do anything else, like copying it for other objects. *HyperCard* will tell you immediately if there's a syntax problem, using a dialog box like the one in Figure 5-3. Sometimes the error boxes give specific hints as to just what the problem is, but other times you'll have to make your best guess. When you go to the script from an error box, the blinking insertion line will be at the location of the problem. Even with an easy-to-use programming language like HyperTalk, expect to see many error boxes on your way to scripting fluency. You'll get the best results if you're careful and methodical in devising your scripts.

Figure 5-3. Script Error Box

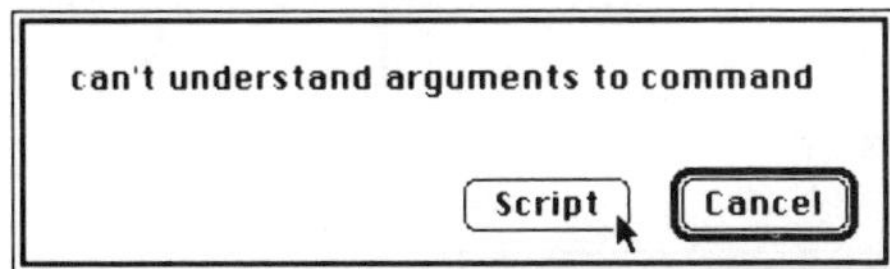
can't understand arguments to command
Script
Cancel

Writing Scripts

Now you have the background necessary to start writing your own scripts. Let's try writing three sample button scripts—a simple navigation button, a button that puts text into a container, and a button to perform some basic math. First, do the following:

- Go to the Home stack and create a fresh card and a blank background.
- Name the card *Scripts.*
- Make three new card buttons and a card field.
- Name the buttons "Next," " Words," and "Math," and make sure the button names are showing.
- Name the field "Test" and size it so that it's most of the width of the screen and is five lines high, with the lines visible.
- Show the message box and tear off the Tools palette.
- Refer to Appendix A for more information on any HyperTalk term you do not recognize.

Writing the Next Button Script

Before writing a script, you should be clear about what the script is to accomplish. The function of the *Next* button is to create a fancy transition to the next card.

You know that the script of a button must begin with a trap for a message. Open the script window for the Next button and you'll see that *HyperCard* assumes the message your button will be looking for is *on mouseUp*—that phrase is already entered in the script window, and so is *end mouseUp,* which has to close the message handler (see Figure 5-4).

Figure 5-4. *Next* Button Script 1

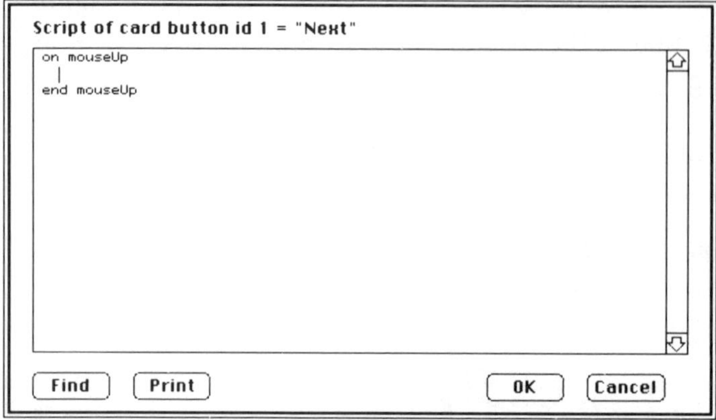
Script of card button id 1 = "Next"
on mouseUp
end mouseUp
Find
Print
OK
Cancel

All you need to do is add one or more command lines to get you from this card to the next. Type

```
go to next card
```

between the two existing lines, and then hit Enter (Figure 5-5). Now test the script so far by clicking on the button.

Figure 5-5. *Next* Button Script 2

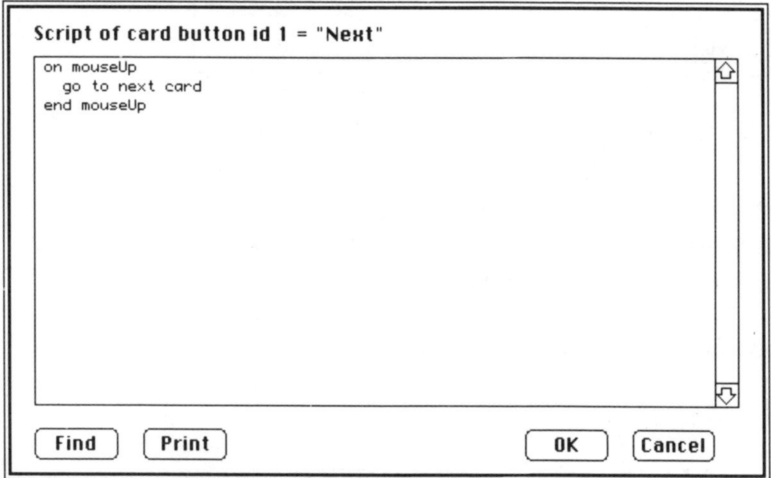
Script of card button id 1 = "Next"
on mouseUp
go to next card
end mouseUp
Find
Print
OK
Cancel

You should be at the next card. (If you got an error box instead, go back to the script and check your spelling.) Return to the previous card and open the Next button script again.

Now you'll add a line to the script that creates a cinematic transition like the ones in the *HyperCard* Intro. Use the visual command to do this. Type in the line

```
visual effect wipe left
```

before the line *go to next card,* as in Figure 5-6.

Now, test the button again. The next card should appear to slide over the card with the button on it. Now you've finished writing your first script. You can copy this button and use it in any stack you create.

Figure 5-6. *Next* Button Script 3

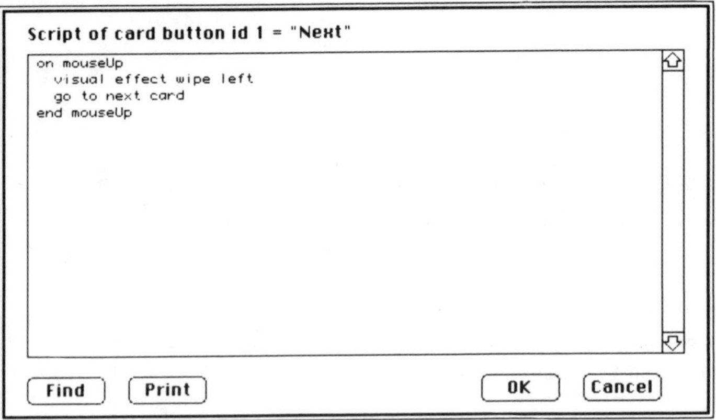
Script of card button id 1 = "Next"
on mouseUp
visual effect wipe left
go to next card
end mouseUp
Find
Print
OK
Cancel

Writing the Words Button Script

With this button, you'll be using the *Words* button to get information from another part of the stack and then insert it in the "Test" field.

Open the script window for the Words button and type

```
go last
```

as the second line of the script (Figure 5-7).

Figure 5-7. *Words* Button Script 1

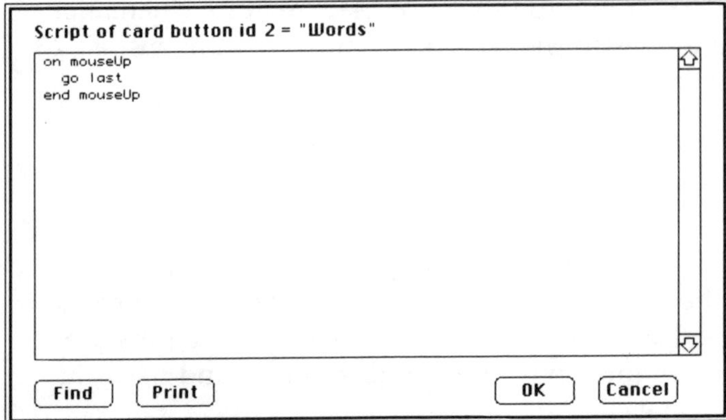
Script of card button id 2 = "Words"
on mouseUp
go last
end mouseUp
Find
Print
OK
Cancel

Figure 5-8. *Words* Button Script 2

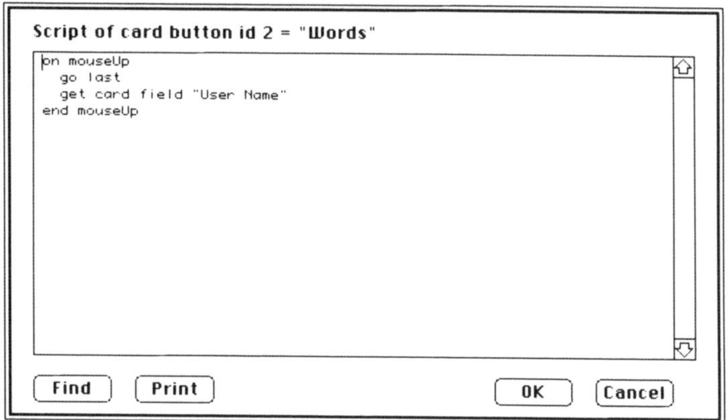
Script of card button id 2 = "Words"
on mouseUp
go last
get card field "User Name"
end mouseUp
Find
Print
OK
Cancel

Press Enter and test the button. You should be at the User Preferences card, the last card in the Home stack. The task is to retrieve the user name from this card. (If you haven't typed your name into the User Name field, do it now.) Return to the Scripts card and open the button script again. Type

```
get card field "User Name"
```

as line 4 of the script (See Figure 5-8.) Test the script again.

Now the contents of the card field "User Name" (should be your name) are in the local variable *It*—the command *get* always puts what it's retrieving into *It*. Now the information in *It* must get to it's destination, card field "Test" on the Scripts card. Return to the Scripts card and open the button script. Type

```
go back
```

as the fifth line, and

```
put it into line 1 of card field "Test"
```

as the sixth line (Figure 5-9).

When you test the button now, you'll be flashed to the User Preferences card, taken back to the Scripts card, and you'll then see your name appear in the "Test" field. Seeing that quick trip is dizzying and would be much worse if *HyperCard* were making

Figure 5-9. *Words* Button Script 3

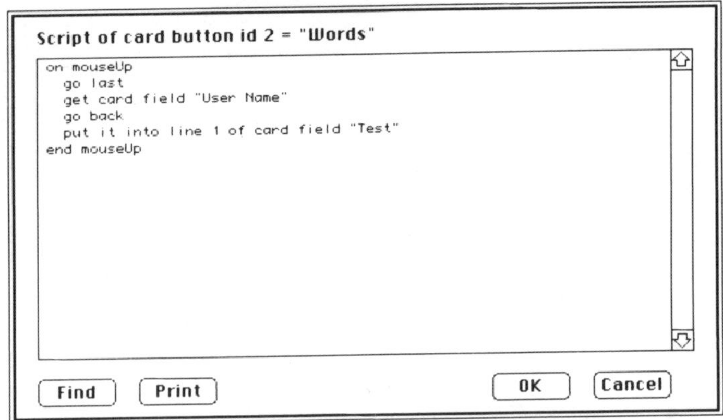
Script of card button id 2 = "Words"
on mouseUp
go last
get card field "User Name"
go back
put it into line 1 of card field "Test"
end mouseUp
Find
Print
OK
Cancel

dozens of trips to retrieve lots of different pieces of information. Fortunately, there's a way to hide all that. Type

```
set lockScreen to true
```

as the second line of the script (Figure 5-10).

Setting the lockScreen property to true (on) means that *HyperCard* shows you only the screen visible when the script starts to run, even though all kinds of "getting" and "putting" are going on behind the scenes. Try the button now, and your name will pop into the "Test" field. The lockScreen property sets itself to false (off) automatically at the end of a script, so you don't have to.

Figure 5-10. *Words* Button Script 4

Script of card button id 2 = "Words"

```
on mouseUp
  set lockScreen to true
  go last
  get card field "User Name"
  go back
  put it into line 1 of card field "Test"
end mouseUp
```

Find Print OK Cancel

Writing the *Math* Button Script

The *Math* button will generate a series of numbers, put them into the "Test" field, total the result, and put it into the message box. You'll be using a repeat control structure for this.

First, you need to clear any text from the "Test" field and the message box. Type

```
put empty into card field "Test"
```

and

```
put empty into msg box
```

as the second and third lines of the script (Figure 5-11).

Putting the constant *empty* into any container, including a field, is the same as erasing everything in the container.

Now, construct the repeat structure. The goal is to put five random numbers into field "Test," one per line, and then add them. Use the function *the random* to generate random integers between 1 and a specified upper limit (we'll use 10 as the upper limit). You could type

```
put the random of 10 into line 1 of card field "Test"
add line 1 of card field "Test" to msg box
```

five different times, changing the line number of the field each time. But a repeat structure lets you save time by writing fewer

Figure 5-11. *Math* Button Script 1

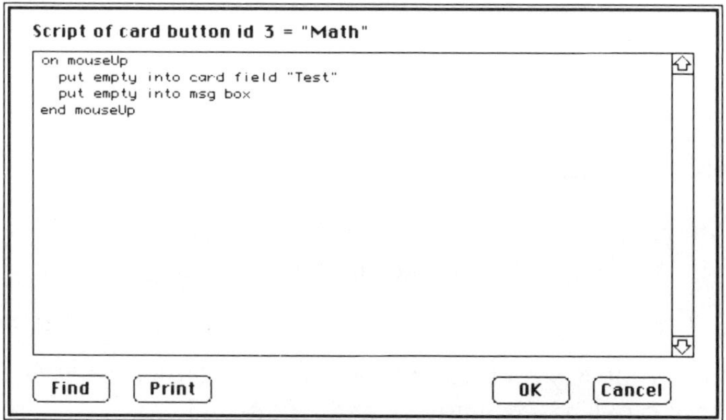
Script of card button id 3 = "Math"
on mouseUp
put empty into card field "Test"
put empty into msg box
end mouseUp
Find
Print
OK
Cancel

Figure 5-12. *Math* Button Script 2

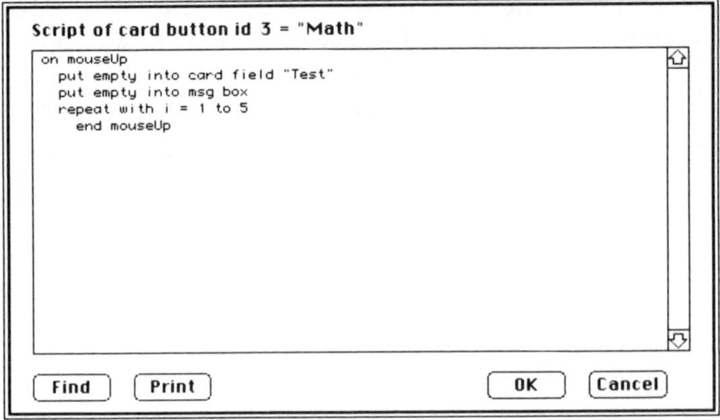
Script of card button id 3 = "Math"
on mouseUp
put empty into card field "Test"
put empty into msg box
repeat with i = 1 to 5
end mouseUp
Find
Print
OK
Cancel

script lines that repeat (iterate) themselves the number of times you specify. Here, we'll use the "repeat with" structure.

The form of the repeat with structure is

repeat with <variable> = <low number> to <high number>

The variable can be any letter or word you want to call it (we'll use the letter *i*). The low number to high number is a number range determined by the number of times you want to repeat the action and/or the numbers of field lines, objects, or what-have-you that you want to perform the action on. In this case, you have a simple range. You want to do something to each of five lines of the field "Test," so the number range is 1–5. Type this as the third line in the button script (Figure 5-12)

```
repeat with i = 1 to 5
```

Now add the actions that will be repeated (Figure 5-13):

```
put the random of 10 into line i of card field "Test"
add line i of card field "Test" to msg box
```

Note two things: One, the lines under the repeat structure automatically indent; and two, the variable i *is substituting in the script for the number range 1–5.*

Now end the repeat structure with *end repeat.* Remember, all control structures must be explicitly closed. (Figure 5-14).

Figure 5-13. ***Math*** **Button Script 3**

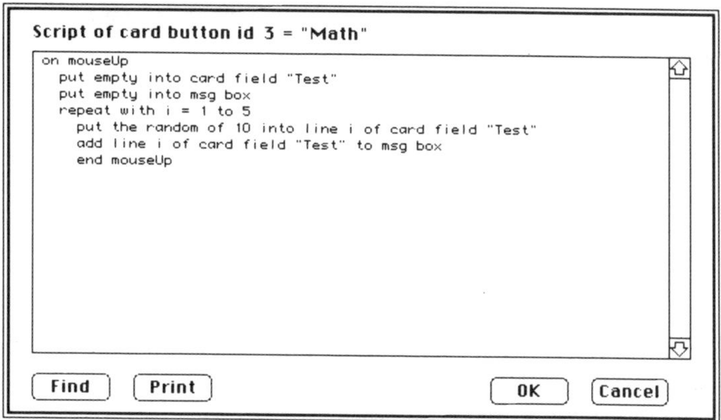
Script of card button id 3 = "Math"
on mouseUp
put empty into card field "Test"
put empty into msg box
repeat with i = 1 to 5
put the random of 10 into line i of card field "Test"
add line i of card field "Test" to msg box
end mouseUp
Find
Print
OK
Cancel

Test the button. The random numbers appear one per line in field "Test," and their total appears in the message box. Every time you click the button, different numbers appear in the field, and a different total appears in the message box.

With these three exercises, you've gained many of the script-writing skills you'll need to tackle your own projects. Part II of this book contains more scripts along with extensive guidelines for planning and making complex stacks.

Figure 5-14. ***Math*** **Button Script 4**

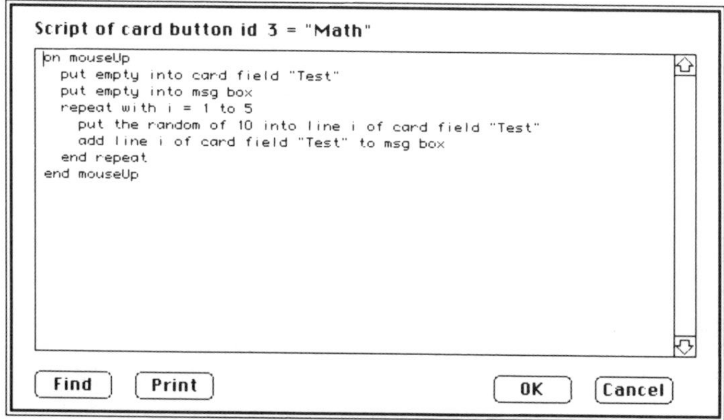
Script of card button id 3 = "Math"
on mouseUp
put empty into card field "Test"
put empty into msg box
repeat with i = 1 to 5
put the random of 10 into line i of card field "Test"
add line i of card field "Test" to msg box
end repeat
end mouseUp
Find
Print
OK
Cancel

TIP: Seeing the Scripts of Other Stacks. You'll probably learn to write scripts faster by studying existing scripts than by using any other method. However, examining all the scripts of a complex stack to find the interesting ones is a time-consuming process; you don't even have the advantage of being able to tell which objects have empty scripts and which don't without opening the script window for each one. Luckily, there's help in the form of public domain and shareware programs that automatically read all the scripts in a stack and prepare a report for you. Appendix D lists several of these; the best is Script Report 1.2 by Eric Alderman, 48 Shattuck Square, Suite 13, Berkeley, California. This essential shareware program, which will even sleuth out the scripts of protected stacks, costs ten dollars and is widely available on bulletin boards and from user groups.

Part II: DESIGNING STACKS

Chapter 6
Designing Your Stacks

You've finished your *HyperCard* apprenticeship and are ready to tackle building your first stack. The prospects are limitless—in fact, so limitless that it's a little frightening. With all the power you control as a *HyperCard* author comes responsibility. You'll be able to design custom *HyperCard* applications to meet specialized information needs that no commercial developer would ever address, but by the same token, you'll now have to do all the hard development work you once could leave to others.

This chapter will help get you started by providing a potpourri of suggestions for how to go about designing your own stacks. Keep in mind, however, that *HyperCard* authoring is an art, not a science—there are no absolute rules to follow, no one best way to design a stack. In this chapter, you'll find design guidelines and methods of working to make stack creation easier and more successful. Even so, you may develop other methods that suit you better.

Making a Plan

Before you set out to design your stack, sit down and outline your goals. As you do, answer these basic questions:

- What do I have to say?
- Who will use it?
- What's the best way to arrange my information?

The design of your stack flows logically from the answers to these questions. We'll look at issues regarding each of these in the following pages.

It may help, in the beginning, to write brief notes to yourself on paper and post them near the Mac as a reminder of your goals. Your planning shouldn't stop there, however; for a complex stack, more extensive notes are helpful to you and to anyone who may be working with you. Draw diagrams or flowcharts, compile lists of sources for data, identify readymade buttons and graphics you may want to use, and talk to those who will be using the stack. It's possible, and in many cases desirable, to work out the important aspects of the stack and avoid possible pitfalls before you ever begin to program. In fact, this type of planning is the first step in the authoring process, and if you plan conscientiously, you'll save yourself a lot of aggravation later, making it more likely that the stack will do what you want it to do.

Organizing Your Information

The obvious first step toward any stack design is deciding what the stack's content will be. Applications can be as simple as a customized address file or as complex as an interactive educational stack with voice synthesis, animation, and branching lessons. Even within *HyperCard*'s own limits as a programming environment, the possibilities for organizing and disseminating information and creative works are nearly infinite. Whether you're designing

- a database for a well-defined body of information that you'll include in the stack (for example, a catalogue of imported clothes from Asia),
- a complete interactive environment for a game or simulation, or
- an information stack that plays without any interaction from the user (such as a trade-show guide),

you must gather and organize your information before you create the stack.

You'll find immediately that most information already appears to possess a natural organization. For example, addresses are logically grouped in an alphabetical list, maps in an atlas by geographic region, electronic parts in a product catalogue by function or features, and events in a narrative by scenes or chapters. That organization, in turn, imposes an order on the stack; in other words, form follows function. A simple address list, for example, can be loosely organized with few or no direct links between cards. Users can get from place to place in the address file quite adequately with just the navigation commands and the Find function. On the other hand, an interactive stack that lets you branch from one part of the stack to another (or to other stacks entirely) based on responses you give to prompts, must be organized much more tightly, probably in a tree-like structure. A play-only trade-show guide will be linear in form, running from one card to the next and looping back to the beginning. Figure 6-1

Figure 6-1. Information Structures

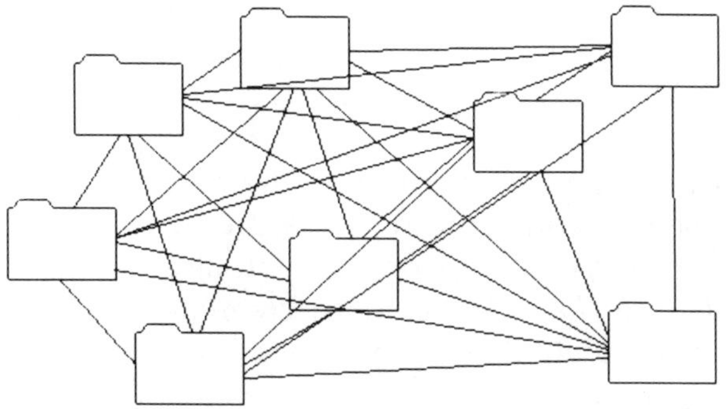

Random structure

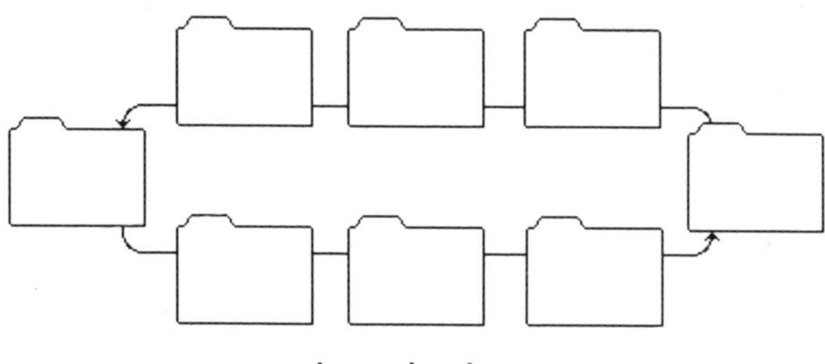

Loop structure

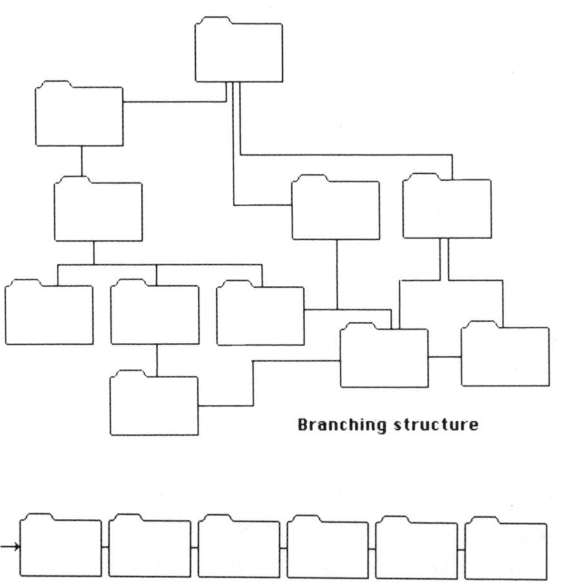

Branching structure

Linear structure

diagrams some possible information structures that, in turn, affect the structures of their stacks.

When it's not immediately obvious how to organize your information, it helps to divide your data up into small pieces. Believe it or not, the easiest way to do this is by making notes on 3 × 5 inch paper index cards and then shuffling the cards until the organization makes sense. You could do the same by making and rearranging temporary *HyperCard* cards, but you face the disadvantage of seeing only one *HyperCard* card onscreen at a time, while you can see and manipulate many paper cards at once (one of the last advantages of paper over *HyperCard*). Creating a flow chart with one of the Mac's planning or outlining programs is another option. Keep in mind that *HyperCard* allows you to display only a screenful of information at once, so information that can't be broken up into modest-sized bites is not well-suited to *HyperCard*. An example of this kind of indivisible information is a large painting or photograph that doesn't fit on a card. It wouldn't be very satisfying to look at a long Japanese painted scroll by having to flip through several cards—you would get no real sense of the painting's composition or total aesthetic impact.

Some stacks contain little information themselves, but function as ways for users to store or manipulate other information. Examples of these types of stacks include templates for information the stack user will store (empty databases) and *HyperCard* utilities that extend the program's abilities.

Identifying Your Audience

Now that you know what you want to say, identify your audience. Is it experienced *HyperCard* users; specialists in a particular field; Mac neophytes, or people who've never worked with a computer; or possibly any and all of these?

It's easy to design a stack for advanced *HyperCard* users because they'll know the *HyperCard* conventions and will be experienced in figuring out how stacks work. You can assume a lot with experienced users and even get by with being a little sloppy in documenting how your stack works. Likewise, if you're presenting data to a group of specialists, you can at least depend on your audience being able to put the information into context and understand your terminology. However, the more kinds of users that will encounter your stack, the more basic your design must be; at the most basic level, you can't even assume the person knows how to use the mouse. Actually, *HyperCard* is ideal for basic users, or *viewers*—it's easy to create a stack that "runs" by itself, almost like a videotape. Typical examples of these kinds of stacks are point-of-sale displays and public-access information systems, where a wide range of people will encounter the stack and use it in a public setting. Educational stacks for young children also fall into this category, and must assume the minimum level of skill possessed by children in the age range you're addressing. You shouldn't, for example, design a stack for four- to six-year-olds that requires them to read instructions. Use language synthesis (see Chapter 9) or pictures instead.

You should also consider where to set the user level of the stack. *HyperCard* gives you the ability to restrict the user level to any of the five settings, using a stack script like the following:

```
on openStack
   set userLevel to <1 through 5, with 1 browsing and 5 scripting>
end openStack
```

In general, you should allow your audience to set its own user level rather than setting one in advance. Knowledgeable users will be able to circumvent any user-level restrictions anyway, and less experienced users should be encouraged to understand more about the program and not be shut out from it. But there are some cases in which it does make sense to restrict the user level to browsing or typing—for the user's own safety. Stacks for children are an example: You may not want young *HyperCardians* to accidentally access and delete your scripts or scribble over carefully designed graphics with the paint tools.

Designing a User Interface

Once you've determined the goals of your stack and who it's intended to reach, the major questions you face are *What does the user expect a HyperCard stack to act like?*, and its corollary, *Do I need to fulfill the user's expectations?*. You'll also have other questions to answer, such as *How should this stack look to have the maximum desired impact?* and *How can I minimize the work I need to do without compromising the usefulness of the stack?*.

Answering these questions involves designing a *user interface.* A user interface (this ugly phrase cries out for an elegant alternative) is basically the way a program looks and the way it asks you to work with it. User interfaces can be friendly, helpful, and intuitive like the Mac's highly visual "human interface," or unhelpful and nonintuitive, like the standard text-only MS-DOS interface. Each does the job, but the Mac interface is much easier to . . . well, interface with.

HyperCard's unmatched programming flexibility means you're not really dependent on the Mac style of iconic interface; you can design nearly any kind of interface you like for your stack, including one that's thoroughly confusing and frustrating. Assuming user anguish is not your goal, you need to give some prior thought to your stack's interface so that it makes sense, works smoothly, and has aesthetic appeal. When actually designing a stack, you'll find that, as with most other construction projects, good design counts. In general, the interface of a well-designed informational stack is functional, clean, easy-to-use, and bug-free. This means you'll be best off adhering to some general conventions of *HyperCard* software design so that users of your stack will have minimal difficulty knowing what to do. For example:

- *Consistency is important.* Make sure familiar objects work the same way, all the time. For example, buttons with house icons should always take you Home, and if the objects are standard items in the Mac interface, use them in the expected way—don't use checkboxes the same way as radio buttons. In fact, you should probably stick close to the Mac interface whenever you have a choice of how to do something. (This doesn't apply for games, hypercomics, and other creative uses for *HyperCard*—gamers and artists can create any interface they choose, with the attendant risk, of course, of artistic failure.)
- *Don't assume the user is experienced or understands what you're trying to do.* Provide online help, explanations, keymaps, stack diagrams, tables of contents, and/or indexes. These guides are *de rigeur* for complex stacks, just as tables of contents and indexes are standard equipment for books. Always design so that an inexperienced user can use intuition to figure out what you intend.
- *Give users all the information they need.* Don't, for example, hide the menu bar without providing other ways to navigate through

the stack, and don't include important information in hidden fields without showing how to get to those fields.

- *Redundancy is helpful.* Provide more than one way to organize or gain access to information.
- *Keep it simple.* Use only the buttons, fields, and graphics the stack needs; never throw in extraneous decorations and functions just because you can; extras are just static interfering with the information you want to convey.

Figures 6-2 and 6-3. Two Interfaces

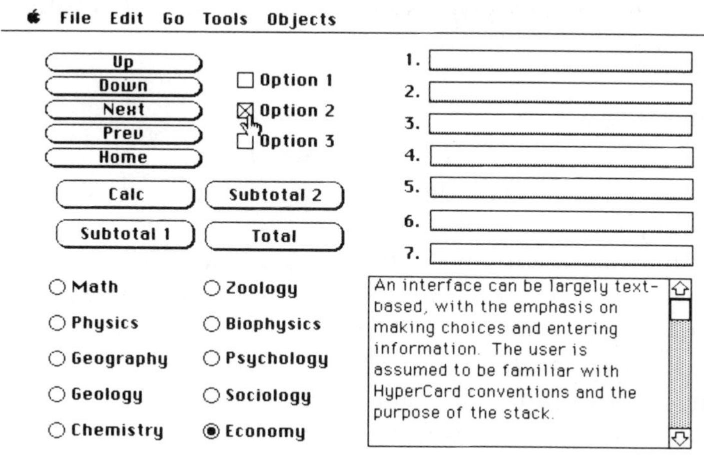

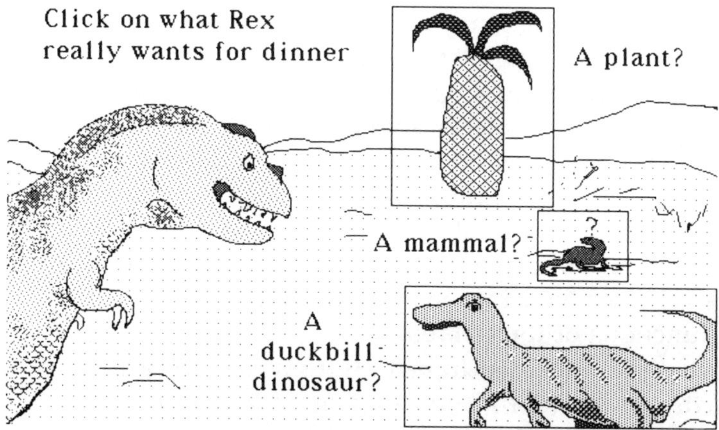

An interface can be simple and graphic, creating a controlled environment that limits the number of options available to the user.

- *Make it look good.* Use screen space efficiently, but don't clutter things up with too many objects. If you have too many objects to fit easily on a card, rethink your stack design, or separate objects by function onto different cards or backgrounds. Symmetrical arrangements of objects are easiest for users to understand. Group related objects together.
- *Weed out the bugs.* Mistakes are not only wrong, they're confusing. No one is perfect, but try to be. Check carefully for minor errors like typos and leftover parts of pictures that should have been erased.

Figures 6-2 and 6-3 give two examples of very different interfaces.

Visual Design Issues

HyperCard's powerful graphic tools can be used to clarify and enhance your information. When designing the look of your stacks, here are some issues to keep in mind.

Settle on a visual metaphor for the stack as a whole—this will help to orient the user of the information. The information you'll be putting into the stack should give you an idea about what metaphor to use. Information that normally is stored on cards (like addresses) suggests an index-card border for the stack. Graphics may call for some sort of picture frame. Don't, however, devote a lot of time to creating an elaborate visual environment at the expense of organizing and clearly presenting your information.

On a large screen, the menu bar doesn't hide the top of a card. If you think your stack may be viewed on a large screen, be sure to tidy up any stray graphics under the menu bar. Even though big screens are increasingly popular, it isn't a good idea to place essential graphics or objects under the menu bar since the old nine-inch Mac screen will be the standard for some time to come, and the user may not know how to hide the menu bar to see what's underneath. If you absolutely must use the menu bar area, you can hide it with a script, but note that you must then provide the stack user with buttons that duplicate at least the navigational functions of the menus.

Decide what sort of visual transition from card to card is appropriate for the information. You can script a variety of cinematic transitions with HyperTalk card or button scripts. *Wipes* (right, left, up, and down) are good for stacks that depend heavily on a card metaphor, or for slideshow-type stacks. Several styles of *dissolves* are available for smooth transitions to different parts of a stack, to indicate the passage of time or a distance traveled, or for animation effects. Use zoom-ins to go to a card that zeroes in on a selected item to show more detail, and use zoom-outs to get back to the big picture. Barn-door transitions should open up and close down new areas of the stack. It's even possible to use blackouts and whiteouts for emphasis, appropriate for a stack that runs by itself or possesses a narrative. Each transition can be slow or fast as well. The visual command is covered in Appendix A, "HyperTalk Glossary."

Try to give all fields and buttons on the screen similar visual properties. A screen with five styles of buttons and four styles of fields will look incoherent. If you do need different styles of objects, group the styles together in separate regions of the screen; for example, along the top, group round-rectangle buttons that have their names showing, and along the bottom, group transparent buttons that have icons and no names.

If you need graphics for your stack but your artistic talent is meager, use clip art or scanned art, or contact experienced Mac artists at user groups or through bulletin boards.

Avoid fancy backgrounds that add no information to your cards and only use up precious screen space. The kind of "stacked cards" graphic used in *HyperCard*'s Help stacks and elsewhere in the program are best used when the density of information on a single card is low, or when the expected audience is unfamiliar with *HyperCard*.

TIP: Installing and Distributing Fonts. If you're distributing stacks with fonts other than the system fonts supplied by Apple, use the Font/DA mover to install the fonts onto your stack disk. Pressing the Option key as you click the Font/DA Mover's Open button will let you add fonts to any individual stack. Before you distribute any font with a commercial product, keep in mind that you may need permission from the individual or company holding the copyright to the font. (This usually isn't an issue with public-domain fonts.) You don't need permission to use any of the Apple-owned screen fonts such as Chicago, Monaco, and Geneva.

Use a minimum number of fonts in field and graphic text. Many different letter sizes and styles make for a confusing, unattractive, and hard-to-read stack. All field text should be in one standard font, like Geneva 12 or New York 10. Restrict the use of shadowed and outlined text styles to card titles, and use only one fancy style throughout a stack. Use an Apple System font—Monaco or Chicago—for text that's associated with buttons or that refers to the Mac system. Try not to mix serif and sans-serif fonts on one card, and use capital letters only for titles or emphasis.

Sound Design Issues

Like graphics, sounds can add to the impact of your stacks. The creation and use of sound effects will be covered in more depth in Chapter 9, but here are a few general items to consider:

- *HyperCard* comes with four sounds—"boing," dialing tones, harpsichord, and silence—stored as sound resources. You can add others with ResEdit or utilities listed in Appendix D. The familiar Macintosh *beep* can be invoked with the beep command; play the built-in sounds with the play command (both covered in Appendix A).
- Sound resources take up a lot of disk space. You can fit only a few moments of uncompressed digitized music on a disk, so you're better off trying to get the most out of using the supplied sounds or adding only a few crucial new sounds very sparingly. If you try to cram a lot of slick sounds onto a disk, you won't have enough room for the rest of the stack.
- Use the beep to alert the user to something important—usually an error, a limit reached, or an action that must be taken. The "boing" sound can be used in somewhat the same way—when a student gives a wrong answer to a question posed in an educational stack, for example. A right answer can be rewarded with a upbeat little tune, perhaps synchronized with a visual effect.
- You can match sound effects to card transitions. Sound resources in the public domain include the sounds of cards being flipped, ripped, and shuffled; switches being turned on and off; and stacks of paper being dropped on a desk.
- As an alternative to text information, consider using voice synthesis. (To do this, you must have the program *MacInTalk* in

your system folder and a special command installed in your stack or Home stack—see Chapter 9). You can write a script that tells *HyperCard* to say any text aloud, including the contents of a field entered by the stack user. Artificial speech is especially appropriate for public access stacks, stacks for young children and the handicapped, and for entertainment and game applications, but speech can also be used to prompt users who may be away from the computer or who are engaged in other activities.

Stack Structures

With some basic design issues settled, you're now in a position to block out the stack design. Several aspects are covered below.

Backgrounds. The basic unit of stack design is the background; for most stacks, that's where the major fields, buttons, and graphics are, and where you'll be spending most of your design time.

Stacks come in two types—homogeneous and heterogeneous. *Homogeneous* stacks contain cards with only one background. The Address stack is an example of a homogeneous stack. *Heterogeneous* stacks contain cards with more than one background. The Home stack is an example of a heterogeneous stack—it has several backgrounds.

The *number of backgrounds* you can have in a stack is limited only by the number of cards in the stack. How do you know how many backgrounds you'll need? Generally, your information will tell you. If your information is all of one type, such as a single list containing product ordering information, a single background will do. If you have several different kinds of information in the stack, such as maps, text articles, artists' renderings, and indexes, then you'll need several backgrounds—one for each type of information. In extreme cases, when each card of the stack contains very different kinds of information, you may opt for a different background for every card, or you may use a single blank background and put all objects and information into the card domain of each card. Even if your stack has many backgrounds, you should try to give each background a similar look, using the same fonts, button icons, and so on, to give coherence to the design of the stack as a whole.

There are two important advantages to using multiple backgrounds in one stack as opposed to creating multiple stacks with one background each and linking them together. The first is that one stack, even with many backgrounds, takes up less disk space than two stacks—a consideration if you're trying to squeeze a large amount of information onto a floppy disk or if you expect users to download your stack from a bulletin board or online service. The other advantage is that it's far easier and faster to search for and move information in a single stack than it is between stacks. For example, using the Find function to search the background fields of a stack different from the one you're in takes several times longer than searching the same stack, and it can only be accomplished with a script, not through the message box. Still, you may have no choice but to create multistack applications; techniques for doing this are discussed in Chapter 8.

> **TIP: Multiple Backgrounds and Print Report.** In current versions of *HyperCard*, the Print Report feature doesn't recognize more than one background in a stack. If you plan to print out many reports of your information, but you need more than one background, create a one-background stack to hold the information and put other backgrounds, such as those for instructions and indexes, into a separate stack. This makes for a somewhat awkward arrangement, but at present, there's no way around it.

Card Order. Do the cards in your stack need to be in a particular order? In most cases, cards can be in any order as long as they're linked correctly. In some stacks, however, the nature of the information requires cards to be arranged either alphabetically, by date, or by number. An example is a stack of invoices. These should always be in either invoice-number order or date order so that the user can flip through the cards as well as search by key words or key numbers. A stack, background, or button script can sort the cards by whatever criteria you specify. Consider also whether your stack will require users to add new cards. Typically, empty databases—such as datebooks and address lists that users are expected to fill with their own information—make provisions for creating new cards or extending the current series of cards, usually with an Extend or New Card button. New cards are normally inserted after the current card no matter where you are in the stack, but it may make sense for all new cards to be automatically placed at the end of the stack by means of a *stack sort script* like the following:

```
on newCard
   doMenu "Cut Card"
   go last
   doMenu "Paste Card"
end newCard
```

Cards introducing the stack should obviously be at the beginning of the stack, even if the rest of the cards are in no particular order. Map and index cards should be well linked to every other card so that the user can always step back for an overview of the stack at any point.

Objects and Domains. Once you've decided how many backgrounds you need and in what order the cards should be, it's time to figure out in which domain, card, or background to put graphics, fields, and buttons. Objects and graphics common to all the cards in a homogeneous stack, or common to all related cards in a heterogeneous stack, should be placed in the background domain (for example, navigation buttons should be in the background domain). One-time-only objects and graphics belong in the card domain. Buttons linking one specific card to another should be in the card domain. Most fields are background fields, but card fields (although rarer) also have their uses. (For example, captions for pictures in a graphic database could be in card fields.)

Hidden Objects and Graphics. Often, you'll want an object or graphic in most of the cards in a stack, but not in all. In this case, the best approach is to put the object or graphic in the background and hide it on the few cards where you don't want it to be seen. Chapter 9 covers hiding and showing objects and graphics in some detail, but here is a brief overview. There are several ways to hide a background object or graphic:

- Cover an object with an opaque, locked-card field or a card button with an empty script.
- Cover a graphic with an opaque, white borderless shape in the card graphics layer.
- Write a card script that hides the selected object or objects and then shows the object again when you go to another card. For example:

```
on openCard
   hide background button 2
end openCard
```

```
on closeCard
    show background button 2
end closeCard
```

You also have the option of using the stack script to automatically hide and show the menu bar, the message box, and the Tools and Patterns palettes. Except in unusual cases, the menu bar should always be shown. If the users of your stack will be using the find function to search through your stack, you should show the message box already set up for a search. Show the Tools and Patterns palettes in stacks that invite users to add their own graphics or create their own objects.

Hidden fields can carry text to be revealed only when a certain action is taken, as when the user clicks on an underlined term to get more information. By hiding fields until they're needed, you can get more onto a card than first meets the eye. A field that appears when needed is called a *pop-up* field. Figure 6-4 shows how pop-up fields can be used. Each field's script hides it again when you click within the perimeter of the field.

Don't, however, assign important functions to hidden buttons and expect users to find them.

Field Design. As stated, fields are the main information holders in your stacks. To maintain the clarity of text in your fields, settle on similarly styled fields per card. A mixture of fields with and without outlines, lines, and scroll bars is not good design, as is mixing more than one or two fonts on the card. (Individual fields cannot have more than one font at a time, which is probably a good thing.) Try using a gray tint in the background to make opaque fields stand out more clearly.

Remember that fields are containers as well as objects, and you can manipulate their contents with scripts. Fields can also perform some of the functions of buttons; for instance, you can write a script that waits for the pointer to cross the perimeter of the field and then puts text into the field. Clever scripting can also reduce the number of fields you may need on a card. Rather than making a little field for each individual piece of text you need to display, create a few larger fields and assign text to individual lines of the fields.

Always put the *I*-beam cursor into the first field of the card so that the card is ready for text entry as soon as it's opened. Use this card script:

Figure 6-4. Hidden Fields

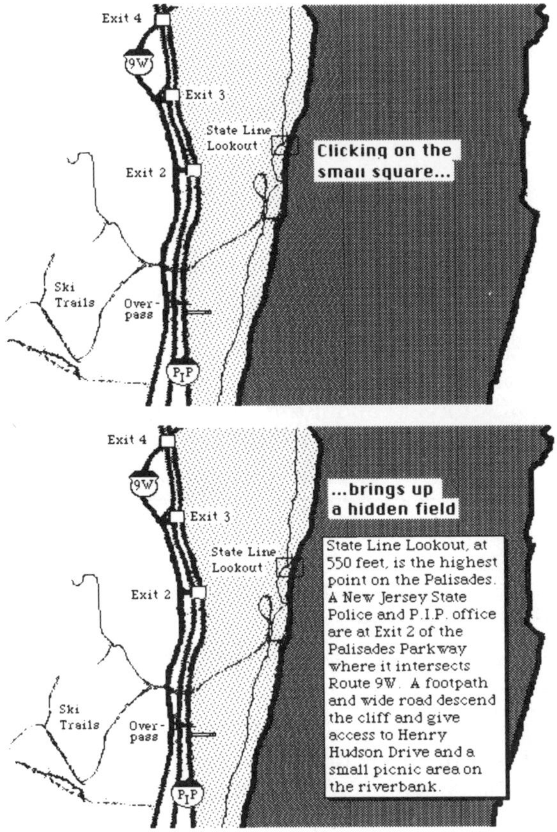

```
on openCard
   tabkey
end openCard
```

Button Design. Set button properties consistent with their functions. For maximum clarity, give the button an icon and a name, and show the name so there's no question about what the button is supposed to do. You can write the button script so a sound effect like a "beep" or "boing" sounds when the button is clicked (although this will slow down the button's response).

Transparent buttons can be placed over graphics or text in a nonscrolling field without interfering with the look of the underlying item. Use radio buttons to offer a choice among various options, and use checkboxes to turn on or off one or more properties or functions at a time. Turn the autoHilite feature on for rectangle, round rectangle, and icon buttons when you want the user to know the button has successfully been triggered.

Provide arrow buttons for navigating the stack, and a Home button to get Home. These buttons can use icons only and can even be rather small, tucked away along the bottom border of the card. Users will soon learn where to find them.

> **autoHilite and Selections.** Don't turn on the autoHilite property of a button that operates on selected text or graphics. When the button autoHilites, the selection will automatically be deselected (autoHiliting is nothing more than briefly selecting the button, and since only one item can be selected at a time, the button autoHilite makes *HyperCard* "forget" about the other selection). The button's script won't be able to find a selection on which to operate.

Prompts. *HyperCard* offers several ways to prompt the user for information or a reply to a question. You have at your disposal two custom dialog boxes—the *ask* box, shown in Figure 6-5, and the *answer* box, shown in Figure 6-6. The ask box contains an area in which the user can type in a short reply to a question, such as a name. The reply is automatically put into the local variable *It* when the OK button is clicked; you can then use the contents of *It* in a script. Users can choose among three alternatives

Figure 6-5. Ask Box

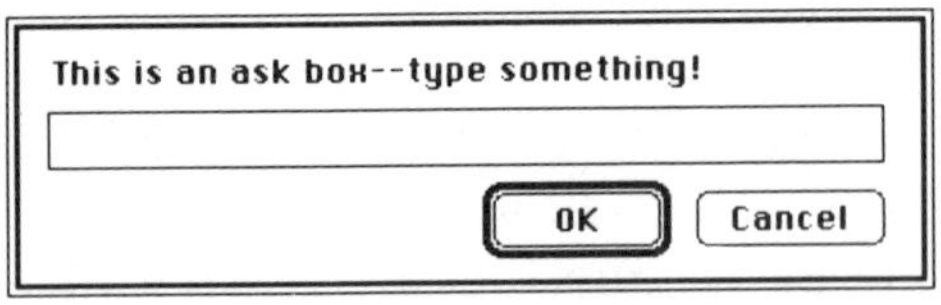

This is an ask box--type something!

OK   Cancel

Figure 6-6. Answer Box

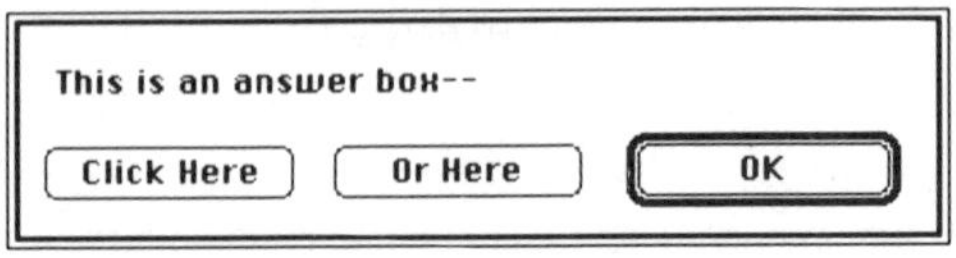

This is an answer box--

Click Here   Or Here   OK

from the answer box by clicking on the relevant button. The use of both boxes is covered in Appendix A.

The message box is also a potential avenue for communication with the person using the stack; for example, Appendix A uses it to show the results of many scripts. However, the message box should usually be reserved for the user's own messages; instead of the message box, consider creating a special prompt field and putting text into it with a script, or have *HyperCard* give the prompt, using speech synthesis.

Scripting Issues

Scripts are as much a part of the *HyperCard* environment you're constructing as any object or graphic. You should assume they'll be examined, so develop good scriptwriting habits accordingly.

The concept of *hierarchy* (see Chapters 3 and 5) has a direct bearing on how you'll write scripts and what objects you'll assign to them. It's especially important to assign a message handler to the proper rung in the hierarchy. This issue tends to arise when you're trying to decide whether to put a message handler in a script for a card, a background, a stack, or the Home stack. For example, you could assign all your message handlers to your Home stack; *HyperCard* will find them there sooner or later, but it will slow down the program's operation considerably. It's much better HyperTalk programming practice to assign a message handler to the lowest rung at which it will still operate successfully. Keep in mind the function of the script you're writing. Do you want it to affect every stack? Put it in the Home stack. Should it change every card in the current stack? Write the script for the background if the stack is homogeneous, or for the stack if it's heterogeneous.

People who use your stack will probably read your scripts. One of the best things you can do for yourself and for anyone who might be reading your scripts is to add explanatory comments about how the script works in the script itself. You can do this by typing a double hyphen (--) after the line you want to annotate and then typing in your comments. Many scripts in this book are annotated in this way; see especially the scripts in Chapter 8. Scripts can also be broken up into sections if that makes them easier to understand. Leave a line space between sections, and insert an explanation before each section. You can list custom messages, functions, and variables at the beginning of the script, as well as your name and address, and a copyright notice (if you've created a magnum opus of a script).

Also, your scripts should be friendly to the user and to the *HyperCard* environment. Include provisions for error handling and error messages in the script so that if the user does something wrong, a prompt will appear, steering him or her toward the right path. If the handler takes a long time to execute, change the pointer to the familiar wristwatch with this command:

```
set cursor to 4
```

right after the handler begins.

Be sure to pass *resume messages* and *other messages* objects up that the hierarchy might need to receive. Set lockScreen to *true* when going back and forth from stack to stack in the course of your script. Don't assume that *push card* and *pop card* operations will work as you expect when you go to another stack—that stack may have a handler that automatically pushes a card in front of one you may have pushed earlier.

Finally, your stack scripts should make sure to reset everything to the previous condition when the stack is closed. For example, if you've hidden the menu bar, show it again. Reset the user level and any other global or painting properties that have been changed.

Quality Control

Stacks are complicated things, with plenty of opportunity for errors. Unlike book authors, you won't have the benefit of editors, copy editors, fact-checkers, designers, and proofreaders to help perfect your project.

Many authors write first drafts of books, and you should consider your first try at the stack as a first draft also. Don't try to finish every detail at once, but test out the stack at an early stage—you may decide to make major changes. When you do feel you're close to a final design, check and doublecheck everything. Test every button, put text into every field, go to every card, and look at every background. Print out the stack as cards and check them for consistency and graphics errors. Print out a report of the stack scripts and edit them, looking for typos and places to add explanations. Check for typos in field text *and* graphic text, something many stack authors seem to neglect. Make sure indexes, maps, and tables of contents are linked to their proper sections, and be sure cards are in proper order if card order is important in the stack. Test the stack while running *MultiFinder* (if you can).

Even so, you won't find all the problems or think of all the things your stack should contain. You have to field-test it before releasing it. Get at least one potential user (preferably a group of potential users) to try out the stack at both first-draft and final stages, and watch how the tester uses it. The feedback you get will be invaluable. Observe whether your tester quickly grasps the point of your stack and learns to use it without trouble, and ask him or her to suggest additional features that would make your stack more useful. Note whether any stack features appear to be unnecessary. You may end up inviting the test users to be your collaborators.

Copyright Considerations

Like books, photographs, paintings, films, or most other creative works, stacks are a form of intellectual property and can be copyrighted. The copyright laws guarantee you, as the stack creator, the exclusive rights to the publication, sale, and reproduction of the stack. Current law does not require you to register your stack with the Copyright Office, but you should put a copyright notice directly on the stack. A line such as the following,

© 1989 by Janet Doe. All rights reserved.

placed in a locked field or in graphic text on a title card should suffice.

When you place a stack in the public domain, you're explicitly surrendering your rights to copyright protection, allowing anyone to copy and distribute the stack without your permission. A shareware stack is a commercial product and should carry a copyright notice. If you're thinking of publishing your stack through a stackware supply house (see below), you may be asked to transfer the copyright of the stack to the publisher. Think carefully before you do this.

TIP: *HyperCard* Trademarks. Stack authors take note: Apple has established trademark rights to the following *HyperCard*-related names:

HyperCard™
HyperTalk™
Stackware™
MacStacks™
AppleStacks™
HyperStacks™

Claris, Apple's software-publishing spinoff company, owns the rights to:

HyperDemo™
HyperTour™

Apple zealously protects its trademarks, so do not use these terms in your stack without the proper trademark symbol (™) and credit if you're planning to release the stack as a commercial product. The word *stack* is generic and can be used freely. These caveats also apply to other Apple-related terms , such as Mac, Macintosh, and so on. You must get permission from Apple to use these terms in your software product title.

To Protect or Not to Protect

Do you want to prevent your audience from tampering with your carefully designed stacks? Do you need to protect sensitive information from unauthorized use? *HyperCard* provides tools to do both.

There are several levels of protection you can apply to your stacks. At the simplest level, you can prevent individual cards and backgrounds from being deleted by checking the *Can't delete card* and *Can't delete background* check boxes in the Card Info and Background Info dialog boxes. You can also lock fields by clicking on the *Lock text* check box in the Field Info dialog box. This prevents editing of any text entered before the field was locked. If you're really anxious about what a naïve user could do to your stack, you may want to restrict the user level to browsing as well (see above). Of course, these measures can be reversed by anyone who knows enough HyperTalk to reset the user level and gain access to the Info boxes again.

Figure 6-7. Protect Stack Dialog Box

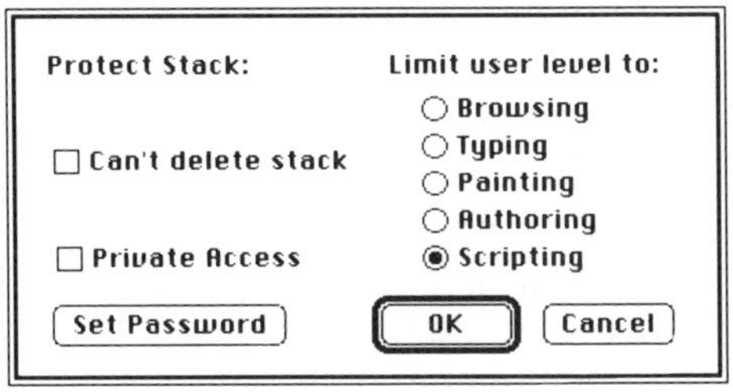

A more extreme step is to restrict access to the stack itself with the Protect Stack . . . option in the File menu. Choosing it brings up the dialog box in Figure 6-7.

Check the *Can't delete stack* box if you want to make sure others won't be able to change or remove the current stack. You also have an alternative way to limit user level to browsing or typing if you don't want to confuse the user with the full authoring environment, or if you want to prevent anyone from reading or modifying the scripts in your stacks. (You'll still be able to get to the Protect Stack . . . menu option—which is only visible at the authoring and scripting user levels—by pressing the Command key while pulling down the File menu.

For the ultimate in protection, check *Private Access* if you want to limit access to the current stack and to the Protect Stack dialog box to someone with the proper password. Here's how to do it:

- Click on Set Password to tell *HyperCard* the password. You'll see the dialog box in Figure 6-8.

Figure 6-8. Password Dialog Box

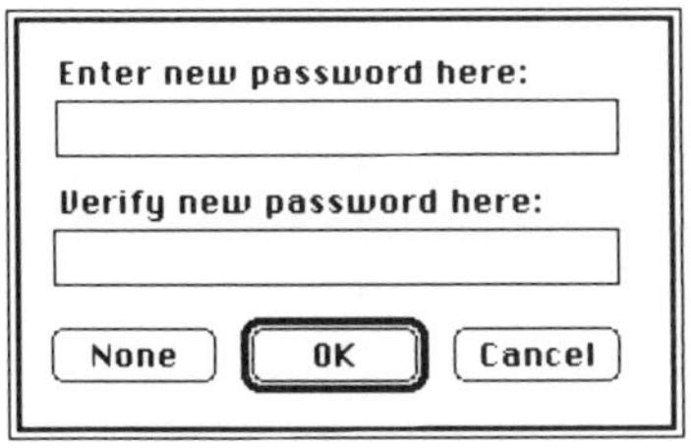

- You must type in the password twice, identically, so that its spelling can be verified. Hit Tab to get to the second entry of the password. Clicking OK protects the stack. To open the stack again, you must provide the password, spelled exactly as it was in the Password dialog box.
- Once you've gained entry to the stack, you can change the password using the method described above.

This form of protection has its drawbacks—the most obvious one is that if you forget the password, you won't be able to open the stack again. So DON'T FORGET THE PASSWORD.

Note: Be sure to copy an important stack to another disk and store that copy in a secure place before password-protecting the original.

> **TIP: Password Protection Bugs.** Two bugs in *HyperCard* version 1.0.1 make password protection rather risky. Always set the Private Access feature BEFORE you assign a password. If you do it the other way around, you may be locked permanently out of your stack. Also, be sure to hit Tab, *not* Return, to get from the first entry of your password in the Password dialog box to the second entry. If you hit Return instead, you may confuse the program into looking for a password that's spelled differently than the one you intended, and you may not be allowed access to the stack.

The problems with password protection make it a less-than-ideal way to protect your stack. Instead, consider more conventional security measures, such as keeping sensitive information on a separate disk that you can physically lock away. If your information is stored on a hard disk, use one of the commercial security utilities to create a locked area on the disk and keep your stacks there.

Consider the philosophical aspects of stack protection, too. Except in specialized circumstances, it makes little sense to protect or restrict access to stacks being offered to the public domain or as shareware. In fact, restriction runs counter to the whole idea of *HyperCard*—freedom of access to information—and is likely to turn your audience away from your product.

Version 1.2 Note: Write Protection and Locked Stacks
Stacks created under version 1.2 can be locked with the following techniques:

- Putting it on a CD-ROM.
- Putting it on a file server in a Read-Only folder.
- Checking the Locked box in the stack's Get Info box in the Finder.
- Flipping the write-protect tab up on the stack's floppy disk.

A small padlock appears at the right of the menu bar of a locked stack. Locked stacks on a file server can be browsed through by more than one user at a time.

Locked stacks are write-protected—users cannot make permanent changes to them. You can also write-protect (but not lock) stacks by

- Checking *Can't Modify Stack* in the stack's Protect Stack dialog box (this is a new option in version 1.2).
- Setting the cantModify stack property to *true* (see Appendix A).

When a stack is locked or write-protected, you can't type into fields and you don't have access to all menu options.

While write-protection and locking are not irreversible, they provide the most convenient and foolproof ways of protecting your stack from casual or accidental modification.

Distributing Your Stack

Once you've created a knockout stack, how should it be distributed to its intended audience? The usual channels for Mac public-domain software distribution are the many Mac special-interest groups on the online information services and electronic bulletin boards. Compact your stack and compress it with a file-compression utility before you upload it. This will save your audience time and money and make them happy. You can place your stack in the library of local Mac user groups. Stackware supply houses distribute your stacks for you and pay a royalty, or you can advertise the stack yourself in Mac-specific magazines. If your stack isn't just for any *HyperCard* user, but contains a specialized body of information, you can distribute it directly to groups that deal with that information or advertise in the relevant journals. If you're developing point-of-sale or other turnkey applications, personal demonstrations to interested organizations are the only way to go. The more narrowly you define your audience, the more focused your energies will be in getting your stack to them.

Chapter 7

Basic Stackbuilding

Sample stack: The Gallery Guide

A very common type of stack is the simple database (address lists, collection and product catalogues, and so on) in which all the information contained in the stack is text held in fields on a single background. The Area Codes stack included with the *HyperCard* package is a good example of this kind of database. If you're using *HyperCard* simply to distribute a homogeneous body of text information, this is the stack format to use. Such stacks are relatively easy to build and make good introductory projects for learning basic stackbuilding.

In this chapter, we'll tackle the design and construction of a sample stack containing information about art galleries. (The choice of subject here is arbitrary—the principles you'll learn can be applied to any other similar information you may want to distribute; simply redesign the stack to suit your needs.) In the process of creating this stack, you'll create and arrange fields and buttons, use the paint tools, write some simple scripts, and enter sample information. This stack was purposely made simple and unadorned, but feel free to alter it as you like.

Plan Your Approach

As mentioned in Chapter 6, it's important to decide what your stack is intended to do and who it's intended to reach before you begin actual construction.

Description: The sample stack in this chapter is called "The 1988 Art Guide." It is an annual description of all the art galleries and museums in the United States and Canada. (For the purposes of this chapter, we'll assume the information is already available and that you're merely putting it into *HyperCard* format. Actually acquiring that kind of information is a far bigger job than creating a stack to hold it, of course.)

Audience: The audience for this stack includes art galleries and dealers, artists, art buyers, and business people offering products and services to the art market. It's assumed that users of the stack already have some familiarity with *HyperCard* and don't have to be told how menus, buttons, and searches work.

Interface: The interface for this stack sticks close to the standard *HyperCard* interface with a visible menu bar, the user level set to scripting, standard arrow buttons, and a minimum of graphics. The stack is not protected in any way, except that the text in some fields is locked.

Structure: This will mainly be a homogeneous stack with two backgrounds. One background is used for introductory and instruction cards only. The main background contains fields for storing information on the gallery's name, address, phone, director, hours, description, artist represented, and catalogues in print. Buttons on the background provide navigation, sorting, scanning, and phone features. There is one card object in the stack. Figure 7-1 diagrams the stack structure.

Figure 7-1. Art Guide Stack Structure

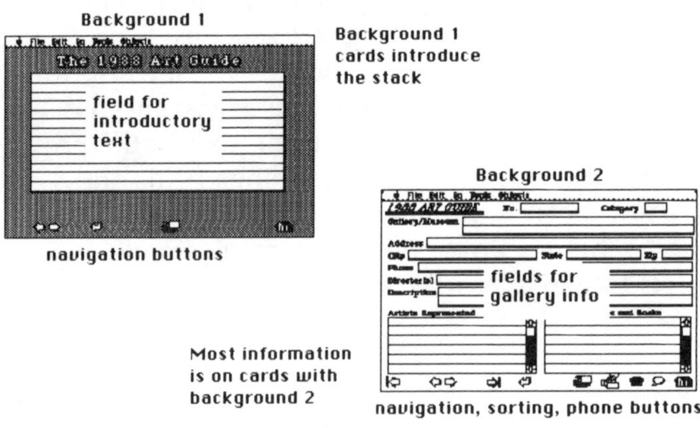

A stack like this would, in reality, be composed of thousands of cards (in this case, over 4000—one per North American gallery and museum). Since this would fill several floppy disks, distributing the stack would be quite unwieldy. Chapter 8 has some hints on handling large stacks by breaking them down into smaller components. If you're adapting your own information, you may want to start with a smaller database that will fit comfortably on one floppy disk.

Creating the New Stack

In the next few pages, we'll go step by step through the process of creating the Art Guide. First, let's start up a new stack.

- Choose New Stack from the File menu.
- Name the stack *Art Guide.* You want a completely clean background, so make sure the *Copy current background* check box is not highlighted.
- Save the stack to the current disk.

The stack has the following script:

```
on openBackground
   show menubar
   hide tool window
end openBackground
```

To be more considerate, when the stack is open, the stack script could store the condition of the menu bar, message box, and palettes in global variables, and then reset these to the values contained in the globals when the stack is closed. This isn't necessary, however, in this simple stack.

Making the Introductory Cards

The stack has two backgrounds. Let's make the first a simple background with one field and several navigational buttons that will serve as the backdrop for two informational cards. Below is a list of the elements you'll need for this first part of the stack. (For this stack, *location* and *rect* coordinates are provided for fields, and *loc* coordinates are provided for buttons.) Refer to Chapter 3 for how to create and manipulate objects.

Background

Name: Titles
Script: empty

Background Graphic Text

Font: New York
TextSize: 24-point
Style: Outline/shadow/underline

Background Graphic Fill

Pattern: 22 (medium gray)

Background Field 1

Location: 257,171

LockText: true
Name: Copyright
Rect: 43,63,471,279
Script: empty
ShowLines: false
Style: shadow
TextAlign: center
TextFont: New York
TextHeight: 16
TextSize: 12
TextStyle: plain
WideMargins: false

Background Button 1

AutoHilite: true
Icon: 1014 (Prev Arrow)
Location: 34,328
Name: Prev
Script:

```
on mouseUp

go to prev card
end mouseUp
```

ShowName: false
Style: transparent
Visible: true

Background Button 2

AutoHilite: true
Icon: 1013 (Next Arrow)
Location: 71,328
Name: Next
Script:

```
on mouseUp
   go to next card
end mouseUp
```

ShowName: false
Style: transparent
Visible: true

Background Button 3

AutoHilite: true
Icon: 1012 (Return Arrow)
Location: 119,328
Name: Return
Script:

```
on mouseUp
   visual effect iris close
   pop card
end mouseUp
```

ShowName: false
Style: transparent
Visible: true

Background Button 4

AutoHilite: true
Icon: 32670 (View)
Location: 285,328
Name: View
Script:

```
on mouseUp
   show all cards
end mouseUp
```

ShowName: false
Style: transparent
Visible: true

Background Button 5

AutoHilite: true
Icon: 1011 (Home)
Location: 463,328
Name: Home
Script:

```
on mouseUp
   visual effect iris close
   go home
end mouseUp
```

ShowName: false
Style: transparent
Visible: true

Card 1

Name: Copyright
Script:

```
on openCard
hide msg box
end openCard
```

Card Button 1

AutoHilite: true
Icon: none
Location:
Name: Introduction
Script:

```
on mouseUp
   visual effect wipe left
   go to card "Intro"
end mouseUp
```

ShowName: true
Style: round rect
Visible: true

Card 2

Name: Intro
Script:

```
on openCard
   show msg box at 19,276
   doMenu "Find . . . "
end openCard
```

Enter background mode and type in the graphic text first. Position it with the selection tool; then fill the background graphics layer with gray, using the bucket. This leaves little enclosed spaces in the *h*, 9, *u*, and *d*; fill these with the bucket in FatBits.

Once the graphics are completed, place the background field and buttons. (Figure 7-2 shows how the completed background

Figure 7-2. Completed Background 1

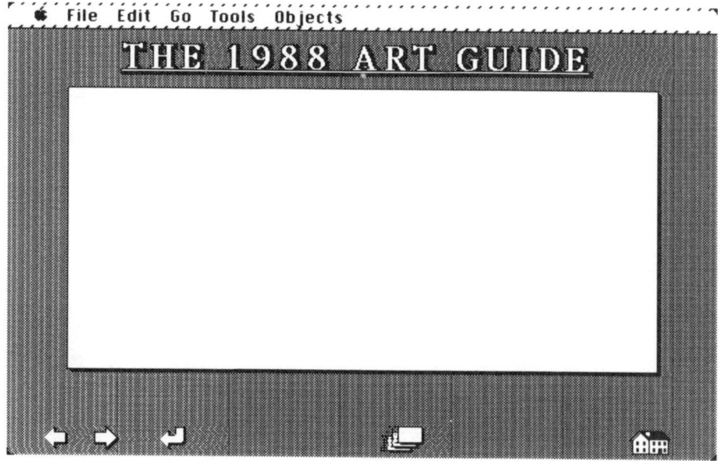

Figures 7-3 and 7-4. Cards 1 and 2

File Edit Go Tools Objects

THE 1988 ART GUIDE

Copyright © 1988 by HyperArt Associates
900 Madison Avenue, New York, New York 10021
(212) 100-0001
All rights reserved.

Introduction

File Edit Go Tools Objects

THE 1988 ART GUIDE

Welcome to the 1988 ART GUIDE, the only complete computerized source for information on North American galleries, museums, art dealers, and consultants. Each listing contains basic information about the art organization and lists the artists represented and catalogues published by the organization in 1988. Information has been supplied by the organizations directly.

Organizations are categorized as follows: G is gallery; M is museum; IG is institutional gallery; D is dealer; and C is consultant.

Type a search word into the message box to look for galleries by state, city, name, director, artist's name, catalogue title, or author.

find ""

looks); then enter card mode and add the card button to the first card. Finally, type in the field text as shown in Figures 7-3 and 7-4. The first card holds a copyright notice; the second card gives general instructions. If additional instructions are needed, more cards with the same background can be created.

TIP: A Script for Cataloguing Background Objects. Wouldn't it be nice to have a summary of the properties of all the background objects in your (or anyone else's) stack? A button with this script pasted on any background will catalogue that background for you, listing all the background buttons and fields and giving the state of several properties for each.

```
                                        --first, catalogue the buttons
on mouseUp
 doMenu "New Card"
 set lockScreen to true
 doMenu "New Field"
 set the name of card field 1 to "Button Info"
 set the style of card field "Button Info" to scrolling
 set the loc of card field "Button Info" to 256,175
 set the rect of card field "Button Info" to 30,30,500,320
                                        --Check spacing
 set the textSize of card field "Button Info" to 10
 set lockScreen to false
 repeat with i = 1 to the number of bkgnd btns
  put the name of bkgnd btn i into item 1 of line i of card field "Button Info"
  put the style of bkgnd btn i into item 2 of line i of card field "Button Info"
  put the icon of bkgnd btn i into item 3 of line i of card field "Button Info"
  put the showName of bkgnd btn i into item 4 of line i of card field "Button Info"
  put the autoHilite of bkgnd btn i into item 5 of line i of card field "Button Info"
  put the loc of bkgnd btn i into item 6 of line i of card field "Button Info"
  put the rect of bkgnd btn i into item 8 of line i of card field "Button Info"
 end repeat

                                        --now, catalogue the fields
 doMenu "New Card"
 set lockScreen to true
 doMenu "New Field"
 set the name of card field 1 to "Field Info"
 set the style of card field "Field Info" to scrolling
 set the loc of card field "Field Info" to 256,175
 set the rect of card field "Field Info" to 30,30,500,320
 set the textSize of card field "Field Info" to 10
 set lockScreen to false
 repeat with i = 1 to the number of bkgnd fields
```

(Continued on page 139)

(Continued from page 138)

```
    put the name of bkgnd field i into item 1 of line i of card field "Field Info"
    put the style of bkgnd field i into item 2 of line i of card field "Field Info"
    put the textFont of bkgnd field i into item 3 of line i of card field "Field Info"
    put the textStyle of bkgnd field i into item 4 of line i of card field "Field Info"
    put the textSize of bkgnd field i into item 5 of line i of card field "Field Info"
    put the loc of bkgnd field i into item 6 of line i of card field "Field Info"
    put the rect of bkgnd field i into item 8 of line i of card field "Field Info"
  end repeat
end mouseUp
```

The script creates a new card and a new scrolling field for background button properties, and then does the same for background field properties. There are a number of ways this script could be improved. First, you could enlarge it to list all the properties of every background object, not just the selected ones chosen here. Second, the script could be modified to automatically catalogue all objects on all backgrounds in a stack. Third, it could be made to handle card objects as well. These improvements are left to you as script-writing exercises.

Making the Gallery Cards

The rest of the stack consists of the actual gallery listings. All the fields containing gallery information are on one background, as are several navigation and other utility buttons. There are no card objects in this part of the stack; the only graphics are graphic text for the labels (see Figure 7-5). Here are the objects used:

Figure 7-5. Galleries Background

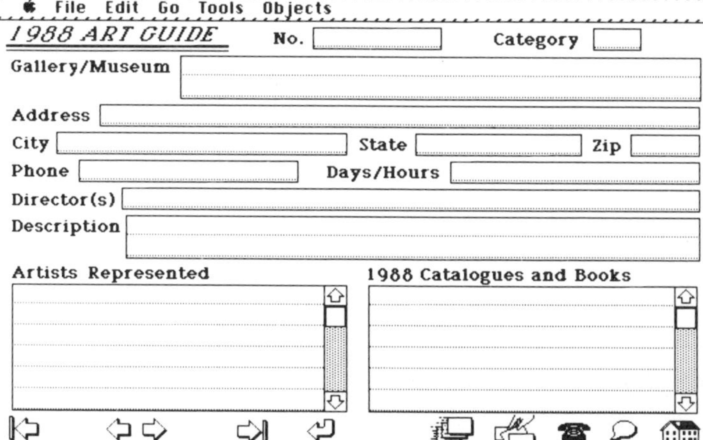

Background 2

Name: Galleries
Script:

```
on openBackground
   hide msg box
end openBackground

on newCard
   tabkey                    --puts the cursor into the first field automatically
end newCard
```

Background Graphic Text Title—Check Hyphens

Font: New York
TextSize: 18-point
Style: Italic

The double rules underneath are drawn with the line tool at two different widths.

Background Graphic Text—Labels

Font: New York
TextSize: 12-point
Style: bold

Background Field 1

Location: 273,32
LockText: false
Name: Number
Rect: 227,24,320,41
Script: empty
ShowLines: true
Style: transparent
TextAlign: left
TextFont: Geneva
TextHeight: 16
TextSize: 12
TextStyle: plain
WideMargins: false

Background Field 2

Location: 446,32

LockText: false
Name: Category
Rect: 429,24,464,41
Script: empty
ShowLines: true
Style: transparent
TextAlign: left
TextFont: Geneva
TextHeight: 16
TextSize: 12
TextStyle: plain
WideMargins: false

Background Field 3

Location: 320,62
LockText: false
Name: Name
Rect: 132,46,508,79
Script: empty
ShowLines: true
Style: transparent
TextAlign: left
TextFont: Geneva
TextHeight: 16
TextSize: 12
TextStyle: plain
WideMargins: false

Background Field 4

Location: 290,91
LockText: false
Name: Address
Rect: 74,83,507,100
Script: empty
ShowLines: true
Style: transparent
TextAlign: left
TextFont: Geneva
TextHeight: 16
TextSize: 12
TextStyle: plain
WideMargins: false

Background Field 5

Location: 147,112
LockText: false
Name: City
Rect: 43,104,252,121
Script: empty
ShowLines: true
Style: transparent
TextAlign: left
TextFont: Geneva
TextHeight: 16
TextSize: 12
TextStyle: plain
WideMargins: false

Background Field 6

Location: 361,112
LockText: false
Name: State
Rect: 301,104,421,121
Script: empty
ShowLines: true
Style: transparent
TextAlign: left
TextFont: Geneva
TextHeight: 16
TextSize: 12
TextStyle: plain
WideMargins: false

Background Field 7

Location: 481,112
LockText: false
Name: Zip
Rect: 456,104,507,121
Script: empty
ShowLines: true
Style: transparent
TextAlign: left
TextFont: Geneva
TextHeight: 16

TextSize: 12
TextStyle: plain
WideMargins: false

Background Field 8

Location: 138,133
LockText: false
Name: Phone
Rect: 59,125,217,142
Script: empty
ShowLines: true
Style: transparent
TextAlign: left
TextFont: Geneva
TextHeight: 16
TextSize: 12
TextStyle: plain
WideMargins: false

Background Field 9

Location: 416,133
LockText: false
Name: Days/Hours
Rect: 326,125,507,142
Script: empty
ShowLines: true
Style: transparent
TextAlign: left
TextFont: Geneva
TextHeight: 16
TextSize: 12
TextStyle: plain
WideMargins: false

Background field 10

Location: 298,154
LockText: false
Name: Director(s)
Rect: 90,146,507,163
Script: empty
ShowLines: true

Style: transparent
TextAlign: left
TextFont: Geneva
TextHeight: 16
TextSize: 12
TextStyle: plain
WideMargins: false

Background Field 11

Location: 300,183
LockText: false
Name: Description
Rect: 93,167,507,200
Script: empty
ShowLines: true
Style: transparent
TextAlign: left
TextFont: Geneva
TextHeight: 16
TextSize: 12
TextStyle: plain
WideMargins: false

Background Field 12

Location: 131,267
LockText: false
Name: Artists
Rect: 10,219,252,315
Script: empty
ShowLines: false
Style: scrolling
TextAlign: left
TextFont: Geneva
TextHeight: 16
TextSize: 12
TextStyle: plain
WideMargins: false

Background Field 13

Location: 286,267
LockText: False

Name: Artists
Rect: 267,219,505,315
Script: empty
ShowLines: false
Style: scrolling
TextAlign: left
TextFont: Geneva
TextHeight: 16
TextSize: 12
TextStyle: plain
WideMargins: false

Background Button 1

AutoHilite: true
Icon: 130557 (First Arrow)
Location: 19,328
Name: First
Script:

```
on mouseUp
   go to first card
end mouseUp
```

ShowName: false
Style: transparent
Visible: true

Background Button 2

AutoHilite: true
Icon: 1014 (Prev Arrow)
Location: 87,328
Name: Prev
Script:

```
on mouseUp
   go to prev card
end mouseUp
```

ShowName: false
Style: transparent
Visible: true

Background Button 3

AutoHilite: true
Icon: 1013 (Next Arrow)
Location: 113,328
Name: Next
Script:

```
on mouseUp
   go to next card
end mouseUp
```

ShowName: false
Style: transparent
Visible: true

Background Button 4

AutoHilite: true
Icon: 26865 (Last Arrow)
Location: 183,328
Name: Last
Script:

```
on mouseUp
   go to last card
end mouseUp
```

ShowName: false
Style: transparent
Visible: true

Background Button 5

AutoHilite: true
Icon: 1012 (Return Arrow)
Location: 233,328
Name: Return
Script:

```
on mouseUp
   visual effect iris close
   pop card
end mouseUp
```

ShowName: false
Style: transparent
Visible: true

Background Button 6

AutoHilite: true
Icon: 32670 (View)
Location: 328,328
Name: View
Script:

```
on mouseUp
   show all cards                    --zips quickly through cards
end mouseUp
```

ShowName: false
Style: transparent
Visible: true

Background Button 7

AutoHilite: true
Icon: 20186 (Sort)
Location: 373,328
Name: Sort
Script:

```
on mouseUp
   sort by first word of bkgnd field "Name"
end mouseUp
```

ShowName: false
Style: transparent
Visible: true

Background Button 8

AutoHilite: true
Icon: 1017 (Phone)
Location: 415,328
Name: Phone
Script:

```
on mouseUp
   dial bkgnd field "Phone" with modem <modem code>
end mouseUp
```

ShowName: false
Style: transparent
Visible: true

Background Button 9

AutoHilite: true
Icon: 19678 (Info Balloon)
Location: 451,328
Name: Info
Script:

```
on mouseUp
   visual effect zoom out
   go to card "Intro"
end mouseUp
```

ShowName: false
Style: transparent
Visible: true

Background Button 10

AutoHilite: true
Icon: 1011 (Home)
Location: 463,328
Name: Home
Script:

```
on mouseUp
   visual effect iris close
   go home
end mouseUp
```

ShowName: false
Style: transparent
Visible: true

Figure 7-5 shows how all these elements are arranged with the fields shown in field mode. Figure 7-6 shows a sample card with information entered.

To create the fields, first make background field number 1 and set the properties listed above. Then clone that field to make the rest of the fields. Move them precisely into alignment with

Figure 7-6. Sample Gallery Card

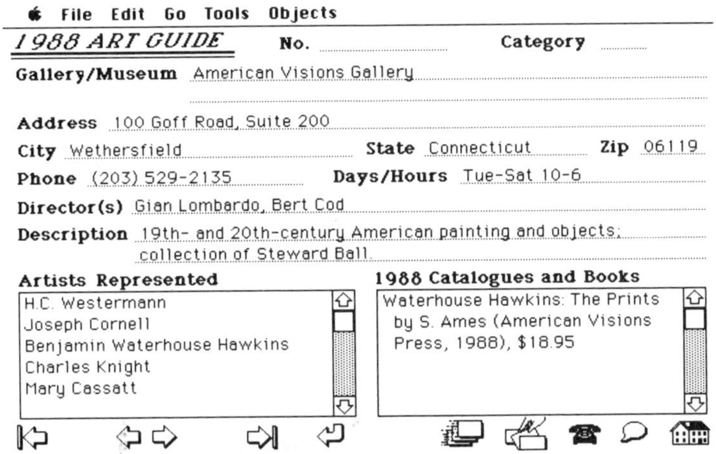

File Edit Go Tools Objects

1988 ART GUIDE **No.** **Category**

Gallery/Museum American Visions Gallery

Address 100 Goff Road, Suite 200

City Wethersfield **State** Connecticut **Zip** 06119

Phone (203) 529-2135 **Days/Hours** Tue-Sat 10-6

Director(s) Gian Lombardo, Bert Cod

Description 19th- and 20th-century American painting and objects; collection of Steward Ball

Artists Represented

H.C. Westermann
Joseph Cornell
Benjamin Waterhouse Hawkins
Charles Knight
Mary Cassatt

1988 Catalogues and Books

Waterhouse Hawkins: The Prints by S. Ames (American Visions Press, 1988), $18.95

the help of the Shift key. Be sure the fields are created in the proper order—sequentially from background field 1 to background field 13—so that you can tab from one to the next. If the fields get out of order, use Bring Closer and Send Farther.

> **TIP: More on Bring Closer and Send Farther.** You may have tried to move an object forward or backward with Bring Closer or Send Farther and obtained bizarre results—the object number wouldn't change or it seemed to change unpredictably. Note that objects have to be moved past all the layers in their domain, not just layers belonging to objects in their class. Thus, if you want to change background field 2 to background field 4, but there happen to be three background button layers in between (as well as one field layer), you would have to invoke Bring Closer five times, not two. Just keep trying until you get the result you want.

With a background of this kind containing a number of small fields, placement of the fields is dictated mostly by how easy it is to read the information, followed by your own sense of aesthetics. There are any number of other ways such fields can be arranged; for example, by aligning the left edge of all fields along a margin and positioning labels above the fields. It's also possible to use fewer fields. Try putting the name, address, and phone number on different lines of one field. Several fields are chosen here so searches can be specified by a small amount of text in one background field. This can really speed up a search when it involves looking at thousands of cards.

Actually, arranging graphic text and fields in the layout shown for this background proceeds somewhat by trial and error. You know approximately where each field and graphic text label should go, but not exactly; you'll need to switch back and forth from paint mode to field mode as you make fine adjustments to the spacing and alignment. One method that saves time is to arrange all the fields first and then fit the graphic text in around them.

Using the Stack

Use of this stack is really quite simple. To create a new gallery card, choose New Card from Edit, or press Command-N. Use the Find . . . option to perform searches or scan cards with the View button until you reach the one you want (click the mouse to stop the scan anywhere). The Phone button lets you dial the number in the Phone field; the button's script can be elaborated to include dialing preambles and modem codes, or you can rewrite the script to take you to the Phone card included with the *HyperCard* package. The Sort button allows you to put the cards in the stack into alphabetical order by the first word in the Name field.

TIP: Sorting and the Alphabet. Sorting can be a great convenience in stacks like this one, putting the cards in a reasonable order for scanning and browsing. But you should realize that sort does have its limitations, especially when alphabetizing names and organization titles. You'll have some cards that just won't alphabetize properly under any sorting criteria. It would be better if you could sort cards by more than one word at a time—for example, if the sort command could look at word 2, then word 1, then word 3, and so on before actually sorting the cards. But true alphabetizing is beyond sort's capacities, at least for now.

One system that works reasonably well is to enter personal names by last name first, and organization names by most important word first, and then sort by first word. (See Appendix A for more on the sort command.) Mark Christopher's *SortLines* stack contains a button that lets you alphabetize text on lines in a field, something that would come in handy for alphabetizing artists' names and catalogue titles in this stack's two scrolling fields.

Making a Home Button

New stacks don't automatically get a button on the Home card. Making a Home button for this stack is quite easy, as shown below.

- Go to the Home card.
- Create a new card button named "Art Guide"—it can be any style you like, but be sure to show the name.
- Link it to the first card of the Art Guide stack using the Link feature on the Button Info box.

If you want a button with a picture instead of plain text, you have two options: You can create a custom icon for the stack, as described in Chapter 3, and then create a transparent card button with that icon and link it to the first card of the Art Guide stack. A simpler, if less elegant, way is as follows:

- Create a card graphic like the one in Figure 7-7 (shown in Fat-Bits) using the paint tools.

Figure 7-7. Art Guide Graphic

- Position the graphic where you want it on the Home card. Create a transparent card button with the name showing and lay that over the graphic.
- Link the button to the first card of the Art Guide stack. The finished button is shown in Figure 7-8. Most of the buttons on the Home card are constructed in the same way.

Figure 7-8. Art Guide Home Card Button

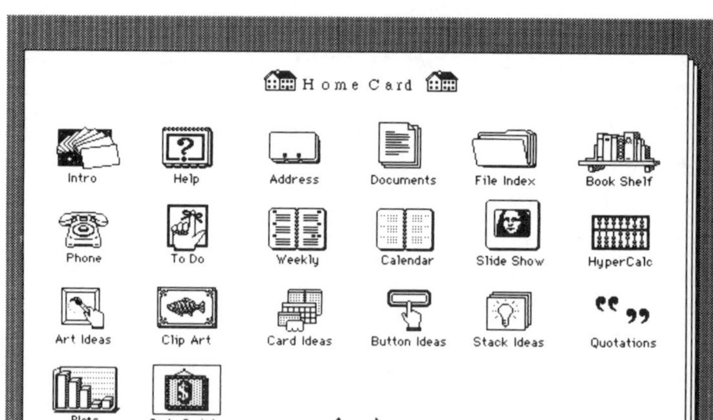

Importing and Exporting Text and Data

Stacks such as Art Guide incorporate large amounts of data. Often this data will be in another computerized form such as a relational database file, spreadsheet file, or word processor file. You need to translate that information to a *HyperCard*-readable format. Likewise, you may have accumulated information in a stack that you want to transfer to a fully relational database, a spreadsheet, or a word processor to take advantage of the powerful features such programs offer.

Initially, it wasn't easy to transfer text and data information between *HyperCard* and other programs. At present, there are still not many applications that will output information in *HyperCard* format, and *HyperCard* is equally unable to read files from other applications. This is not much of a problem when you just want to transfer a paragraph of text to or from *HyperCard*—the Clipboard is perfect for that. But suppose you want to pour a few hundred database records into a stack? Life is too short to do that through the Clipboard.

HyperCard versions 1.1 and 1.2 include three new buttons—Import, Export Text, and Export Data—that make importing and exporting text and data much easier. You can paste these buttons into any stack.

These buttons move text or data to and from the current stack and any ASCII text file. Data is defined as any text document separated into fields and records, as is usually done in databases. Almost always, a Tab character (ASCII 9) is used to delimit (end) a field, and a Return (ASCII 13) character to delimit a record. Text is not divided in this way.

Each button brings up a series of dialog boxes with questions for you to answer, and then it takes actions based on your answers. When you import data, a new background and new cards are created for each record and the contents are dumped into scrolling background fields, one for each field in the record. (These fields are piled one on top of the next, so they have to be separated later.) Imported text is put into a single card-sized scrolling field on a new background and card; there's a limit of about 16–18 pages (32K) per field, so if you want to import a longer text file (the first chapter of your *HyperCard* novel, for example), break it up first into files that are smaller than 32K. *HyperCard* doesn't accept typical word processor files, such as those generated by *Microsoft Word* or *WriteNow;* you must convert these files to ASCII format first. These programs, and most other Mac word processors, provide a translator feature to do the conversion.

The Export Text button sends ASCII text from one or more background fields of the current background to a new or existing document (the imported text will write over any text in an existing file). The Export Data button sends ASCII text from one or more background fields of the current background to a new or existing document (the text is sent with delimiting characters for input into databases and spreadsheets that use them). Again, imported data will write over any data in an existing file.

> **TIP: Import-Export and Pathnames.** These buttons are not kind enough to display the standard open file/open stack dialog boxes. Instead, you'll be shown an *ask dialog* in which you must type in the pathname of the stack, file, and/or folder you want to import from or export to. Be sure to jot down the path name before you initiate the process.

Now you've created a custom database. Nothing fancy, but it beats index cards. In the next chapter, you'll take on a more elaborate application with many automatic features and information-swapping among two stacks. In Chapter 9, you'll look at some advanced special effects that truly tap into *HyperCard*'s higher capabilities.

Chapter 8

A Multistack Business Application

Sample stack: A mail-ordering system

If you've ever struggled with the thousands of paper forms required to run even a small business, you've probably longed for a simple computer business system. The problems with most computerized business management systems—even those for the Macintosh—are that they're hard to customize and may demand that you move faster than you're ready into automating your business; also, such packages are expensive and sometimes difficult to learn.

HyperCard provides a relatively painless path to computerization for many small businesses. Since *you* are actually doing the programming, you can proceed at your own pace and customize your stacks to suit your business, using analogs of the paper forms you already use. The learning curve for authoring your own stacks isn't likely to be much steeper than one for mastering a dedicated business-management or accounting system.

Below, we'll look at the design of two core parts—an online catalogue and an invoicing stack—of a small, fictional, direct mail/phone retail business. The main purpose is to investigate how to create multistack applications. While the stacks discussed don't comprise a complete small-business management system, they do provide examples of creating related stacks for different audiences, trading information between stacks, and designing scripts that perform chains of calculations, all of which are applicable to a larger and more comprehensive program. The scripts in these stacks are more elaborate than those you worked with in previous chapters; also, the catalogue stack contains some sophisticated graphics.

The Stacks

Description: The two stacks in this application are "Ends of the Earth, Inc., Online Catalogue, " a retail catalogue distributed by mail on disk and via information services, and a *linked invoicing* *system* used at the company offices to take phone and mail orders and to print invoices. Information from an in-house copy of the product catalogue is retrieved automatically by the invoice stack when an order is taken; the information is then used to generate a complete invoice to include as a packing slip when the order is shipped.

Audience: The catalogue is designed to be used by anyone with basic *HyperCard* knowledge. The invoice stack is to be used by employees who aren't necessarily proficient with *HyperCard*, but who should be familiar with basic Mac operations.

Interface: The catalogue stack is designed to be visually appealing. The user environment is controlled so that users cannot mistakenly alter the information in the stack. The invoice stack is primarily text-based and offers a standard *HyperCard* environment.

Structure: The catalogue stack has a cover card, two introductory cards, and product listings cards. Except for the cover card, the other cards share a similar background design. Standard navigation buttons and a special search button are provided. The cards are put into subject groups by the stack author.

The invoice stack has one background only. This contains the fields for the invoice information, and buttons to perform navigation, calculation, search-and-retrieve, and printing functions. Figure 8-1 is a diagram of the application showing linkages between the stacks.

In Chapter 7, property descriptions of every object were provided to help you recreate them, if you so chose. In this chapter, we'll concentrate on the *scripts* of the objects rather than on their properties.

Figure 8-1. Application Diagram Showing Linkages Between Stacks

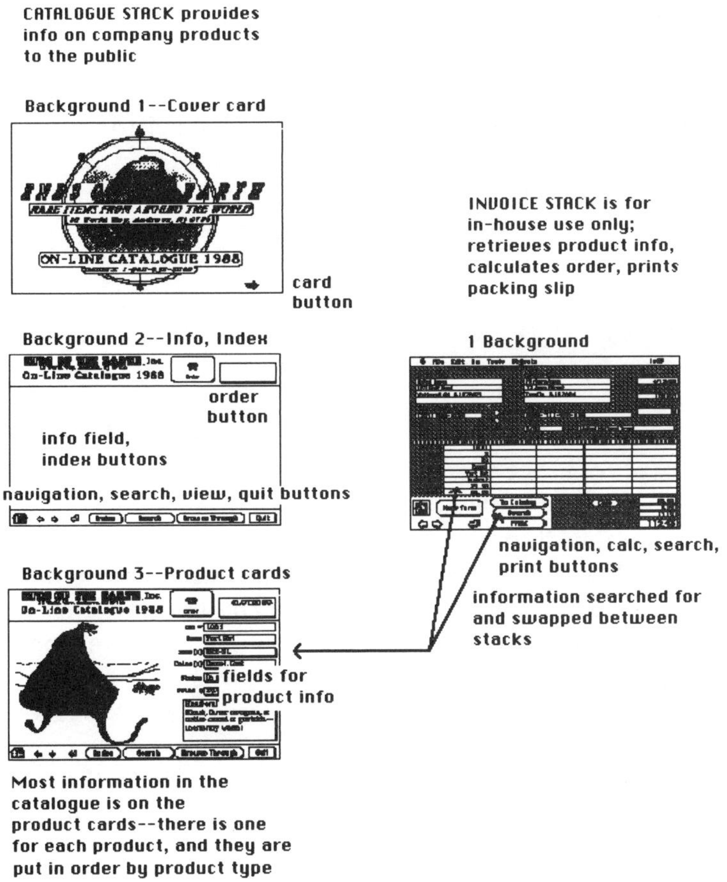

CATALOGUE STACK provides
info on company products
to the public

Background 1--Cover card

card
button

INVOICE STACK is for
in-house use only;
retrieves product info,
calculates order, prints
packing slip

Background 2--Info, Index

order
button

info field,
index buttons

navigation, search, view, quit buttons

1 Background

navigation, calc, search,
print buttons

information searched for
and swapped between
stacks

Background 3--Product cards

fields for
product info

Most information in the
catalogue is on the
product cards--there is one
for each product, and they are
put in order by product type

Making the Catalogue Stack

In concept, this stack is much like the one described in Chapter 7. It begins with some introductory cards, and the main body of information is contained on cards with one background. One difference is that the cards in this stack have been grouped by subject—for example, all cards showing clothing are contiguous—making it easier for casual browsers to find what they want.

First, create a new stack with a blank background, called *Mail Order Catalogue*. Give it this simple script:

```
on openStack
   hide msg box
   hide menubar
end openStack
```

```
on closeStack
   show msg box
   show menubar
end closeStack
```

Using the Protect Stack feature, the user level is set to browsing and the *Can't delete stack* option is checked. In addition, all fields will be separately locked; this is so information cannot accidentally be changed by someone browsing through the stack.

The Cover Card

A slick retail catalogue calls for a slick cover. Here's how to create the graphics shown in Figures 8-2 through 8-4.

- Make sure you're in the card domain. Enter *painting* mode by choosing the oval tool. Set the line width to 1, set the pattern to black, and choose *Draw Centered* from the Options menu.
- Place the crosshairs in the center of the screen and make a small mark; you'll use this as the center of three concentric circles that will form the basis for a compass card. Draw the two inner circles, pressing the Shift key as you drag to make a circle and not an ellipse; then change to line width 2 and draw the outer circle. The diameter of the outer circle should be about 300 pixels (Figure 8-2).
- Draw the points of the compass using the line tool, with the line width set to 1 and Draw Centered still on. Make four lines

Figure 8-2. Ends of the Earth Cover 1

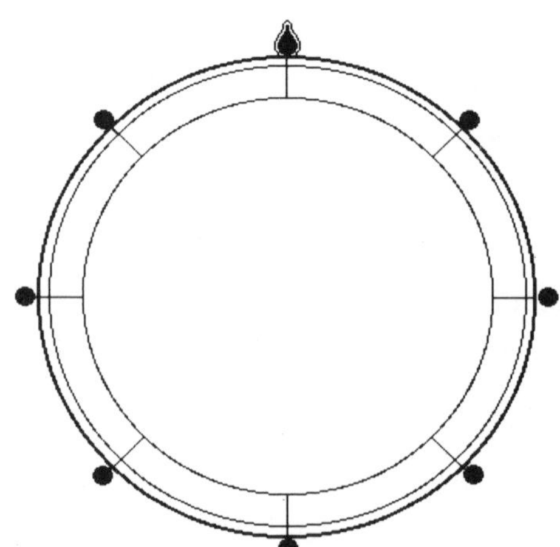

to divide the set of circles into eighths: Starting at the center of the circles and dragging straight, draw one horizontal line, one vertical line, and two lines at 45-degree angles (Figure 8-2).

- Switch to the brush tool and choose a large circular brush. Place markers on the outside of the outer circle where the lines intersect it. Make the upper (North) marker a little fancier, as shown in Figure 8-2. Finally, erase the parts of the lines within the inner circle, either using the eraser or by drawing a borderless circle filled with white (by pressing the Option and Shift keys as you drag) that is centered on the same spot as the other circles.
- Within the compass card, create a painting of a snowcapped mountain using the brush and spray tools and several patterns. Give the mountain a three-dimensional look by using lighter patterns on the left side, becoming gradually darker on the right (Figure 8-3).

Figure 8-3. Ends of the Earth Cover 2

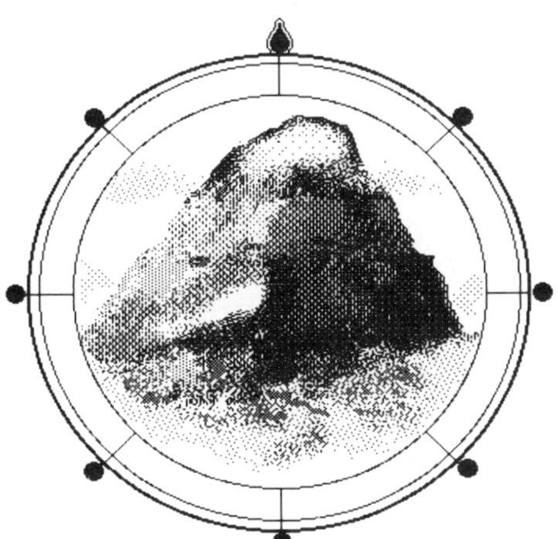

Options to the snowcapped mountain for conveying the corporate identity might be a world map or an old Ford Tri-Motor. If you're designing a real logo or cover, draw several versions and have your company choose the best one.

- Now for the text. First make a new card to use as a scratch pad; you'll design the text parts on this card and then paste them on top of the compass mountain later. When you're through with the scratch card, delete it.
- The font used throughout the catalogue is New York—the author's candidate for best-looking Mac screen font. First type the

main title, "Ends of the Earth," in 24-point italic, shadowed, extended New York, with an extra space between letters. Select the text and enlarge it about 25 percent by dragging a lower corner while pressing the Command and Shift keys. Try to gauge the resizing so the letters don't look too ragged.

- The first subhead ("Rare Items . . . ") is 20-point italic, bold, extended, and 14-point italic, bold, extended. The second subhead ("On-Line Catalogue") is 24-point bold, extended, and 14-point italic, bold, extended. Use centered alignment for both subheads. Make the borders for the text with the round-rectangle tool; surround each line with a round rectangle, and then use the eraser in FatBits to erase the lines between them.
- Finally, use the lasso tool to copy the lines of text from the scratch card to the compass card, (Figure 8-4). If the middle letters of "Ends of the Earth" don't show up well against the mountain, enter FatBits and use the pencil tool to darken the outline around each letter.

Figure 8-4. Ends of the Earth Cover 4

At bottom left, add a Next card button with this script:

```
on mouseUp
 visual effect wipe left
 go to next card
end mouseUp
```

Figure 8-5. Background Template

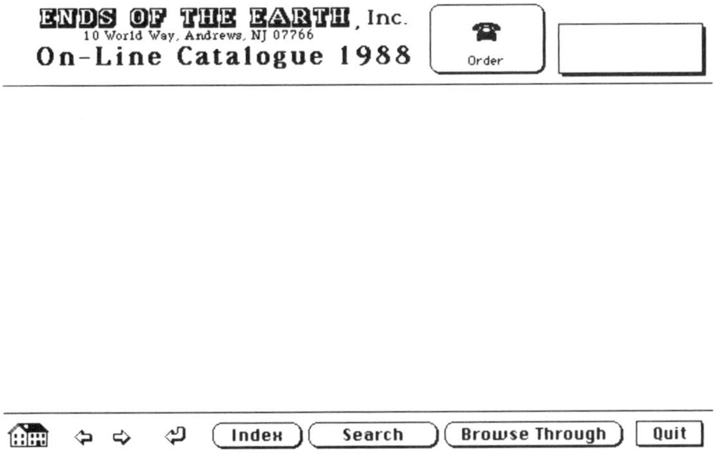

ENDS OF THE EARTH, Inc.
10 World Way, Andrews, NJ 07766
On-Line Catalogue 1988
Order

Index Search Browse Through Quit

The Background Template

The rest of the cards in this stack are based on the background design shown in Figure 8-5. The top contains a header in graphic text, a button that dials the order number automatically if your Mac is hooked up to a modem or handset coupler, and a small shadowed field ("Index") to hold subject keywords for searching. Along the bottom are navigation buttons: a button that takes you to a special index card (see below), a button that lets you perform dialog-based searches, a modified View button, and a Quit button. (Since the menu bar is hidden, basic functions like *quitting* have to be supplied by the stack designer; you shouldn't assume the user knows how to restore the menu bar or use the Command-Q key combination.) Thin lines set off the top and bottom "service areas." The middle of the card will contain different types of information as the function of the card changes.

The background itself has an empty script. Here are the background button scripts:

Background Button 1: Order

```
on mouseUp
  dial "1 800 932 8000"
end mouseUp
```

Background Button 2: Home

```
on mouseUp
  visual effect iris close
  go "Home"
end mouseUp
```

Background Button 3: Prev

```
on mouseUp
  visual effect wipe right
  go to previous card
end mouseUp
```

Background Button 4: Next

```
on mouseUp
  visual effect wipe left
  go to next card
end mouseUp
```

Background Button 5: Return

```
on mouseUp
  push recent card
  pop card
end mouseUp
```

Background Button 6: Index

```
on mouseUp
  visual effect zoom out
  go to card "Index"
end mouseUp
```

Background Button 7: Search

Allows you to search any field in the stack by responding to a dialog box (some users won't know how to use the Find command).

```
on mouseUp
  ask "Search for . . . ?"              --creates an ask dialog box
  if it is "Cancel" then
    exit mouseUp                        --if Cancel is clicked then quit the handler
  end if
  put it into searchWhat
  if searchWhat is empty then           --if nothing was typed into the ask box
    exit mouseUp
  end if
  set lockScreen to true
```

```
  push card                                   --so you can return later
  find searchWhat
  if the result is "not found" then           --error handling
    answer "Can't find it—check your spelling" with "OK"
    pop card                                  --go back
  end if
end mouseUp
```

Background Button 8: Browse Through

Cycles through the cards at one-second intervals.

```
on mouseUp
  repeat with i = 1 to the number of cards
    show 1 cards
    wait 1 secs
  end repeat
end mouseUp
```

Background Button 9: Quit

Included so you can quit *HyperCard.*

```
on mouseUp
    doMenu "Quit HyperCard"
end mouseUp
```

The Introductory Card and the Index

Use this background as the basis for the second card in the stack (Figure 8-6), which is simply an information card, and the third

Figure 8-6. Catalogue Info Card

The ENDS OF THE EARTH, Inc. ON-LINE CATALOGUE 1988 brings you a unique selection of the rarest and most unusual items the world has to offer. You'll find everything you never knew existed, from Tortuga mambu pipes to pure iridium meteorites from Antarctica to still-warm echidna eggs from Queensland. All items are authentic, not manufactured for the tourist trade. Your complete amazement and satisfaction is 100% guaranteed.

* Toll-Free Ordering, 24 Hours a Day, 7 Days a Week

* Express Shipment--Next Day Delivery

* 100% Satisfaction Guaranteed

* Customer Service 1-800-932-9000

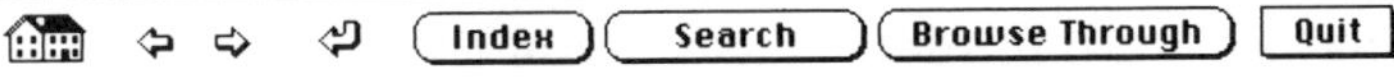

Figure 8-7. Catalogue Index

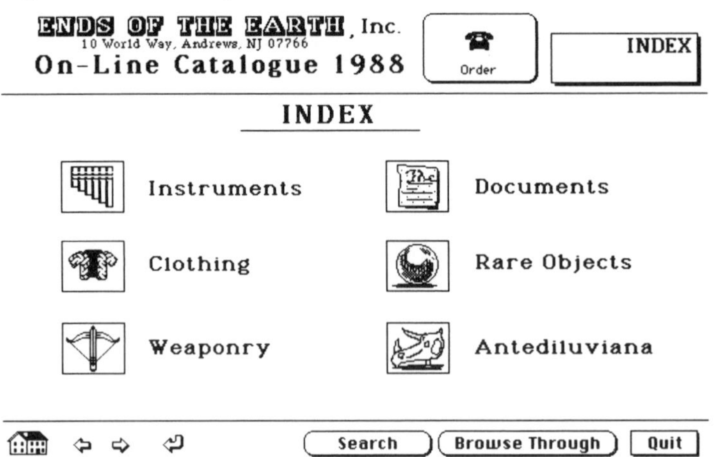

card (Figure 8-7), which is an index. These can be made simply by invoking the New Card menu option, or pressing Command-N.

The information card contains a large card field to hold text. The Index card contains buttons that go to the first card in each subject section, using a simple find operation like the following:

```
on mouseUp
   visual effect zoom in
   find "Clothing" in bkgnd field "Index"
end mouseUp
```

You could also create a simple link to the relevant card with the Link To . . . feature. Note, by the way, that the background Index button appears to be missing on the Index card; in fact, it's hidden by an opaque card button. Since you're already at the Index card, there's no need to confuse things by showing a button that offers to take you there.

The Product Cards

For the cards actually holding product information, you'll need to copy the background template and then add some background fields to it. This is more involved than it seems because *HyperCard* provides no simple way of using an old background to make a new one. If you create a new card with the background and then add additional fields, the fields will show up on all cards with that background. The same thing occurs if you cut a card with that background and paste it to another location in the stack—

cutting and pasting do not affect a card's background. You could create a new blank background with New Background from the Objects menu, and then cut and paste all the objects from the background template onto it, but there's an easier way.

TIP: Many Backgrounds from One. To solve the problem of adding new fields to an old background, try the following:

- Use *Copy Card* to copy a card with the desired background to the Clipboard.
- Enter background mode and choose the pencil tool. Make a one-pixel mark in an inconspicuous place on the background—it doesn't need to be visible.
- Exit painting mode and check the current background's I.D.
- Paste the card from the Clipboard wherever you want it in the stack. Check the background I.D. of this card; it will be different from that of it's "parent" card. With the exception of that one-pixel mark, the backgrounds will be identical in every other way.
- You can now modify the new background anyway you like without affecting the other background. Repeat the operation as many times as necessary.

Now that you've created a duplicate background, add background fields named *Cat#, Item, Size, Color, Status, Price,* and *Description.* These will contain information for the invoice stack to use in preparing orders. A complete catalogue entry is shown in Figure 8-8. The Index field at the upper right holds a keyword

Figure 8-8. Catalogue Product Card

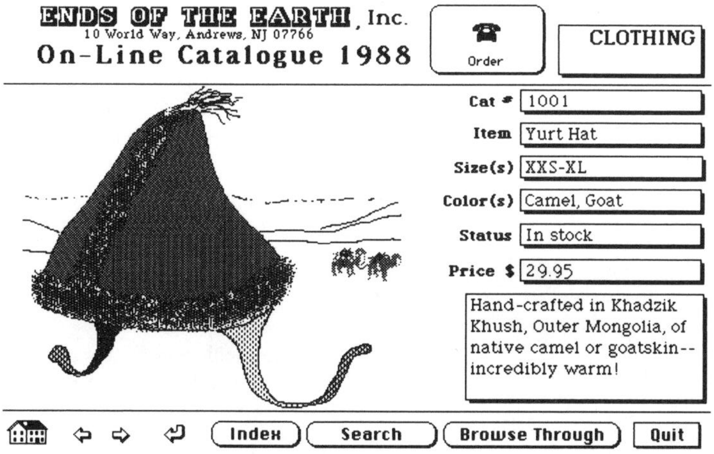

that indicates to which general category of goods the product belongs.

Making the Invoice Stack

The invoice stack is homogeneous. Its duties are to keep a record of incoming phone and mail orders, to aid the order-taker in calculating and retrieving information, and to print out the invoices. A sample card is shown in Figure 8-9.

Figure 8-9. Invoice Card

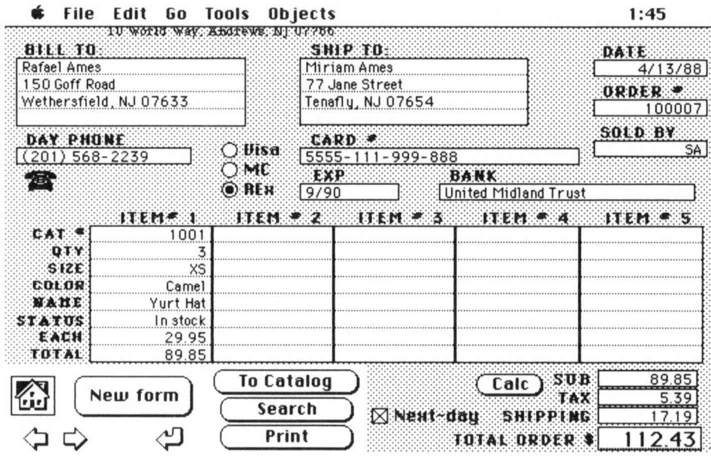

The stack is named *Mail Order Invoices* and has the following script:

```
on openStack
  hide msg box
end openStack
```

The one background is named *Mail Order Form*. It performs a number of automatic functions for each card:

```
on newCard
  sort ascending by bkgnd field "order #"          --puts cards into numerical order
  put the short date into field "Date"             --dates each card
  put the number of cards + 100000 into field "order #"
                                                   --gives each card a unique order number
  tabKey                                           --puts the text cursor into the first field
end newCard
```

```
on idle
  repeat with j = 5 to 15
    if the visible of bkgnd button j is false then
      show bkgnd button j
    end if
  end repeat
  pass idle
end idle
```

This has to do with making sure hidden buttons are shown again if printing is aborted; we'll get back to this handler later.

All objects and graphics in the stack are in the background domain. The background has a light gray pattern with the same head as the catalogue cards at upper left. All field labels are in bold Geneva graphic text. The fields are numbered from upper left to lower right and are given names to correspond to their labels. The five "item" fields are numbered 7–11.

Background Buttons

The buttons are numbered according to which buttons are to be hidden and which have to work together, rather than by their locations on the card. Following are the background button scripts with annotations.

Background Button 1: Next-Day

```
empty script
```

This check box is used merely to show whether express mail service has been ordered. A handler in the Calc button script (below) looks for the state of the hilite of this button, and then adds express charges accordingly.

The next three radio buttons work as a group, indicating which credit card is being used to pay for the order. If you click on one, setting its hilite to true, the hilite of the others is automatically set to false—which is how groups of radio buttons always should act. The three buttons all have the same script. Note that for this to work, the radio buttons have to have consecutive numbers (background buttons 2, 3, and 4).

Background Button 2: Visa

```
on mouseUp
  set the hilite of me to true               --me is the object with the current handler
  repeat with k = 2 to 4                     --the button numbers of these buttons
    if k is not the number of me then
      set the hilite of bkgnd button k to false
    end if
  end repeat
end mouseUp
```

Background Button 3: MC (MasterCard)

```
on mouseUp
  set the hilite of me to true
  repeat with k = 2 to 4
    if k is not the number of me then
      set the hilite of bkgnd button k to false
    end if
  end repeat
end mouseUp
```

Background Button 4: AEx (American Express)

```
on mouseUp
  set the hilite of me to true
  repeat with k = 2 to 4
    if k is not the number of me then
      set the hilite of bkgnd button k to false
    end if
  end repeat
end mouseUp
```

When several objects require similar scripts, it's often possible to put one script a step or two higher in the hierarchy that handles the work of all the object scripts. Can you think of a way to do this with the radio buttons above? Hint: You need to pass the mouseUp message up to the background level and create a handler for it there.

Version 1.2 Note: More on Me and the Target
The script for background buttons 2, 3, and 4 use the term "me" when referring to the object with the current handler. This could be a button, a field, or any other object. With 1.2, you can also use *me* as a container when *me* is a field. For example,

```
get the id of me
```

returns the id of the object. With 1.2, you can also say,

```
put "a new me" into line 1 of me
put me into the msg box
```

in effect, manipulating the contents of the field referred to by *me*.

The same is true of the *target*, the term used to refer to the currently selected object or the object that was the recipient of the most recent message. The target refers to the object itself, as in:

```
put the name of the target into the msg box      --returns the name
```

With 1.2, you can manipulate the contents of the target when the target is a field. For example:

```
put target into field "Target Practice"          --puts the contents/value of
                                                 --the target in the field
put "bull's eye" into line 2 of target
```

Before we look at the next script, here's a little information on how to write scripts to search another stack. A search can be initiated by a find command or by another action. To search another stack with the find command, use a skeleton script like the following:

```
on mouseUp
   set lockscreen to true
   get the selection                  --or the msg box, a field, etc.
   go to stack "StackName"            --provide the full pathname if necessary
   find it
   if the result is empty then        --error handling
    go back
    answer "Can't Find It" with "OK"

    set lockScreen to false
   end if                             --now you're back in the original stack
end mouseUp
```

In many cases, you'll want to search for an item in another stack and then retrieve some associated information and return to where you were. Use the following modification of the above script to do this:

```
on mouseUp
   set lockscreen to true
   get the selection                        --or the msg box, etc.
   go to stack "StackName"
   find it
   if the result is empty then
     go back
     answer "Can't Find It" with "OK"
   else get bkgnd field 1                   --contains the information you want to retrieve
   go back                                  --now you're in back in the original stack
   put it into the msg box
   set lockScreen to false
end mouseUp
```

The first part of the following script searches the catalogue stack, using a variation of the handler just described. It also calculates subtotals, tax, and shipping, and figures out the total order cost. The script is broken into functional parts for clarity.

Background Button 5: Calc

Long and involved, the Calc button script takes time to execute, especially if much information has to be fetched from the catalogue stack.

```
                                    --this part gets information from the catalogue and puts
                                    --it into the "item" fields on the invoice; the assumption is
                                    --that the order-taker has been given a catalogue item
                                    --number over the phone or on a mail-order form
on mouseUp
  set lockScreen to true
  push card
  repeat with h = 7 to 11                        --the numbers of the invoice "item" fields
    put line 1 of field h into catNumber         --get the catalogue number
    if line 1 of field h is empty then
      next repeat                                --skip to the next field
    else go to stack "Mail Order Catalogue"
    find catNumber
    if the result is "not found" then            --error handling
      answer "Can't find it—check catalogue number" with "OK"
      pop card
    end if
```

```
    put field "item" into itemName                --get the info in these
                                                  --catalogue fields

    put field "price" into itemPrice
    put field "status" into itemStatus
    pop card
    set lockScreen to false
    put itemName into line 5 of field h           --put info into invoice
    put itemStatus into line 6 of field h
    put itemPrice into line 7 of field h
  end repeat

                          --this part calculates the subtotal of each "item"
                          --field and adds it to the "sub" field
set numberFormat to "0.00"                        --for handling money
  put empty into total1                           --clear things from possible previous
                                                  --calculation

  put empty into total2
  repeat with i = 7 to 11
    put line 2 of field i * line 7 of field i into total1 --quantity times price
    if total1 is 0.00 then                        --if the field is empty
      next repeat
    else put total1 into line 8 of field i
    add line 8 of field i to total2               --add the totals of
                                                  --each "item" field

    put total2 into field "sub"
  end repeat                                      --now figure the sales tax; tax is
                                                  --being charged only in the
                                                  --home state of New Jersey

  put empty into field "tax"
  repeat with j = 2 to 5
    repeat with k = 3 to 4
      if word j of line k of field "bill to" is "NJ" then    --looking for New Jersey in
                                                             --specific parts of the address
        put field "sub" * 0.06 into field "tax"              --calculate sales tax
      end if
    end repeat
  end repeat
```

You could dispense with the nested repeat structure above and say "If 'NJ' is in field 'bill to,' " but you might possibly pick up an 'nj' combination that doesn't refer to New Jersey.

```
                          --this part calculates shipping
put empty into field "shipping"
  if the hilite of bkgnd button "Next-day" is false then
    if field "sub" < = 50.00 then
      put 4.00 into field "shipping"              --a minimum shipping charge
```

```
    else put field "sub" * 0.08 into field "shipping"
  end if
  if the hilite of bkgnd button "Next-day" is true then        --if express is ordered
    if field "sub" < = 50.00 then
      put 12.00 into field "shipping"                          --minimum next-day charge
    else put field "sub" * 0.08 + 10.00 into field "shipping"
  end if

                                     --finally, calculate the total order
  put empty into field "total order"
  put field "sub" + field "tax" + field "shipping" into field "total order"
end mouseUp
```

The next four buttons are standard navigation buttons.

Background Button 6: Home

```
on mouseUp
  visual effect iris close
  go "Home"
end mouseUp
```

Background Button 7: Prev

```
on mouseUp
  visual effect wipe right
  go to previous card
end mouseUp
```

Background Button 8: Next

```
on mouseUp
  visual effect wipe left
  go to next card
end mouseUp
```

Background Button 9: Return

Use this to toggle back and forth from the catalogue.

```
on mouseUp
  push recent card
  pop card
end mouseUp
```

Background Button 10: New Form

```
on mouseUp
  visual effect wipe left fast to black
  visual effect wipe right fast               --looks like one card is being
                                              --removed and another inserted
  doMenu "New Card"
end mouseUp
```

The elaborate visual effect gives you an extra cue that a new card is being created so you won't think you're just going to another card that already exists.

Background Button 11: To Catalogue

```
on mouseUp
 go to stack "Mail Order Catalogue"
end mouseUp
```

The search button below is a variation of the one contained in the catalogue—it gives you a choice of stacks to search.

Background Button 12: Search

```
on mouseUp
 answer "Search where . . . ?" with "Invoices" or "Catalogue" or "Cancel"
                                              --where do you want to search?
 put it into searchWhere                      --store the answer
 if searchWhere is "Cancel" then
  exit mouseUp
 end if
 ask "Search for . . . ?"                     --asks for the search word
 put it into searchWhat                       --store the answer
 if searchWhat is empty then
  exit mouseUp
 end if
 set lockScreen to true
 push card
 if searchWhere is "Invoices" then
  find searchWhat
  if the result is "not found" then           --error handling
   answer "Can't find it—check your spelling" with "OK"
   exit mouseUp
  end if
 else go to stack "Mail Order Catalogue"
 find searchWhat
 if the result is "not found" then
  answer "Can't find it—check your spelling" with "OK"
  pop card
 end if
end mouseUp
```

If the search is successful, you'll end up in the right stack at the card with the searched-for item.

The Print button hides selected buttons on the card, so when it's printed, a text message is revealed at lower left. An opaque

Figure 8-10. Invoice Ready for Printing

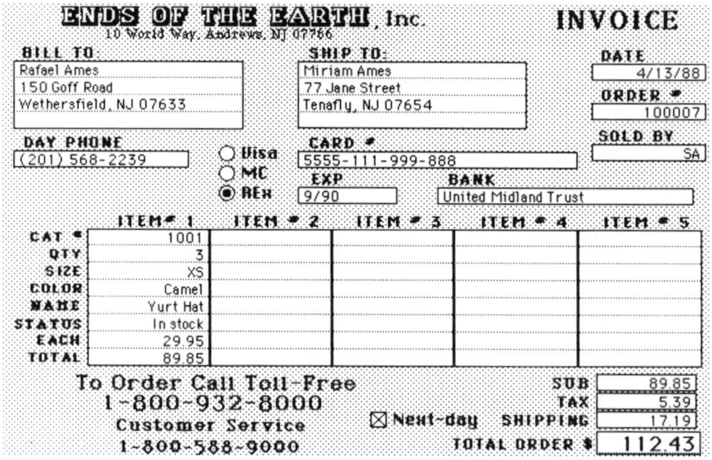

ENDS OF THE EARTH, Inc. INVOICE
10 World Way, Andrews, NJ 07756

BILL TO:	SHIP TO:	DATE
Rafael Ames 150 Goff Road Wethersfield, NJ 07633	Miriam Ames 77 Jane Street Tenafly, NJ 07654	4/13/88

ORDER #: 100007

SOLD BY: SA

DAY PHONE: (201) 568-2239

Visa / MC / AEx (selected: AEx)

CARD #: 5555-111-999-888

EXP: 9/90

BANK: United Midland Trust

	ITEM # 1	ITEM # 2	ITEM # 3	ITEM # 4	ITEM # 5
CAT #	1001				
QTY	3				
SIZE	XS				
COLOR	Camel				
NAME	Yurt Hat				
STATUS	In stock				
EACH	29.95				
TOTAL	89.85				

To Order Call Toll-Free
1-800-932-8000
Customer Service
1-800-588-9000

☒ Next-day

SUB	89.85
TAX	5.39
SHIPPING	17.19
TOTAL ORDER $	112.43

button hides the message during normal use of the stack—that's why there's a white rectangle behind the lower left group of buttons. Figure 8-10 shows an invoice card ready for printing.

Background Button 13: Print

```
on mouseUp
  repeat with i = 5 to 15
    hide bkgnd button i                    --hides unwanted buttons
  end repeat
  print this card
  repeat with j = 5 to 15
    show bkgnd button j                    --shows them again
  end repeat
end mouseUp
```

If the printing operation is aborted halfway through by typing Command-. (period), the entire handler is also aborted at that time. This means the part of the script that makes the buttons visible again won't execute, which is very inconvenient. That's why there's an "on idle" handler in the background script that shows any hidden buttons.

Background button 14: Opaque Button

```
empty script
```

This is the opaque button that hides the background graphic text at lower left.

Background Button 15: Phone

```
on mouseUp
  dial field "Day phone" with modem <modem codes>
end mouseUp
```

> **TIP: More on Modems.** A good place to learn more about how to handle phone dialing with HyperTalk is the *Phone SetUp* card. The button scripts in that card include features for dialing preambles and eliminating area codes for local calls. If you need those features, you can add them to the dialing scripts in your stacks, using Phone SetUp as a model.
>
> To dial without a modem, connect your touch-tone phone with an acousitc coupler (or try holding the phone up to the Mac's speaker) and click a button that issues a dial command without modem codes. To dial a voice call with a modem, pick up the handset, and then click a dial button that issues a dial command with the proper modem codes.
>
> A peculiar aspect of *HyperCard*'s telephone handling is that it doesn't hang up automatically when you get a busy signal. To hang up the modem after getting a busy signal with the dial command, create a button with this script:
>
> ```
> on mouseUp
>    dial "7" with modem "ATDT"
> end mouseUp
> ```
>
> Click the button and the modem will hang up.

Note how often the "repeat with" structure is used in these scripts. It is one of the most powerful HyperTalk structures, invaluable for taking care of repetitive actions within parameters that you can set.

How This Application Works

To see how the two stacks mesh and work together, let's run through a typical session with them.

- The customer—let's say her name is Alice—receives a copy of the catalogue disk by mail or downloads it from a bulletin board.
- After browsing and searching through the catalogue, Alice decides to make a purchase. She clicks on the *To Order* button, and her modem dials up the Ends of the Earth toll-free order number.

- An order taker—let's call him Ray—is sitting in front of a Mac running the invoice stack and takes the call. He creates a new invoice card by clicking on the *New Form* button. The new invoice is automatically numbered and dated.
- Ray asks Alice for her billing and shipping addresses; daytime phone; credit card information; the order numbers, quantities, sizes, and colors of the first five items she wants to order; and whether she wants express shipment. He types this all into the relevant fields, tabbing to get from field to field. If she wants to order more than five different items, he completes the first card and creates a new one for the rest of the order.
- Once Ray has all the information he needs from Alice, he clicks the *Calc* button to total up her order. At that time, he can tell her if any item she wants is out of stock. If she wants more information about an item, Ray can zip to his own copy of the catalogue, which might contain additional information for in-house eyes only.
- The order taken, Ray prints out a copy to be used as a packing slip when the order is shipped.

The Ends of the Earth online catalogue and invoice stacks by no means comprise a full-fledged business management application. Among the many improvements that could be made to this system are:

- A linked inventory stack that keeps track of stock levels as items are purchased from suppliers and sold to customers, and that signals when inventory is low.
- A separate mailing list of customers with their histories of purchasing and returning merchandise.
- Other stacks for accounts payable and receivable, purchase orders, cash disbursements, employee records, payroll, financial report generation, and more, with information updated automatically among stacks.

Even without creating additional stacks, the invoice stack described above could benefit from a number of improvements, including more comprehensive handling of tax and shipping options, and a way to extend the order to a second card without having to retype billing information. An alternative field arrangement might allow information for more than five items to be entered on one card. There should also be some way of handing backorders. As an exercise, you can try scripting these improvements yourself.

If you've ever set up on-paper accounting for a business, you have the know-how to tackle the design of a *HyperCard* business system. The easiest approach is to create one part of the system at a time; for instance, design a stack to display and keep track of inventory, and then build out from there to a complete system. Another approach is to use a dedicated accounting application to take care of that part of the business, and use *HyperCard* for product catalogue and other applications in which the program's hypermedia abilities can come into their own. This works well if your business is already partially computerized, but you need to add capabilities that your present software doesn't offer. You may be able to use *HyperCard*'s Import and Export buttons (discussed in Chapter 7) to move data between the accounting system and your *HyperCard* stacks.

Merging Stacks

Suppose Ends of the Earth's online catalogue contained not a few-dozen cards, but a thousand. This could easily be the case with the parts catalogue of an electronics supplier, or a large database like the one for the 1988 Art Guide, described in Chapter 7. Large stacks like those just won't fit on one floppy; they have to be broken up into several stacks and distributed on a number of floppy disks. This makes it a hassle for floppy disk users—and even for hard disk users who may have the storage capacity for a multimegabyte stack, but who would still receive the catalogue or database as several stacks. Of course, you can always live with having to browse and search through several stacks and/or floppies, but that could drive you crazy. (Those who are trying to run *HyperCard* with floppy drives and no hard disk are already going crazy.)

It would be nice if *HyperCard* had a built-in stack division and merging feature so that large stacks could be broken down and distributed on as many floppies as necessary, and then conglomerated back into one large stack on a hard disk. It would even be helpful if you could cut and paste an entire stack, or at least a group of cards, all at once. However, current versions of *HyperCard* don't have these features. Instead, if you want to break up and reconstitute a large stack, you face the laborious prospect of cutting and pasting individual cards: once, when you (the author) break it into smaller stacks, and a second time when the stack user puts all the stacks back together. The following shows you how to speed up both processes with a button script. The assumption is that you and the stack user are using hard disks with enough capacity to hold two versions of your large stack.

To break up a large stack into smaller stacks on individual disks:

- Once you've created the large "mother" stack on a hard disk, compact it and check the size of the stack by calling the stack's size property (see Appendix A) or by looking it up in the Finder; also get the number of cards in the stack.
- Divide the size in bytes by 700,000 (an 800K disk minus 100K, for a margin of safety) to get the number of floppy disks you'll need for the broken-up stack. Divide the number of cards by the number of disks to find out how many cards should go on each disk (round all fractions up to the next highest whole number).
- As an example, say your stack is 7,000,000 bytes in size and contains 1000 cards. Divide 7,000,000 by 700,000 to get the number of disks you need: in this case, ten. Divide the number of cards by the number of disks to get the number of cards per disk: 1000 ÷ 10 = 100 cards per disk.

Now create as many new stacks as you'll need disks. Name these "daughter" stacks 0, 1, and so on (be sure to start with 0 and not 1—you'll see why from the following script); give them blank backgrounds, and save them to the same folder as the mother stack. Each of the daughter stacks will get a portion of the cards from the mother stack.

Create a "Divide" button on the mother stack and give it this script:

```
on mouseUp
  set lockScreen to true
  set lockMessages to true                --freezes openStack, openCard, etc.
                                          --messages
  set lockRecent to true                  --speeds things up a little
  set cursor to 4
                                          --the wristwatch
```

```
 push card
 repeat with i = 0 to <the number of the last daughter stack>
  repeat with j = 1 to <the number of cards to be pasted into each daughter stack>
   go to stack <Mother Stack>
   go to card (j + (i * < the number of cards to be pasted > ) )

                                --this statement "ratchets" the card numbers up for each
                                --successive daughter stack; for example, if there are 100
                                --cards per daughter stack and the script is now starting to
                                --put cards into the third daughter stack (in other words, is
                                --beginning the third iteration of the variable i), this copy-
                                --and-paste cycle begins with mother stack card number
                                --(1 + (3 * 100) ), or 301.
end if
   doMenu "Copy Card"
   go to stack i
   go to last card
   doMenu "Paste Card"
  end repeat
  doMenu "Compact Stack"
  go to stack i
  doMenu "Delete Card"                   --gets rid of the blank first card
                                         --in the stack

 end repeat
pop card
beep
end mouseUp
```

This button will conveniently paste the requisite number of cards into each daughter stack while you sit back and relax—it even beeps when it's done. Expect it to take some time—for a thousand-card stack, you can make a sandwich and watch the news. If you want to be sure the script is working correctly, don't set lockScreen to *true* at the beginning of the script (however, this will cause the script to run even slower).

Once the script is finished, check each stack to make sure you got the correct results. If there weren't enough cards to fill the last daughter stack, the script will paste in extra copies of the last card to fill out the requirements of the repeat structure. Leave them there—the merge script will take care of them. Then, you can *Save A Copy* of each stack to a separate formatted floppy, or use the Finder to do the same thing.

Now, how should the users of your stack merge the separate daughter stacks back into one large mother stack? First, users should load all the daughter stacks into one folder. Along with the daughter stacks, provide an empty mother stack containing a "merge" button to reverse the divide process. Here is the script:

```
on mouseUp
  set lockScreen to true
  set lockMessages to true
  set lockRecent to true
  set cursor to 4
  push card
  repeat with i = 0 to <the number of the last daughter stack>
    repeat with j = 1 to <the number of cards in each daughter stack>
      go to card j of stack i
      doMenu "Copy Card"
      go to the last card of stack <Mother Stack>
      doMenu "Paste Card"
    end repeat

    doMenu "Compact Stack"
  end repeat
```

This part is applicable only if there are extra cards from the last daughter stack.

```
go to <Mother Stack>
  go to card <number of first extra card>
  repeat <number of extra cards> times          --make sure to get this number right!
    doMenu "Delete Card"
  end repeat
pop card
beep
end mouseUp
```

This script will paste cards to the end of the mother stack, creating a unified stack with no effort on the part of the user of your stack. Make sure you run through the entire divide and merge process before you distribute your stack, testing to make sure you got all the numbers right.

Linking Stacks with Other Applications and Files

With *HyperCard,* it's possible not only to link stacks together, but also to link applications together. Even if you aren't using *Multi-Finder,* you can open and close other applications like word processors, database managers, spreadsheets, and paint programs from within *HyperCard;* you can move certain kinds of information back and forth from these applications and *HyperCard;* and you can exit from other applications directly to *HyperCard* without paying a visit to the Finder. This is one major area where *HyperCard* has the potential to supplant the Finder entirely (although as yet, the Finder is much more versatile and requires less effort to use).

Opening and Closing Non-*Hypercard* Files

Chapter 7 covered techniques for importing and exporting information; now, we'll take a brief look at opening and closing non-*HyperCard* applications and files. *Document Representatives,* a stack supplied on the *HyperCard* and Stacks disk, offers one way to do this. The stack tells you to list all your application and folder names on the Document cards in your Home stack, and then provides a button that prepares an info card on each document and application. A sample card is shown in Figure 8-11. Each of these info cards contains a button that opens the application or document (assuming it's available on a currently mounted disk). When you quit any document or application you've opened from within *HyperCard,* you go directly back to the last card you saw without stopping at the Finder. One slightly cumbersome way to get in and out of applications from *HyperCard* is to go to the proper Document Representatives info card and click on the Open button.

You may think a good alternate method is to paste the Open

Figure 8-11. Document Representatives Info Card

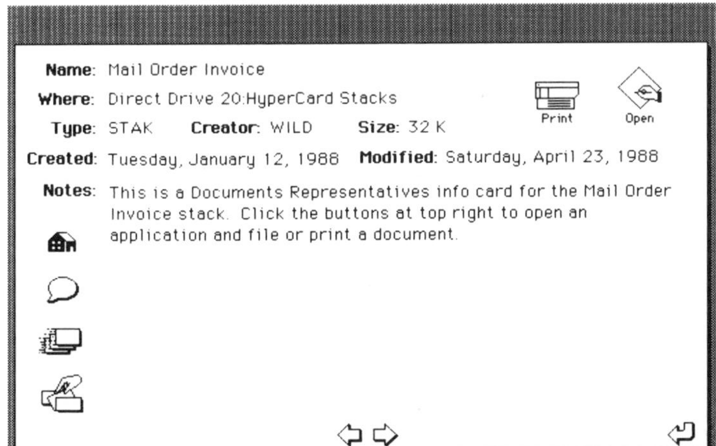

button into your own stack. Take a look at the button script before you do—it looks like this:

```
on mouseUp
  if field "Type" is "STAK" then go to stack field "Name"
  else if field "Type" is "APPL" then open field "Name"
  else
    put GetCreator(field "Creator") into appName
    if appName is not empty then open field "Name" with appName
  end if
end mouseUp
```

This script depends on the contents of fields on the Document Representatives info card and uses a custom function—getCreator(field "Creator")—to boot (see Appendix A for more on custom functions). You would have to paste the entire card into your stack, plus find the custom function handler and put it into your stack script. It's much easier to use the open and close commands in your own scripts.

Open opens an external application, or application and document. Be sure to specify the complete pathname of the application you're accessing, as in this sample button script:

```
on mouseUp
    open "Direct Drive 20:WP:MacWrite"
end mouseUp
```

HyperCard finds *MacWrite* in the folder WP on the disk Direct Drive 20 and takes you there. If you want to go to a particular *MacWrite* document, use this form:

```
on mouseUp
    open "Direct Drive 20:WP:Chapter 8" with "MacWrite"
end mouseUp
```

Quit *MacWrite,* and you're back in *HyperCard* at the last card you viewed—the one with the Open button. With this setup, you can toggle back and forth between your application or document and *HyperCard* much faster than if you had to go to the Finder on every switch. It still isn't as fast or as versatile as *MultiFinder,* but you don't need two megabytes of memory, either.

Also look at the *open file, read from file, write to file,* and *close file* commands, covered in Appendix A. These work in conjunction to let you construct your own import text and export text scripts. Keep in mind that these work only with ASCII (text-only) files.

> **TIP: Application Names as Literals.** Application names are *literals* (see Chapter 5 for a definition of a literal) and must be entered into scripts *exactly* as they appear in the menu or Finder; they often include version numbers or trademark signs. Go to the Finder and check the application's icon to see the correct form of the application's name, or use Get Info from the File menu. The Mac keyboard offers the ™ (Option-2), ® (Option-R), and © (Option-G) symbols.

Chapter 9

Special Effects

Sample stack: DinoCards

Much of a stack's impact derives not only from clever and intricate scripting, but also from the visual and aural impression it makes. This is especially true in stacks for training and education, where special effects are the vehicles by which information is impressed quickly and vividly on the student.

This chapter describes some basic *HyperCard* special effects—including animation techniques, sound and music synthesis, and computer speech—within the context of an example stack, called *DinoCards,* that teaches children about dinosaurs. By the end of this chapter, you should know how to create and score what is, in effect, a small, interactive *HyperCard* slideshow. We'll also look at using global variables and try some message passing, as well as discuss aspects of how to design stacks for children.

By now it's assumed that you've mastered object creation, basic painting operations, and the crafting of common button, card, and stack scripts. Therefore, unlike earlier chapters, this chapter doesn't describe the example stack in full detail. Instead, individual aspects of the stack are examined to shed light on how useful special effects can be achieved.

DinoCards

Description: *DinoCards* is an interactive educational stack about dinosaurs, presenting information about their lives and habits in an easy-to-understand format. The stack's approach to the subject is almost gamelike, incorporating music, synthesized speech, detailed graphics, and simple animations. There's an emphasis on interactivity as well; the stack has the ability to "learn" things about the stack user and then tailor itself accordingly.

Audience: *DinoCards* is aimed at children between 6 and 12 years old. Younger children can use it with supervision. There are really two versions of the program: one for children 8 years old and younger, and one for children older than 8 years. The version for older children contains longer text on topics of special interest that would be beyond the reading abilities of younger children.

Interface: The interface is simple and redundant, with every effort made to make choices and options as "bulletproof" as possible. There is maximum use of graphics, sound, and animation, and a minimum of instructions and text. Fields are locked; the stack, backgrounds, and cards are protected; *powerkeys* is off; and the menu bar is hidden. Most operations are handled automatically by openCard handlers or by clicking on cards or buttons. All text (except for the text in the special-topic articles) is spoken using speech synthesis (see below). Stack users are encouraged to interact with the stack; questions are asked and the answers are stored in other parts of the program.

Structure: The stack has an introduction that plays whenever the stack is opened. An introduction card gets information from the stack user and sets certain aspects of the program accordingly. A contents card gives access to different parts of the stack, as shown in the structure diagram in Figure 9-1.

Figure 9-1. *DinoCards* Structure

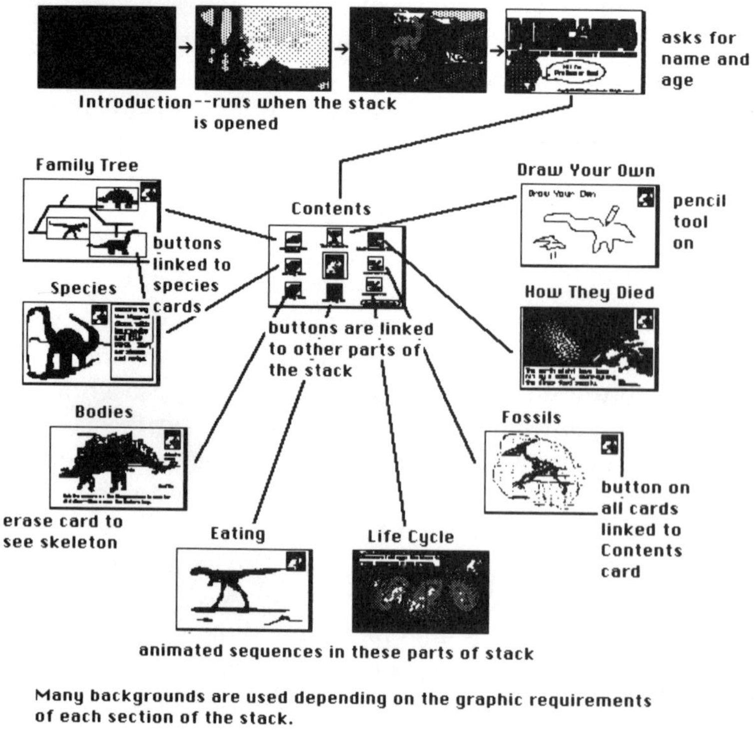

The Stack Script

The stack script for *DinoCards* is the most elaborate one in this book. It handles special functions for speech synthesis (see below), sets up a controlled environment for the stack user, and saves previous *HyperCard* settings in globals for restoration when the stack is closed.

```
                              --the first part of the stack takes care of speech synthesis
on openStack
 global theSpeech
 if theSpeech is empty then
  TurnSpeechOn
 end if

                              --this part saves settings in four global variables
 global saveLevel, saveMenu, saveMsg, saveTools
 put the userLevel into saveLevel
 if the userLevel < 3 then
  set userLevel to 3—"Painting"              --so some graphic tricks
                                             --can be performed later
 end if
 put the visible of the menu bar

into saveMenu                                --saves these settings
 hide menu bar

 put the visible of the msg box into saveMsg
 hide msg box
 put the visible of the tools window into saveTools
 set powerKeys to false
end openStack

                              --now the speech functions have to be switched off
on closeStack
 global theSpeech
 TurnSpeechOff

                              --this restores previous settings
 global saveLevel, saveMenu, saveMsg, saveTools
 set userLevel to saveLevel
 set the visible of the menu bar

to saveMenu
 set the visible of the msg box to saveMsg
 set the visible of the tools window to saveTools
```

```
 set powerKeys to true
                                        --this compacts the stack
   get the freeSize of this stack
   if it > 10000 then doMenu "Compact Stack"    --that's about 10K
end closeStack
```

TIP: Autocompacting Stacks. Stacks can automatically compact themselves if you include an "on closeStack" handler to the stack script:

```
on closeStack
   doMenu "Compact Stack"
end closeStack
```

The stack compacts every time you leave it. If you want the stack to compact only when there is more than a certain amount of free space (unused bytes in the stack), use the form from the stack script above:

```
on closeStack
   get the freeSize of this stack
   if it > 10000 then doMenu "Compact Stack"
end closeStack
```

Another option is to use the undocumented functions, "the diskspace" and "the stackspace." Scripts might look like this:

```
on closeStack
   if the diskspace < 20000 then
     doMenu "Compact stack"
   end if
end closeStack

on closeStack
   if the stackspace > 760000 then
     doMenu "Compact stack"
   end if
end closeStack
```

Having stacks automatically compact is worthwhile when the stack offers the user the ability to add and delete objects and graphics. (*DinoCards* includes a feature allowing the child to add his or her own pictures and to label them with new fields.) After regular use, the stack may accumulate an appreciable amount of free space.

The Introduction

Figures 9-2 through 9-5 show the introductory cards and the contents card. The first three cards "play" automatically when the stack is opened, dissolving from one card to the next. The effect is that of a slideshow with musical accompaniment (a dinosaur theme) and animated text. Clicking the mouse takes you to two further cards, which give more information and provide buttons to get to other parts of the stack.

The first card in the stack is completely black. It dissolves slowly to Card 2, shown in Figure 9-2.

Figure 9-2. Introduction Card 2

The painting is actually the top half of a paper collage digitized with a scanner, saved as a *MacPaint* document, and then completely repainted with the paint tools. A low-cost scanner like *ThunderScan* from ThunderWare, Inc. (21 Orinda Way, Orinda, California 94563) provides an excellent way to add photographic realism to your stacks.

Note: You should be aware that digitizing and using copyrighted photographs and art in a commercial product ***without permission from the copyright owner*** *is illegal.*

The text (24-point, New York, bold, outlined, shadowed, and extended) is held in a transparent card field. Rather than just appearing when the card is opened, it types itself onto the screen as the stack theme plays, using the type command (see more on music later in this chapter).

Here's the card script:

```
on openCard
  play "boing" tempo 200 a3q dq dq cq dq rh rq aq dq dq fq gq a4w      --the theme
  get the loc of card field 1
  click at it
  type "When the earth was very young . . . "     --shows the text being
                                                   --typed in letter by letter
  visual effect dissolve fast
  go to next card
end openCard

on closeCard
put empty into card field 1                          --so that the field is empty
                                                     --for the next openCard handler
end closeCard
```

To get the type command to work, you must first send a click message to the coordinates of a specific field. That's why the script gets the loc of the field and clicks at it before typing in the text.

Card 3 (Figure 9-3) is the lower half of the same scene, but this time it includes pictures of dinosaurs.

Figure 9-3. Introduction Card 3

DINOSAURS ruled
the Earth!

Here's the script:

```
on openCard
  play "boing" tempo 200 a4h g3h fh eh dq dq cq bbq aw     --second half of
                                                            --the theme

  get the loc of card field 1
  click at it
  type "DINOSAURS ruled the Earth!"
  wait until the sound is "done"
. . . wait until the mouseClick                        --click the mouse to
                                                       --see the next card

  visual dissolve
  go to next card
end openCard

on closeCard
  put empty into card field 1
end closeCard
```

Figure 9-4. Introduction Card 4

Introduction Card 4 (Figure 9-4) contains the title and copyright notice, and does a few other interesting things. You'll find its script in the section on speech synthesis. The *DinoCards* lettering, Geneva 24-point, was made even larger by grabbing it with the selection tool and resizing it. A copy of the lettering was made and then traced several times with Trace Edges. Finally, the original solid letters were picked up with the lasso, made transparent, and then placed to fit over the traced letters.

Figure 9-5. Contents Card

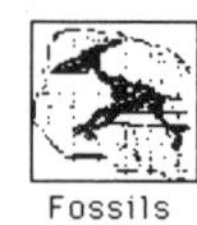

The contents card (Figure 9-5) is the hub of the stack and provides a way to exit from the program. Transparent buttons, linked to the appropriate cards, cover the pictures. The picture of Professor Rex, the program's host, appears on all cards in the stack; it's always under a transparent button that leads back to the contents card, and it provides further information about the program's operations.

A preprogrammed introduction like this offers a familiar and entertaining way to get started with an educational program; it also provides an excuse to show off some flashy graphics and effects.

Sounds and Music

HyperCard contains a built-in synthesizer that allows you to write simple or complex monophonic (one-note-at-a-time) melodies. All *HyperCard* composing involves the *play* command, which acts on digitized sound resources either in the stack or *HyperCard* itself.

The basic form of play is:

play "<sound name>"

HyperCard comes equipped with four digitized *sounds: "boing," harpsichord, dialing tones,* and *silence.* If you put the statement

play "boing"

into a script, you'll hear the "boing" sound whenever the statement executes. You could, as an example, construct a script so that "boing" plays if a wrong answer is given to a query the script poses. A number of scripts in Appendix A use the play command in just that way. You're not limited to the sounds supplied with *HyperCard*. Using ResEdit or a similar program, you can load any sound from another stack (as an *snd* resource, see below), or you can use a sound digitizer to create your own sounds and add them to your stacks.

That's just the beginning, though. *Play* has a number of parameters that let you take any sounds, including sounds you add to the stacks yourself, and use them as the basis for music. Basically, you take the sound and turn it into a series of notes. Here's the complete parameter format for play:

play "<sound name>" mpo <speed>] [<notes>] [# (sharp) b (flat)] [octave] [duration]

And as an example,

```
play "harpsichord" tempo 400 c#3h fb rw g#
```

A little musical knowledge will help you to understand these parameters, but it isn't absolutely necessary.

The *sound name* is the name of the instrument or sound you're manipulating—in the example, it's the harpsichord sound. Any sound resource available to your stack can be used here.

Tempo, the general speed at which the music plays, is always a number. The default value is set at 200 (neither fast nor slow); 400 is faster than 200. Experimentation helps in this area: The same melody can have an entirely different feel depending on whether it's played fast or slow. You may set the tempo yourself, or leave it at 200, the default setting.

Individual notes are specified by the letters *a, b, c, d, e, f,* and *g,* as in the musical scale, and can be designated sharp or flat, with the # symbol for sharp and *b* for flat. For example, c# is C sharp, and fb is F flat. You can also use note numbers, if you prefer. Middle C is 60. Rests are designated by *r.*

The first note in the melody should have an octave number attached. An *octave* is a musical interval that spans all the notes from one note to its next occurrence. For example, on a piano keyboard, an octave is the span of notes from Middle C up to the next C on the scale. There are 12 keys (eight white and four black) in a piano octave. *HyperCard* octaves 3, 4, and 5 correspond to the middle octaves on a piano and have the best sound. Once you set the octave with the first note, the melody remains in that octave until you change it by inserting a new octave number after a later note. The octave in the example is 3.

Notes and rests also need a duration; the duration range is a whole note to a thirty-second note. Whole notes and rests are designated by *w*, half notes and rests by *h*, quarter notes by *q*, eighth notes by *e*, sixteenth notes by *s*, thirty-second notes by *t*, and sixty-fourth notes by *x*.

The play command differs from other HyperTalk commands in that it can continue to execute even while other messages are sent. In other words, while your music is playing, other scripts can run, and you can still use buttons, fields, and tools. (You cannot run more than one play command at a time, so symphonies using the "boing" sound are only a pipe dream.) Disk access while sounds are playing makes for lousy sound plus the occasional error message, so don't design a script to go to other cards or stacks until the music is finished. Test for this with the sound function (see Appendix A), as in the following:

```
on mouseUp
   play "boing" tempo 100 a4w bw cw dw ew fw gw
   wait until the sound is "done"
   go to next card
end mouseUp
```

We'll use the play command to add a dinosaurian theme melody (courtesy of Janet Podell) to the *DinoCards* stack. You can also find it in the script for cards 2 and 3, listed above. Here's the theme again; type it into a button script and try it for yourself:

```
play "boing" tempo 200 a3q dq dq cq dq rh rq aq dq dq fq gq a4w
play "boing" tempo 200 a4h g3h fh eh dq dq cq bbq aw
```

The play command doesn't cope well with soft returns (neither does the *say* command; see below), so if your melody goes on for more than one line, break the line in the middle and begin a new play command on the next line. You won't hear a pause at the end of each line.

TIP: More on Digitized Sounds. Many other sounds are available in other stacks available online or from user groups. These range from card flipping and shuffling sounds, to musical instrument sounds, to animal roars, to unusual synthesized noises. You can use ResEdit or another public-domain program (see Appendix A) to transfer these sounds to your own stacks, or you can use a sound digitizer like *MacRecorder* (see Appendix A) to add your own sounds to your stacks. When you invoke the sound name in the play command parameter, *HyperCard* checks for the sound as an *snd* resource in the resource fork of the stack, the Home stack, *HyperCard*, or the System file, so the sound must reside in one of these—preferably in the stack itself. Keep in mind, however, that digitized sound requires large amounts of memory—ten seconds may consume as much as 300K on a disk. Be sparing with sound—it's more efficient to use the parameters to the play command to warp and tailor a few well-chosen digitized sounds than it is to include many different sounds on a single disk.

Speech Synthesis

Your Mac can synthesize speech as well as music, providing you've got the right resources. While the state-of-the-art in Mac speech synthesis doesn't allow for very attractive voices as yet, speech does humanize your stacks and makes them much friendlier to children and others who don't read easily. *DinoCards* makes extensive use of speech synthesis.

To make your Mac speak, you need two programs. One is the speech synthesis utility, *MacinTalk,* which is supplied with recent updates of the Mac system software; it can also be obtained from user groups, bulletin boards, and Apple dealers. Keep *MacinTalk* in your System folder, and forget about it. The other program you need is a stack called *HyperMacinTalk* by Dennis C. DeMars; it's highly recommended as a good introduction to all aspects of Mac speech synthesis. It can also be obtained through user groups, bulletin boards, and stack supply houses. *HyperMacinTalk* contains the external commands and functions (XCMDs and XFCNs) that let you access *MacinTalk* from *HyperCard*. There is also a button in *HyperMacinTalk* that automatically installs these XCMDs and XFCNs as resources of any stack, including your Home stack. If you plan to distribute a stack that uses *MacinTalk,* you must install the XCMDs and XFCNs as resources for that stack.

Once you've installed the external commands and functions, you must include the following handler in your stack, preferably as part of the stack script, as follows:

```
on openStack
  global theSpeech
  if theSpeech is empty then
    TurnSpeechOn
  end if
end openStack

on closeStack
  global theSpeech
  TurnSpeechOff
end closeStack
```

These are part of the *DinoCards* stack script, as you saw above. With these preparations taken care of, you can have *HyperCard* utter any string of English words using the undocumented "say" command. Here's the format:

say <the English words>

The text to be spoken must be in quotation marks, like any literal. For example:

```
say "The only thing we have to fear is fear itself."
```

What you hear will sound rather robotic and uninflected (that's not too surprising), but it should be understandable. You can modify inflection by using the standard punctuation marks, such as periods, commas, and question marks; adding extra spaces between words and letters can aid in comprehension, too.

Try a few more phrases, however, and you'll begin to notice that there are some distinct problems with *MacinTalk*'s renderings of English. English is notorious as the language with the most bizarre inconsistencies of spelling, so it's not surprising that a low-level speech synthesizer can't cope with every spelling and pronunciation quirk, although there are some things you can do about it. To remedy the inadequacies of *MacinTalk*'s English, *HyperMacinTalk* supplies a way to write phrases with a special phonetic alphabet using the *phoneme* function and the *sayPhonetic* command. Phoneme rewrites any English phrase into its *MacinTalk* phonetic equivalent.

For example, try this button script:

```
on mouseUp
   put phoneme("The only thing we have to fear is fear itself") into msg
end mouseUp
```

In the message box, you'll see:

DHIY OW4NLIY THIH1NX WIY /HAEV TUX FIY5R IHZ FIY5R IH1TSEH1LF #

That's certainly easy to read. You can then tweak the phrase with several dozen phoneme, punctuation, stress, and intonation symbols. (Coverage of these is beyond the scope of this book, but excellent explanations are provided in the *HyperMacinTalk* stack itself, as well as in the *MacinTalk* documentation available from Apple.) To utter the revised phonetic string, use the *sayPhonetic* command in just the same way that the say command is used.

There is no doubt that phonetic spelling yields more understandable speech, especially when it comes to stress and intonation, but you can go far with a little creative mispelling without having to resort to phonetics. Say the sentence youself; then listen to how the Mac renders it with the Say command. Words that are not pronounced correctly can be respelled in the script to sound better. For example, the Mac can't cope too well with the word *mouse;* it makes it sound like "muss." Simply respelling it as *mouwse* improves the pronunciation. Try alternative ways to spell problem words until you find one that works well; you can even set up a pronunciation table of your own for future reference.

You'll find that the speech scripts in this chapter contain deliberately misspelled words. Let's look at the script for Card 5, the last card in the introduction part of *DinoCards.* This script not only makes use of speech, but also gathers information from the user, puts that information into global variables, and stores the information in a hidden field for retrieval the next time the stack is opened.

```
on openCard
  wait 1 secs
  say "Greetings. I am Professor.Rex. Welcome to dyno cards."   --this part gets the user's
                                                               --name
  global userName, userAge                                     --initializes 2 globals
  say "Please type your name in the box."
```

```
ask "What's Your Name?"                         --shows an ask dialog
put it into userName
if it is empty or it is "Cancel" then           --error handling
  put empty into userName
  say "Try agenne."
  ask "What's Your Name?"
  if it is empty or it is "Cancel" then
    put empty into userName
    say "hello"
    say "To keep going, press the mouwse button."
    hide bkgnd button 2                         --a button on all cards that shows
                                                --fields with advanced information
    exit openCard
                                                --leave the script
  else put it into userName
end if

                                  --this part compares the user's name with the name, if any,
in the hidden field
if userName is item 1 of card field 2 then      --the hidden field
  say "Hello"
  say userName                                  --let's hope it's a
                                                --pronounceable one
  say "To keep going, press the mouwse button."
  put item 2 of card field 2 into userAge       --gets the age that was stored
                                                --with the name
  if userAge < 8 then
    hide bkgnd button 2
  end if
  exit openCard
else put userName into item 1 of card field 2   --stores the name
say "Please type your age in the box"
ask "How Old Are You?"
put it into userAge
if it is empty or it is "Cancel" then
  put empty into userAge
  say "Try agenne."
  ask "How Old Are You?"
  if it is empty or it is "Cancel" then
    put empty into userAge
    say "hello"
    if userName is not empty then
      say userName
    end if
    say "To keep going, press the mouwse button."
    exit openCard
  end if
end if
```

```
  put userAge into item 2 of card field 2          --stores the age
  if userAge < 8 then
    hide bkgnd button 2
  end if
  say "hello"
  say userName
  say "To keep going, press the mouwse button."
end openCard
```

At the end of the script, you have the name and age of the user in globals that you can use in other scripts and any other time the stack is opened. If no answers are given to the queries, the stack automatically sets itself to a lower level of sophistication by eliminating the button that provides additional text articles on more advanced topics. Of course, it's possible to obtain much more information from the user and to put it to more extensive use than shown here, but the principles are the same.

> **TIP: Another Way to Talk.** If *MacinTalk* doesn't give you the speech quality you want, you can always digitize real speech and include it in your stacks as a sound resource. Unlike music files, speech files can be compressed without serious loss of integrity. *MacRecorder,* among other commercial sound digitizers, offers a compression utility that lets you shrink the size of a speech sound file to a manageable size. You might be able to fit up to several minutes of compressed speech into your stack, depending on the available space on your disk. Invoke each spoken sound with the play command, like any other sound.

Pop-Up Fields, Buttons, and Graphics

Pop-up fields (fields that are hidden until some action makes them visible; see Chapter 6) are great for providing additional information, answers to questions, or text that just won't fit onto a crowded card. Pop-up fields can be used liberally in an education stack like *DinoCards;* children like the surprise and feel rewarded when they reveal the field by doing the right thing.

The script for a pop-up field varies according to just how the field is supposed to act. If you want it to pop up when a button is clicked, give the button a script like this:

```
on mouseUp
   show card field 1
   wait until the mouse is down
   hide card field 1
end mouseUp
```

Clicking the mouse again anywhere on the card hides the field. Since you can't depend on the user to click, give the card a closeCard handler,

```
on closeCard
   hide card field 1
end closeCard
```

so that the field will be invisible the next time the card is opened. If no button is involved, you can make the field sensitive to mouse actions with this field script:

```
on mouseEnter
   show me
end mouseEnter

on mouseLeave
   hide me
end mouseLeave
```

As long as the pointer is within the field's rectangle, the field will be visible. Once the mouse leaves, the field disappears again. Use the closeCard handler above to make sure the field is hidden for the next session, or use the wait command within the field script to set a maximum time for the field to be visible, and then have it hide automatically:

```
on mouseEnter
   show me
   wait 10 secs
   hide me
end mouseEnter
```

The pop-up fields in *DinoCards* use another factor to limit their onscreen visibility: the length of time it takes for the program to speak the contents of the field. For example, there's a pop-up field (Card Field 1) on the Contents card, triggered by clicking on the Instructions button. Figure 9-6 shows the field.

Figure 9-6. Pop-Up Field

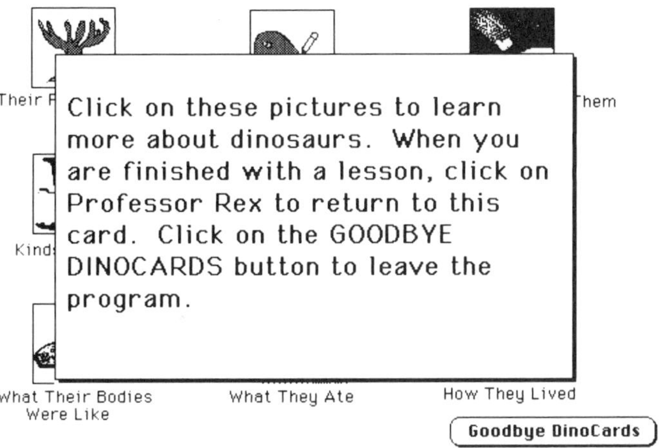
Click on these pictures to learn more about dinosaurs. When you are finished with a lesson, click on Professor Rex to return to this card. Click on the GOODBYE DINOCARDS button to leave the program.
What Their Bodies Were Like
What They Ate
How They Lived
Goodbye DinoCards

This is the button script:

```
on mouseUp
  show card field 1
  say "Click on these pictures to learn more about dynosores."
  say "When you are .finished with a .lesson, click on Professor Rex"
  say "to return to .this card."
  say "Click .on the .goodbuy dynocards .button to leave .the program."
  wait 1 secs                                    --so hiding the field won't be too abrupt
  hide card field 1
end mouseUp
```

The speech goes slowly enough that even slow readers have time to read the words in the field as they are being spoken. It's possible to make speech go even more slowly by adding more space between words, or by breaking the text up into smaller sentences.

You could also use the script form

```
on mouseUp
  show card field 1
  say card field 1
  wait 1 secs                                    --so hiding the field won't be too abrupt
  hide card field 1
end mouseUp
```

but this doesn't allow for creative misspellings that increase the comprehension of the synthesized speech. (You don't want to use phonetic spelling in the field text itself.) However, you can use the above form when you want to say a field whose contents change according to input from the user.

Pop-up buttons are not as common or as useful as pop-up fields, but they have their specialized uses. One way to use them is in the context of a game or puzzle. For example, if the child clicks on the correct sequence of buttons, a new button could appear, leading to another card and another series of challenges. Pop-up button scripts are essentially the same in concept as pop-up field scripts.

Pop-up graphics are a bit more elaborate. There are several ways to accomplish the trick of making an image suddenly appear on the card. One is to cover the image with an opaque field or button so it can't be seen. When some action is taken, such as clicking on a button, a script hides the field or button to reveal the graphic and then shows the field or button again when the graphic has to disappear. With this method, nothing is actually done with the graphic. A related technique is to put the pop-up graphic on the background and cover it with an opaque card graphics layer. To reveal the graphic, a script puts *HyperCard* into background mode with the *editBkgnd* global property, as in this button script:

```
on mouseUp
   set editBkgnd to true            --enters background mode, shows the
                                    --graphic
   wait until the mouseClick        --waits for you to click the mouse
   set editBkgnd to false           --exits background mode, hides the graphic
end mouseUp
```

This works best if the menu bar isn't visible in your stack; otherwise, the striped pattern on the menu bar in background mode is a dead giveaway to how the effect is being accomplished, taking the magic out of it.

One card in *DinoCards* makes use of card and background graphics in a slightly different way. In this case, a card graphic (a painting of a stegosaur) is used to hide a background graphic (a labeled picture of the stegosaur's skeleton). The stack user is invited to erase the card painting to reveal the background skeleton underneath, as Figures 9-7 through 9-9 show. Card and button scripts take care of the details.

Figure 9-7. Stego Card Graphic

Rub the square on the Stegosaurus to see her skeleton--then press the Return key.

Figure 9-8. Erasing the Card Graphic

Rub the square on the Stegosaurus to see her skeleton--then press the Return key.

Figure 9-9. Stego Background Graphic

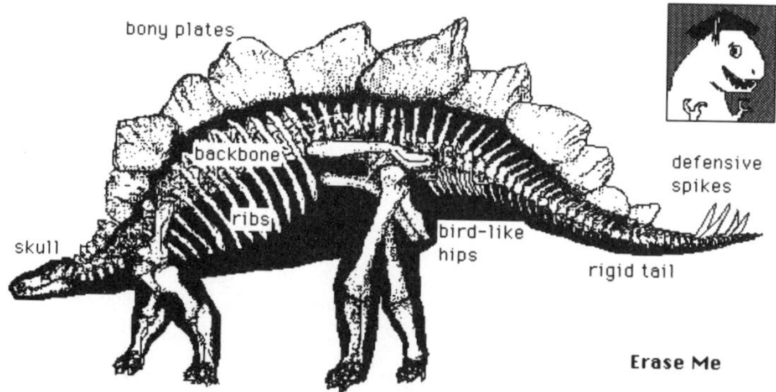

Rub the square on the Stegosaurus to see her skeleton--then press the Return key.

The Erase Me button script:

```
on mouseUp
  choose eraser tool
end mouseUp
```

The card script:

```
                                  --this reads the field at the bottom of the card
on openCard
  say "Click on the erase me button."
  say "then rubb the eraser square on the .Stegosaur to see her skeleton."
  say "When you are done, press the .Return key."
end openCard

                                  --this restores the card graphic after it's been erased
on returnKey
  doMenu "Select All"
  doMenu "Revert"                 --to the last saved version
  choose browse tool
end returnKey

                                  --this is in case the user tries to exit the card without
                                  --pressing the Return key
on closeCard
  doMenu "Select All"
  doMenu "Revert"
  choose browse tool
end closeCard
```

Another method for restoring the card graphic involves keeping a copy of the graphic on another card. The script copies the graphic from the storage card, then pastes it onto the original card, as in:

```
on returnKey
  set lockScreen to true
  go to card "Card Graphic Storage"
  choose select tool
  doMenu "Select All"
  doMenu "Copy Picture"
  go back
  doMenu "Paste Picture"
end returnKey
```

The card script assumes that the user is a child who may not know how to use the menus or the Tools palette, so tools are chosen through buttons and the keyboard. One of the problems the script has to solve is how to best get out of painting mode. Here it's done with a keypress, but a more intuitive way would involve clicking on a button; however, buttons are inactive in painting mode. A logical alternative might seem to be an "on idle" handler in the card script that tests for whether erasing is still in process (for example, by looking to see whether the mouse button is down, or the pointer is over the picture area, or both) and restores the card graphic according to the results of the test. However, you can't do this either because *HyperCard* doesn't send idle messages while it's in painting mode. This is a case in which having to do work in different modes limits the kinds of choices you can offer the user of your stacks. Can you think of a way to get out of painting mode without pressing a key or clicking on a menu item or palette choice?

Suppose you don't want the graphic to just pop on or off, but you want it to wipe or dissolve into or out of view. One way to accomplish this is through a transition from one card to another. Here's how:

- Create the first card. If you want the graphic to *disappear,* put it on this card; if you want it to *appear,* don't put it on this card. If you want to modify the graphic in some other way, put the first version here.
- Copy the card and paste the copy right after the original or anywhere else you like in the same stack.
- Change *only* the graphic on the second card. If you want the graphic to disappear, erase it. If you want it to appear, put it in. If you want to modify it, put the modified version on this card.
- Using one of the visual transitions available with the visual command (a dissolve, a wipe, and so on), write a card or button script for the original card that links it to the copy.
- When you run the script, you'll go from the original card to the copy, but the only change you'll see is in the graphic—it will either appear, disappear, or change.

DinoCards contains a sequence showing how this transition works (Figure 9-10). In the first card, the foot of a *Deinonychus* ("terrible claw") is shown with the ripping claw in the raised position. A dissolve to the next card shows the claw in the down

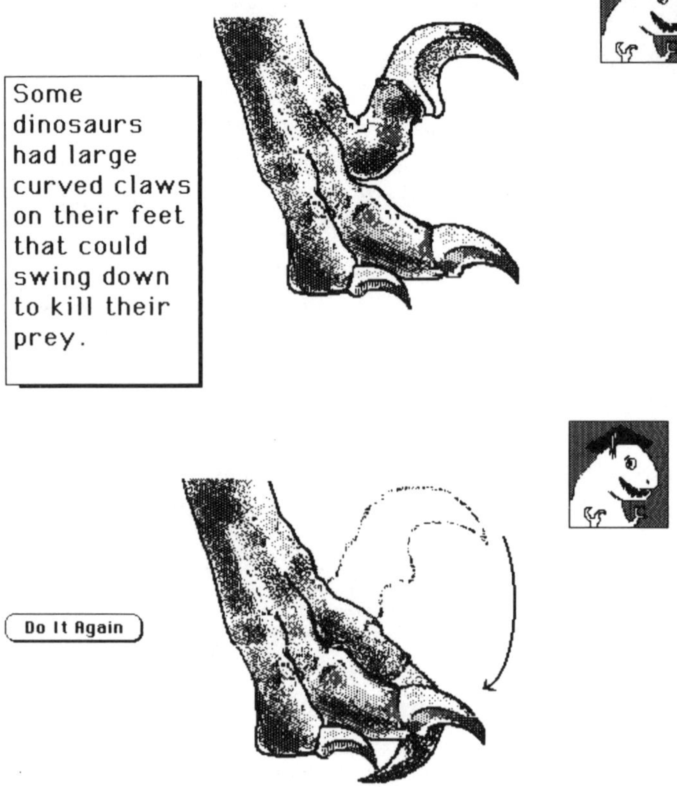

Some dinosaurs had large curved claws on their feet that could swing down to kill their prey.
Do It Again

Figure 9-10. Claw 1 and Claw 2

position. The transition is initiated with a mouse click in the card script of the first card:

```
on mouseUp
   visual dissolve
   go next
end mouseUp
```

A "Do It Again" button on the second card lets you replay the sequence by passing a mouseUp message to the first card.

```
on mouseUp
   go prev
   wait 1 secs                --so the replay doesn't start too abruptly
   mouseUp                    --is intercepted by the card script and
                              --triggers it
end mouseUp
```

Version 1.2 Note: Hide Picture and Show Picture
New commands in 1.2 let you hide or show a card or background graphic with a single line in a script. Here are the forms:

```
hide picture of <card or background name, number, or ID>
hide card picture                    --of the current card
hide background picture              --of the current background
show picture of <card or background name, number, or ID>
show card picture                    --of the current card
show background picture              --of the current background
```

A simple button script could hide and show any picture as follows:

```
on mouseDown
   hide card picture
   show background picture
end mouseDown

on mouseUp
   hide background picture
   show card picture
end mouseUp
```

As long as the mouse button is down, the background picture is shown. When the mouse button is released, the card picture shows again. You can toggle back and forth from card to background picture, or just switch pictures on and off. This new capability offers some interesting possibilities for simple animation.

If you try to paint or paste over a hidden picture, *HyperCard* will ask you if you want to make the picture visible.

Animation

The Deinonychus claw example, which is nothing more than a two-frame cartoon, leads to the subject of *HyperCard* animation. One kind of *HyperCard* animation involves showing in rapid succession a sequence of cards containing an image that changes incrementally for each card. Think of these cards as being like the frames of a movie or the pages of a flip book: As they whizz by, the images take on the appearance of motion. If the frames or cards change fast enough to fool the eye (around 15 images per second or faster), the images they contain seem to move smoothly, an effect called *persistence of vision.* It would be nice if

HyperCard could flip cards that fast, but it doesn't; it takes somewhere between a quarter to a half second for a plain transition, which isn't nearly fast enough for smooth animation. You can, however, still devise card-by-card animations that, while jumpy, do an adequate job of indicating motion.

Suppose you want to zip through all the cards in a stack to create a card-by-card animation. The easy part is the script. Create a title card with this card script:

```
on mouseUp
   show all cards              --or you can specify a particular number of cards
end mouseUp
```

When you click the mouse, this script flashes every card for only as long as *HyperCard* takes to go to the next one (like flipping the pages in a flip book) and takes you back to the first card at the end. The hard part is creating the graphics, since you have to create a slightly different drawing for each card, and the drawings must impart a believable sense of movement when animated. The more cards you use, the longer the animation will be, but the more drawing you'll have to do. If the animation is for instructional purposes only, rather than for a work of animated art, it pays to keep the drawings as simple and easy to make as possible.

Figure 9-11 shows a short animated sequence from *DinoCards*. The first drawing was created for the first card in the sequence; then several copies of the card were made and inserted after the

Figures 9-11. Animation Sequence

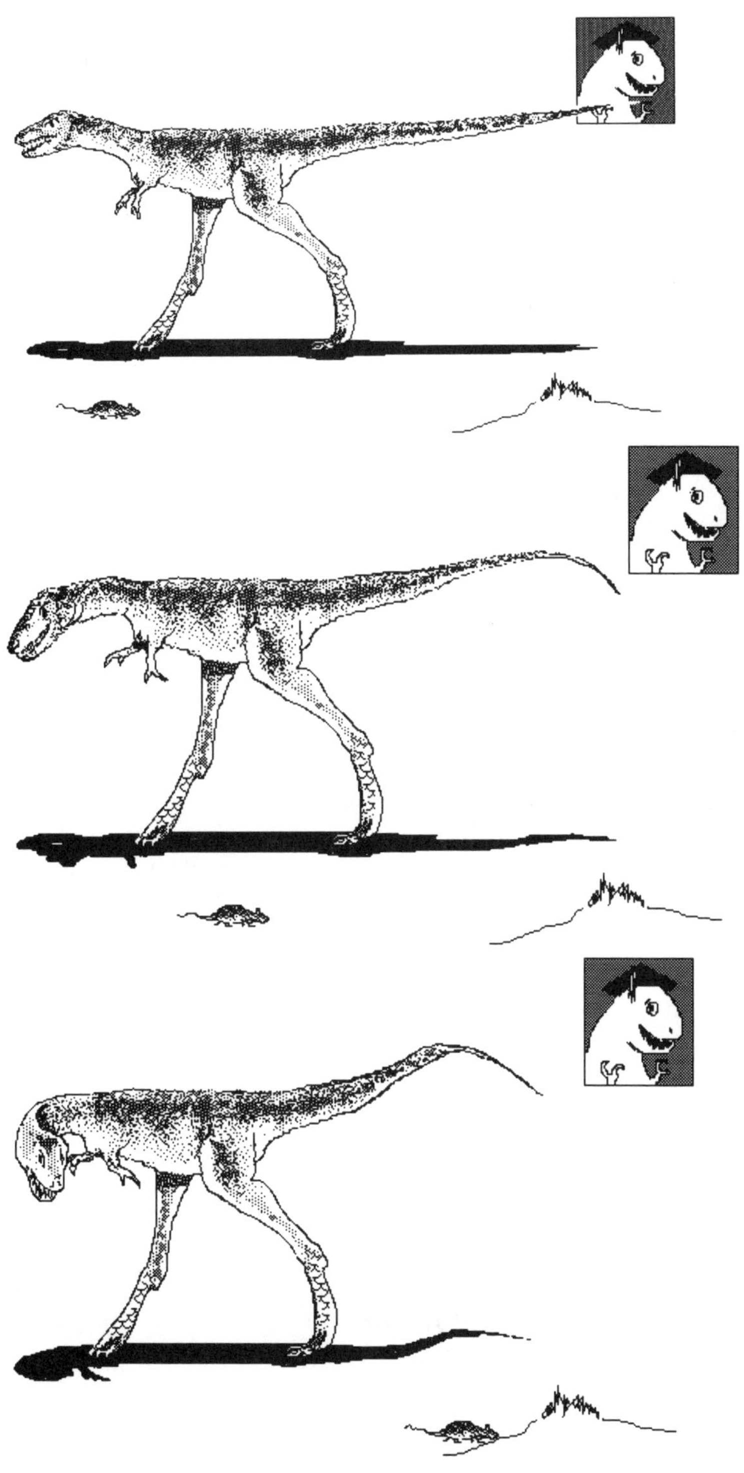

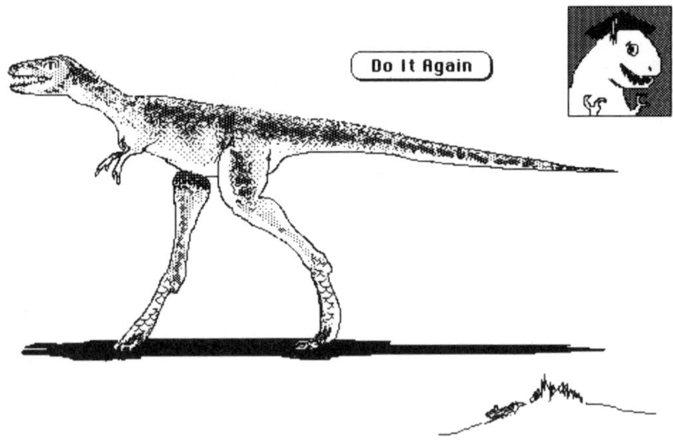

original card. Finally, the graphics on each card were redrawn. When seen in sequence, the effect is of the dinosaur turning its head to follow the mammal, which scurries into a burrow. Note that the body and legs of the dinosaur stay the same through the sequence; only the head, tail, and shadow (an important thing to add if you want to create the illusion of a 3-D moving object) are redrawn each time. (*MacPaint*-compatible drawing programs with free rotate, distort, and perspective features may make the incremental modification of drawings easier. Create the drawings in the paint program; then use *HyperCard*'s Import Paint menu option to bring them into your stack.) A "*Click Me*" button on the first card starts the animation, and a "Do It Again" button on the final card loops you back to the beginning so you can see the sequence again by passing a mouseUp message to the Click Me button:

```
on mouseUp
  set lockmessages to true                    --blocks any openCard messages
  visual dissolve
  go to card "Animation Start"
  send mouseUp to card button "Click Me"
end mouseUp
```

Unfortunately, the show command goes in only one direction—forward by ascending card number. If you want to play an animated sequence backward, create a button with a script like this:

```
on mouseUp
   repeat for the number of cards          --or repeat n times, with n the number of
                                           --cards you want to replay
     go prev
   end repeat
end mouseUp
```

A useful addition to a stack with extensive animation would be a simulated VCR remote control with forward, reverse, fast-forward and reverse, pause, and slow-motion buttons. This remote would reside in the background domain of all cards. You may want to try your hand at creating one; you can find similar controls in some public domain stacks.

An alternative method of animation involves the drag command (see Appendix A). With its help, you can direct drawings to "create themselves" on the screen, or you can move a selected part of a painting around on the screen. The kinds of animation you can produce are more limited, and you can work with only one selection at a time on only one card at a time. However, dragging selections yields much smoother motion and requires much less disk space than the card-by-card animation method described above.

There are two aspects of the drag command you should know about. One is that you can only drag in straight lines (although the lines can be of any length). The other is that you must specify the exact coordinates of the beginning and end points of a drag action. You can obtain these by doing a test drawing or movement path with the mouse and the line tool, using the message box to ask for the mouseLoc at the beginning of the drawing and at the end of each line segment you draw.

Set the dragging speed with the dragSpeed property. The fastest drag speed is 0; otherwise, drag speed is measured in pixels per second, with low numbers being slower than high numbers.

Here's an example that has nothing to do with dinosaurs. To make a pyramid draw itself in the center of the screen (Figure 9-12), use this button script:

```
on mouseUp
 choose line tool
 set lineSize to 1
```

Figure 9-12. Pyramid

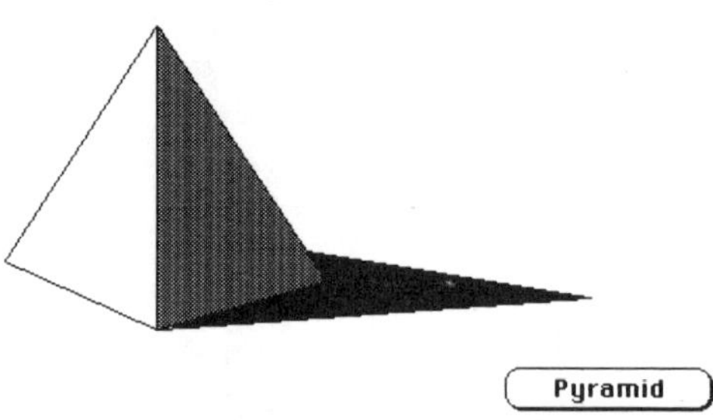

```
  set dragSpeed to 200                          --a moderate speed
  drag from 168,203 to 240,85
  drag from 240,85 to 321,213
  drag from 321,213 to 240,237
  drag from 240,237 to 168,203
  drag from 240,237 to 240,85
  drag from 240,237 to 449,221
  drag from 449,221 to 312,198
  choose bucket tool
  set pattern to 22                             --solid gray
  click at 260,175                              --fills the right side of the pyramid
  set pattern to 12                             --black
  click at 340,220                              --fills the shadow
  choose browse tool
end mouseUp
```

You can drag any selection using the same principle. This script takes the pyramid above and bounces it back and forth on the screen until you click the mouse:

```
on mouseUp
  set dragSpeed to 150                          --a slow dragSpeed works a little smoother
                                                --with selections
  choose select tool
  doMenu "Select"                               --grabs the pyramid with the Lasso
  drag from 280,190 to 73,190                   --gets the selection to one edge
  repeat until the mouseClick
    drag from 73,190 to 303,190
    drag from 303,190 to 73,190
  end repeat
end mouseUp
```

Note that every drag has to start from within the selected area. If you try to run this script when the pyramid isn't at the center of the screen, it won't work. You can find out just where to drag by marking a center point on the object to be selected and then moving it around on the screen and noting the mouseLoc of the centerpoint at each location. (Here's an exercise for you to try: Modify the script to consistently return the pyramid to the center of the screen.)

Use this technique for bouncing balls and molecules, flying birds (or pterosaurs), sailing clouds, and moving any other well-defined object along a linear path.

These are just some of the special effects you can achieve with *HyperCard*. As you become more proficient, you'll discover other effects and will learn how to combine the ones described here in new ways. Filmmaking is a good area to study. How are scenes organized and transitions managed, and how is action scored? The more cinematic your educational or creative stack, the more impact it will have. The possibilities are sufficiently rich that you're not likely to exhaust them for some time—and by then *HyperCard* will have gained new effects for you to explore.

A Final Note on Authoring and Scripting

Like any skill, authoring has an aesthetic dimension. Stacks can take on nearly any form—lean to ornate, trivial to profound—and can serve almost any purpose. On the other hand, scripts should above all be functional; they should also be simple, clean, shapely, and efficient or, to use a more difinitive term, *elegant*. The scripts in this book have sacrificed some elegance for the sake of readability; most of the longer scripts could be rendered in more compact code. You're invited to rewrite and improve any scripts in this book. As you do, you'll discover that there is usually more than one way to perform any *HyperCard* task, and that any scripts, including your own, can be made more elegant. It takes practice and some hard thought to perfect a script, but a well-wrought result is a bit like poetry, and is nearly as satisfying to create.

Appendix A

HyperTalk Glossary

A quick-reference guide to HyperTalk

In this glossary, which is intended as a quick reference to *HyperCard*'s programming language, HyperTalk, you'll find concise descriptions of the categories of HyperTalk terms and hints on how to use them. Also listed, in alphabetical order by category, is every HyperTalk command, constant, control structure, function, operator, property, and system message. Included for each term are the parameter or argument format(s), a definition of each term, and one or more examples—either one-line statements you can test from the message box, or complete scripts you can attach to objects (in most cases, buttons) you create yourself.

To test scripts, you need to create a card with a blank background and create a new background field and background button. The message box and Tools and Pattern palettes should be visible. Some scripts call for the Home or arrow buttons to be on the card as well.

In some cases, hypothetical or generic names of objects are used in the examples (for example, "field 1" or the filename *Writings:Rambles:June 2, 1974*); you can substitute any valid name of a real object in your stack or system.

> **Version 1.2 Note: Version Compatibility**
> A number of new terms have been added to HyperTalk for *HyperCard* version 1.2, which brings up some compatibility problems. Scripts written only with terms contained in versions 1.0.1 and 1.1 will run under any version of *HyperCard,* but scripts using terms introduced in version 1.2 will not run under the earlier versions. To be safe, get version 1.2 and run all your stacks with it. Terms introduced with version 1.2 are included in this glossary, clearly marked as "1.2 and later versions only."

Parameter Notation

The standard notation for describing the parameter(s) or argument of a HyperTalk statement is:

term <parameter or argument>

In the statement

go [to] <destination>

go is the command, *[to]* is an optional word (all optional parts of a statement are enclosed in square brackets), and the word within the arrow brackets, *<destination>*, is a description of the parameter. In an actual HyperTalk statement, you would replace the parameter description *<destination>* with a real destination, such as

```
go to card id 345
```

Often, you'll have to choose among various modifiers; you'll see these separated by vertical lines:

```
put <source> [into | before | after | <container> ]
```

Commands

The terms you'll be using most often are *commands*. A command is one of the instruction words such as *go, find, put, sort, open, play,* and so on. Almost all commands can easily be tested from the message box.

add

Format: add <source> to <container>
Action: Adds a number to another number in a container, or adds the number in one container to the number in another container. Any expression or formula that evaluates to a number can be added to a number in a container.
Example:

```
on mouseUp
   get field "Subtotal 1"
   add it to field "Subtotal 2"
   add field "Subtotal 2" to total              --total is a local variable
   add total to field "Grand Total"
end mouseUp
```

This script adds the contents of three containers—field "Subtotal 1," field "Subtotal 2," and the variable *total*—and adds the amount in *total* to field "Grand Total," where the sum of all the addition is displayed.

answer

Format: answer <question> [with <reply> [or <reply> [or <reply>]]]

Action: Shows a dialog box that asks a question, and offers up to three replies in buttons. The question must be 40 characters or less, and the suggested replies must be very short. The last reply is put in a heavily outlined button on the right. A default reply of "OK" is supplied by *HyperCard* if replies aren't specified in the script. The reply is automatically put into the local variable *It*. Answer works especially well with *if. . .then. . .else* control structures.

Example:

```
on mouseUp
  answer "Are you happy?" with "Yes" or "No" or "Not Sure"
  if it is "No" then
    answer "I'm sorry to hear that" with "OK"
  else if it is "Not Sure" then
    answer "Do you have trouble making up your mind?" with "Yes"
      or "No" or "Not Sure"
      if it is "Not Sure" then
        answer "I think we better stop here" with "OK"
      end if
  end if
end mouseUp
```

ask

Format: <question> [with <reply>]

Action: Displays a dialog box asking for a typed reply of about 40 characters and puts the reply into the local variable *It*. You can also prompt the user with a partial reply, as demonstrated below.

Example:

```
on mouseUp
  ask "How old are you?" with "I'm    years old."
  if word 2 of it < 7 then
    set userLevel to 1
  else set userLevel to 2
end mouseUp
```

ask password

Format: <question> [with <reply>]

Action: Displays a dialog box that asks the user to type in the proper password. This password is stored separately from the Protect Stack password. The stack author can craft a stack script so that if the password does not match an encrypted version already stored within the program, the user will be denied access to the stack.

Example:

```
on mouseUp
  ask password "What's the password"
  if it is not codeword then                    --an encrypted password
    answer "Sorry, that's restricted information"
  else go to card "Further Information"
end mouseUp
```

beep

Format: beep [<number of beeps>]
Action: Makes the specified number of beeps. Use the beep to warn the user that something is about to happen or that a wrong choice has been made. Vary the rate of beeping by inserting wait commands between the beep commands.
Examples:

```
beep
beep 10
on mouseUp
  repeat until the mouse is down
    beep 2
  end repeat
end mouseUp
```

choose

Format: choose <tool name> tool
Action: Selects a tool in the Tools menu. This is the same as selecting the tools with the pointer.
Example:

```
on mouseUp
    choose pencil tool
    drag from 0,0 to 500,300
    choose rect tool
    drag from 0,300 to 500,0
    choose browse tool
end mouseUp
```

click

Format: click at <horizontal coordinate, vertical coordinate> [with <modifier key> [, <modifier key>]]
Action: Clicks on the specified location. This works like clicking the mouse (and pressing a modifier key, if desired). You need to have the coordinates of the object—usually a button—that you want to click on. Use "get the location of <object name>" to find out a valid location for the object.

Example:

```
on mouseUp
  choose button tool
  get the loc of bkgnd button "ShowMyScript"     --puts the coordinates into it
  click at it with shiftKey
end mouseUp
```

Repeating the click command is the same as double-clicking on the target, the background button "ShowMyScript," while pressing the Shift key. This displays the script of "ShowMyScript."

convert

Format: convert <container> to <desired format>
Action: Transforms date and time information to one of the seven date/time formats:

Date/Time	Format
seconds (secs)	The seconds from 12.00.01, January 1, 1904
long date	Sunday, June 2, 1974
short date	6/2/87
abbreviated date (abbr date)	Sun June 2, 1974
long time	12-hour clock, 12:01:45 AM, or 24-hour clock, 24:01:45
short time	12:01 AM, 24:01
dateItems	year, month, day, hour, minute, second, and weekday starting with Sunday, in this form: 1974, 6,2,12,01,45,1)

Use the convert command to help you add or subtract dates and times. If you need to add or subtract dates, it's easiest to convert them to seconds, perform the operation, and then convert them back to more familiar formats.

Example:

```
on mouseUp
   put the long time into templ
   convert templ to secs
   get templ
   put it into the msg box                        --it will be a very long number
   wait 10 secs
   put the long time into temp2
   convert temp2 to secs
```

```
    get temp2
    put it into the msg box
    wait 2 secs
    put temp2 – templ into the msg box          --10 should appear
end mouseUp
```

delete

Format: delete <item>
Action: Eliminates specified text from a field or container.
Example:

```
on mouseUp
    put "one, two, three" into the msg box
    wait 2 secs
    delete item 3 of the msg box
    wait 2 secs
    delete item 2 of the msg box
    wait 2 secs
    delete item 1 of the msg box
end mouseUp
```

dial

Format: dial <phone number> [with [modem] <modem settings>]
Action: Dials the specified phone number through a modem or other device. The default modem setting for "with modem" is ATS0 = 0DT, a standard Hayes modem command-set.
Example:

```
on mouseUp
    put "568-2515" into the msg box
    dial the msg box                        --you'll hear dialing tones
    dial the msg box with modem             --dials the selected number; no dial tones
end mouseUp
```

divide

Format: divide <container> by <source>
Action: Divides the number in a container by the source number, which can be a number in another container.
Example:

```
on mouseUp
  put the secs into the message box
  divide the message box by 60 * 60 * 24        --number of days since Jan. 1, 1904
end mouseUp
```

do

Format: do <source>
Action: Executes a command or the first line of a script in a container. You can enter any command into a container (usually a field) and use *do* to run the command.
Example:

```
on mouseUp
    put "go home" into field 1
    do field 1
  end mouseUp
```

The text in field 1, "go home," is treated as a command by *do*. The script will take you home.

doMenu

Format: doMenu <menu option>
Action: Makes a menu choice. Any menu option can be called with doMenu. Make sure the option is specified *exactly* as it appears in the menu, including the ellipsis.
Example:

```
on mouseUp
  doMenu "Print Card"
  doMenu "Next"
  doMenu "Card Info . . . "
end mouseUp
```

drag

Format: drag from <location> to <location> [with <modifier key> [, <modifier key>]]
Action: Mimics dragging with the mouse and any modifier keys. You can do any kind of drawing (except freehand drawing) with *drag*.
Example:

```
on mouseUp
  choose line tool
  set lineSize to 1
  drag from 100,100 to 200,100
  drag from 200,100 to 200,200
  set lineSize to 4
  drag from 200,200 to 100,200
  drag from 100,200 to 100,100
  wait 20
  choose round rect tool
```

```
    doMenu "Draw Filled"
    set pattern to 38
    drag from 2,2 to 500,330 with optionKey
end mouseUp
```

edit script

Format: edit script of <target>
Action: Shows you the script window for the target object. Use this only if you want users to be shown the scripts of your objects for editing.
Example:

```
on mouseUp
    edit script of this stack
end mouseUp
```

find

Format: find [char[acter]s | word] <source> [in <field>]
Action: Performs a text search in the current stack or in a specified field. Most useful for retrieving the text in fields in different cards or stacks and then using that text in a script. If you just want to search a stack for a specific word, use Find from the message box.
Example:

```
on mouseUp
    go to stack "Address"
    find "Katie" in bkgnd field 1
    get bkgnd field 2                    --the phone number
    go back
    put it into the message box
end mouseUp
```

find chars
find word
find string (version 1.2 only)
find whole (version 1.2 only)

Format: find chars "<search characters>"
find word "<search word>"
find string "<search string>"
find whole "<whole search word or search phrase>"
Action: *Find chars* finds the searched-for characters anywhere inside a word or words. *Find word* finds whole words only (strings of characters set off by spaces at either end); if there's a space in the searched-for string, *HyperCard* will find each occurrence of the

words in the string, even if they're in a different order. *Find whole* (Shift–Command-F) finds only the exact searched-for word or phrase, matching whole words. *Find string* finds the exact string you're looking for within any word or phrase, including spaces. Searched-for strings have to be on the same card, but not necessarily in the same field.

Example:

```
on mouseUp
   find chars "the flag"          --finds letters "the" and "flag" everywhere
                                  --inside words
   find word "the flag"           --finds words "the" and "flag" in any order
   find string "the flag"         --finds string "the flag" even if within
                                  --other words
   find whole "the flag"          --finds only the words "the flag"
end mouseUp
```

flash

Format: flash <number of times>

Action: Creates a flashing visual effect on the entire current card. Use flash as the visual equivalent of a gong or buzzer.

Example:

```
on mouseUp
   flash 1
   wait 20
   flash 6
end mouseUp
```

get

Format: get <expression>
get <property> [of <target>]

Action: *Get* obtains the value of a function or the property of an object. Functionally, getting an expression or property is the same as putting the expression into the local variable *It*.

Examples:

```
on mouseUp
   get the time
   put it into the msg box
   wait 2 secs
   get location of bkgnd button "Home"
   put it into the msg box
end mouseUp
```

global

Format: global <variable name(s) >

Action: Creates a global variable or variables with the specified name(s). You can reuse the global and whatever it contains by declaring it at the beginning of any handler.

Example:

```
on mouseUp
   global aleph, beth, gimel              --creates three global variables
   put field "User Name" into aleph
end mouseUp
on mouseUp
   global aleph                           --redeclares the global, which still contains
                                          --the contents of field "UserName"
end mouseUp
```

go

Format: go [to] <destination>

Action: Takes you from card to card and from stack to stack.

Example:

```
on mouseUp
   push card
   go home
   go to last card                        --of the current stack, which is the
                                          --Home stack
   go to stack "Area Codes"
   go back
   pop card
end mouseUp
```

help

Format: help

Action: Takes you to the Help stacks.

Example:

```
on mouseUp
   help
end mouseUp
```

hide

Format: hide menu bar | <window> | <field> or <button>

Action: Makes the specified object(s) disappear. Buttons and fields are deactivated, so they can't be used. However, you can still type into the hidden message box if the blind typing option is checked on the User Preferences card in the Home stack.

Use the hide command in conjunction with the show command (see below). It's good form to show the menu bar or the message box again when a stack is closed.

Examples:

```
on mouseUp
   hide menubar
   hide msg box
   hide bkgnd button "Home"
   wait 2 secs
   show bkgnd button "Home"
   show msg box
   show menubar
end mouseUp
```

hide picture (version 1.2 only)

Format: hide picture of <card name | number | id>
hide picture of <background name | id>
hide card | background picture

Action: Hides the picture of the specified card or background, or hides the picture of the current background or card.

Example:

```
on mouseUp
   repeat until the mouse is down
     hide card picture
     show background picture
     hide background picture
     show card picture
   end repeat
end mouseUp
```

lock screen (version 1.2 only)

Format: lock screen

Action: Freezes the current screen so other script actions can go on unseen; does essentially the same thing as *set lockScreen to true.* Lock screen should be reversed at the end of a script with "unlock screen" or by setting lockScreen to false.

Example:

```
on mouseUp
   lock screen
   go home
   go back
   unlock screen
end mouseUp
```

multiply

Format: multiply <container> by <source>

Action: Gives the product of the number in a container times another number or a number in another container.

Example:

```
on mouseUp
   put the secs into the msg box
   multiply the msg box by 10
   wait 2 secs
   multiply the msg box by .1
end mouseUp
```

open

Format: open [<document> with] <application>
Action: Starts another application and document from *HyperCard*. Be sure to give the full pathname of the application and file you want to open. Also, you must give the *exact* name of the application. Sometimes the name of an application will include a version number and/or trademark character.
Example:

```
on mouseUp
   open "HD20:Pictures:TRex" with "HD20:GraphicsApps:MacPaint"
end mouseUp
```

open file
close file

Format: open file <filename>
close file <filename>
Action: Opens an external text file for reading or writing and closes it afterward. Be sure to specify the complete path name of the file you're accessing.
Examples:

```
on mouseUp
   open file "Writings:Rambles:June 2, 1974"
   read from file "Writings:Rambles:June 2, 1974"until return
   close file "Writings:Rambles:June 2, 1974"
end mouseUp
```

open printing/print/close printing

Format: open printing [with dialog]
print [all <number> cards] | [this <card>]
close printing
Action: Controls printing of any group of cards in the order you specify. You can also work the print commands through the message box. Type in *open printing with dialog,* and then go to the cards you want to print and type in *print this card.*

Example:

```
on mouseUp
  open printing with dialog
  print card 1
  print card 6
  print card id 4321
  print next card
  close printing
end mouseUp
```

This button script sets up a printing task. First it shows you the Print Stack dialog box; then it prints the cards specified. *Close printing* shuts down the printing task.

play

Format: play <voice> mpo <speed>] [<notes>] [# (sharp) | b (flat)] [octave] [duration]

Action: Plays digitized sounds at specified tempo, notes, pitch, octave, and duration.

There are four sounds in *HyperCard*'s resources: "boing," dialing tones, harpsichord, and silence. Many other sounds are available in other stacks; you can use ResEdit or other public-domain programs to transfer these sounds to your own stacks, or you can use a sound digitizer to add your own sounds to your stacks.

Tempo is a number, with the default value set at 200; 400 is faster than 200.

Notes are specified by *a, b, c, d, e, f,* and *g,* as in the musical scale, and can be sharps or flats. You can also use note numbers; middle C is 60. Use *r* for rest.

The first note in the parameter should have an octave number attached; octaves 3, 4, and 5 correspond to the middle octaves on a piano and sound the best. Any notes in the parameter will be in the same octave until you change the octave by putting in a new octave number.

Notes can range from a whole note to a 32nd note in duration. Whole notes are designated by *w,* half notes by *h,* quarter notes by *q,* eighths by *e,* sixteenths by *s,* and thirty-seconds by *t* and sixty-fourths by *x.*

Example:

```
on mouseUp
  play "boing"
  play "harpsichord" tempo 400 "c3w"
  play "boing" tempo 400 "at3 b c dw e f gq aw4 b c dt e f gw"
end mouseUp
```

pop

Format: pop card [into <container>]
Action: Retrieves the most recent card marked with the push command. You can push as many cards as you like; the last card pushed is the first card popped.
Example:

```
on mouseUp
   push card
   go home
   pop card                              --shows you the pushed card
end mouseUp
```

print

Format: print <filename> with <application>
Action: Lets you print a file made with another application. The print command closes *HyperCard,* opens the application, prints the file, quits the application, and returns you to *HyperCard* at the place from which you exited. It differs from the *open printing/print/close* printing commands, which act only on cards.
Example:

```
on mouseUp
   print "Writings:Rambles:June 2, 1974" with "WriteNow*"
                                  --use the exact name of the application
end mouseUp
```

push

Format: push [this | recent] card
Action: Earmarks a card for later retrieval using the Pop command. You can push as many cards as you like; the last card pushed is the first card popped.
Example:

```
on mouseUp
   push recent card                      --pushes the card most recently seen
                                         --before the current card
   go home
   pop card                              --shows you the pushed card
end mouseUp
```

put

Format: put <source> {into | before | after | <container>]
Action: Takes information from one source or container and moves it to another container. If you don't specify a target container (as in the statement "put the time"), the information is put into the message box.

Use *into, before,* and *after* to put text or numbers into a another text string. If the text in field id 5656 is "was a theropod," then putting "TRex" *before* word 1 of the field will change the text to "TRex was a theropod." Putting "TRex" *into* word 1 of the field would yield "TRex a theropod" (*TRex* is substituted for *was).* Putting "TRex" *after* word 1 of the field would give you "was TRex a theropod."

Examples:

```
    put the long date                           --puts the date into
                                                --the message box
    put field 1 + field 2 into field 3
on mouseUp
    put the script of button "Home" into field 1
    put "back" into word 2 of line 2 of field 1
    put field 1 into script2                    --a local variable
    set the script of button "Home" to script2
end mouseUp
```

read file

Format: read from file <filename> until <delimiting character> | for <number of bytes>

Action: Reads text from an external text file and puts it into *HyperCard* fields. Read (and the write command, below) must be used in conjunction with the *open file* and *close file* commands. Be sure to specify the complete pathname of the file from which you want to read.

Example:

```
on mouseUp
    open file "Writings:Rambles:June 2, 1974"
    read from file "Writings:Rambles:June 2, 1974" until return      --a return
character
    put it into field 1                         --the read material is automatically put
                                                --into It, the local variable
    close file "Writings:Rambles:June 2, 1974"
end mouseUp
```

reset paint

Format: reset paint

Action: Sets all the paint tools and menu options to their default values. Use *reset paint* at the end of a script in which you've changed many of the tool settings and painting properties.

Example:

```
on mouseUp
   choose rect tool
   set brush to 4
   set polySides to 9
   set lineSize to 3
   doMenu "Draw Filled"
   reset paint
end mouseUp
```

select (version 1.2 only)

Format: select <button> | <field>
select [before | after] <chunk> of <field> | msg box
select [before | after] text of <field>
select empty

Action: Selects a button or field; selects text in a field; positions the I-beam cursor in a field. Select only works if the user level is set to 4 (authoring) or 5 (scripting)

Example:

```
on mouseUp
   select card field "Gettysburg Address"
   select before text of me          --me is the current field, "Gettysburg Address,"
                                     --and I-beam is put before first char in field
   select before word 4 of me           --the I-beam is before word 4, "seven"
   select word 4 to 9 of me             --highlights "seven years ago our
                                        forefathers"
end mouseUp
```

send

Format: send <message> to <target>

Action: Issues a message to any specified object (the target). The message should be in quotation marks. You'll use *send* most often to send a system message to trigger another script.

Example:

```
on mouseUp
   send "mouseUp" to bkgnd button "Home"
   send "mouseUp" to bkgnd button "Prev"
   send "tabKey" to field 1
end mouseUp
```

set

Format: set <property> [of <target>] to <desired setting>

Action: Changes the property of an object to a desired setting.

Example:

```
on mouseUp
   set location of the message box to 100,200
   set autoHilite of button "Home" to true        --switches on the autoHilite feature if it is off
   set name of button "Prev" to "Verp"
end mouseUp
```

show

Format: show menubar | <window> | <field or button> [at <location>]
show {<number> | all} cards

Action: Reveals at a desired location any screen object that may have been hidden; also shows specified number of cards belonging to the current stack. Use the show command in conjunction with the hide command (see above).

Examples:

```
on mouseUp
   hide menubar
   wait 10
   show menubar
   hide tool window
   wait 10
   show tool window at 100,100
   hide message box
   wait 10
   show message at 50,300
end mouseUp
```

```
on mouseUp
   push this card
   show all cards                  --in the stack
   show 4 cards                    --the next four cards
   pop card
end mouseUp
```

show picture (version 1.2 only)

Format: show picture of <card name | number | id>
show picture of <background name | id>
show card | background picture

Action: Shows the picture of the specified card or background, or shows the picture of the current background or card.

Example:

```
on mouseUp
   repeat until the mouse is down
     hide card picture
     show background picture
```

```
    hide background picture
    show card picture
  end repeat
end mouse
```

sort

Format: sort [ascending | descending] [te | numeric | international | dateTime] by <container>
Action: Puts cards into an order according to the item specified in the container. Using the *text parameter* sorts by the ASCII value of the character; *numeric sort* sorts by number value; *international sort* looks for non-English ligatures and diacritical marks and sorts them into proper order; *Date Time* sorts by any valid date and time format, such as 12/25/87, as long as the date is after January 1, 1904 (see the entries for the functions "the date" and "the time" for descriptions of the valid date and time formats); the *default sort* is alphabetically ascending (*a*, *b*, *c* . . .). The *ascending parameter* is the default for the other types of sorts as well.
Examples:

```
on mouseUp
  sort by last word of first line of field 1          --typical sort for an address card
end mouseUp

on mouseUp
  sort descending numeric by field "Count Down"
end mouseUp
```

subtract

Format: subtract <source> from <container>
Action: Subtracts a number from a number in a container, or subtracts the number in one container from the number in another. Any expression or formula that evaluates to a number can be subtracted from a number in a container.
Example:

```
on mouseUp
  put 100 into the message box
  wait 20
  subtract 50 from the msg box
  wait 20
  subtract 49 from the msg box
  wait 20
  subtract −99 from msg box
end mouseUp
```

type

Format: type <source>
Action: Types text into a container, usually a field. *Type* only operates from a script, not the message box. In the script, first select the field to receive the text by clicking at it with the *click* command. Generally, if you want to just put text into a field, use the *put* command.
Example:

```
on mouseUp
   get the loc of field 1
   click at it
   type "Miriam" & return
   type "Less" & return & "Is more"
end mouseUp
```

unlock screen (version 1.2 only)

Format: unlock screen [with [visual] [effect] <effect name>
[<speed>] [to white grey black card inverse]]
Action: Unfreezes the screen if it has been locked by lock screen or by setting lockScreen to true. You can optionally attach one visual effect to the unlock screen command (see visual effect, below).
Example:

```
on mouseUp
   lock screen
   go to card "Info Storage"
   get card field 1
   go back
   put it into card field 1
   unlock screen with wipe left fast
   go to next card
end mouseUp
```

visual

Format: visual [effect] <type of effect> [<speed>] [to image]
Action: Creates a cinematic transition from one card to the next. Put the *visual* command statement before the *go* command statement that actually takes you to the destination card. Note that *visual* doesn't operate from the message box. These are the visual effects available:

- plain (simple jump-cut to the destination card)
- barn door open close

- dissolve checkerboard venetian blinds
- iris open close
- scroll right left up down
- wipe right left up down
- zoom open in close out

Five speeds are available: *very slow(ly), slow(ly), normal* (the default), *fast,* and *very fast.* The image parameter can be *black, gray, white,* or *the next card* (the default).

The *flash* command is also a kind of visual effect, but it has little use as a transitional device.

Example:

```
on mouseUp
   visual effect dissolve to white
   visual barn door close fast to black
   visual wipe left slow
   go to next card
end mouseUp
```

wait/wait until/wait while

Format: wait [for] <length of time> ticks | seconds
wait until <true/false condition>
wait while <true/false condition>

Action: Makes the script wait for a specified time, until an event occurs, or until a condition returns true or false. The wait commands will not work from the message box.

Example:

```
on mouseUp
   put 100 into the msg box
   wait 2 secs
   add 50 to the msg box
   wait until the mouse is down
   add 50 to the msg box
   if the mouse is down then
     wait while the mouse is down
     add 50 to the msg box
   end if
end mouseUp
```

write

Format: write <source> to file <filename>

Action: Writes *HyperCard* text from the specified source (a container) to an external text file. You must first open the file with the *open file* command, and then you must close it with the *close file* command. See also *read file.*

Examples:

```
on mouseUp
   open file "Writings:HyperCardInfo"
   write card field 1 to file "Writings:HyperCardInfo"
   close file "Writings:HyperCardInfo"
end mouseUp
```

Constants

A *constant* is a word which substitutes for a predefined value that never changes. HyperTalk constants can be used to enter values from the mouse and keyboard, such as *up, down, quote,* and *return,* or to test whether certain values are *true* or *false.* For example:

```
if the tabKey is down then go to next card

read from file "TRex" until return

if answer1 is false then go home                --answer1 is a local variable
```

Usually you'll be using the true/false constants within control structures.

down

Action: Returns a down value for a key or the mouse button.

Example:

```
on mouseUp
   if the mouse is up then
     beep 2
   end if
   if the shiftKey is down then
     beep 3
   end if
end mouseUp
```

empty

Action: Returns the null or empty value. *Empty* can be placed in a container, such as a field or global, to clear it for the next use.

Example:

```
on mouseUp
   put "full" into the msg box
   wait 1 secs
   put empty into the msg box
end mouseUp
```

false

Action: Returns the opposite of true. Many properties can be set to true or false as a way of switching them on or off. Also use true or false in a variable as a flag to point the script in a certain direction. For example, if a function returns a certain value, you can put true into a variable. Later, the script will look to see whether the variable is true or false and branch in a certain direction, depending on what it finds.

Example:

```
on mouseUp
   set autoHilite of bkgnd button "Home" to false     --turns autoHilite property off
   get the autoHilite of bkgnd button "Home"
   put it into the msg box                            --returns "false"
end mouseUp
```

formFeed

Action: Returns ASCII value 12 (move paper to top of next page) for sending to a printer. Generally, you'll use this when writing text to an external file (for example, so you can put the content of a field on its own page).

Example:

```
on mouseUp
   open file "Rambles"
   write field 1 to file "Rambles"
   write formfeed to file "Rambles"
   close file "Rambles"
end mouseUp
```

lineFeed

Action: Returns ASCII value 10 (move cursor or paper to next line) for sending to terminal or printer. When transferring text to an external file, you can use the return constant to accomplish much the same thing.

Example:

```
on mouseUp
   open file "Rambles"
   write field 1 to file "Rambles"
   write linefeed to file "Rambles"
   close file "Rambles"
end mouseUp
```

quote

Action: Lets you include quotation marks in a text string. Note how using *quote* is different from just enclosing a text string in quotation marks.

Example:

```
on mouseUp
   put "What fools these mortals be!" into msg box
   wait 3 secs
   put quote & "What fools these mortals be!" & quote into msg box
end mouseUp
```

return

Action: Lets you include the equivalent of a return keypress in a script.

Example:

```
on mouseUp
   put "Ready for return?" into line 1 of bkgnd field 1
   wait 2 secs
   put return & "This is a new line" after word 3 of line 1 of bkgnd field
end mouseUp
```

space

Action: Lets you include the equivalent of a space bar keypress in a script.

Example:

```
on mouseUp
   put "Add a space?" into line 1 of field 1
   wait 2 secs
   put space & "There it was" after word 3 of line 1 of field 1
end mouseUp
```

tab

Action: Lets you include the equivalent of a tab keypress in a script. See also tabKey under System Messages.

Example:

```
on mouseUp
   put "Go to next field" & tab into line 1 of bkgnd field 1      --tabs you to next field
   put "Keep going" & tab into line 1 of bkgnd field 2
   put "Stop here" into line 1 of bkgnd field 3
end mouseUp
```

true

Action: Returns the opposite of false. Many properties can be set to true or false as a way of switching them on or off. Also use true or false in a variable as a flag to point the script in a certain direction. For example, if a function returns a certain value, you can put true into a variable. Later, the script will look to see whether the variable is true or false and then branch in a certain direction depending on what it finds.

Example:

```
on mouseUp
   set autoHilite of bkgnd button "Home" to true     --turns autoHilite property on
   get the autoHilite of button "Home"
   put it into the msg box                            --returns "true"
end mouseUp
```

up

Action: Lets you put the *key* or *mouse-button up* value into a script.

Example:

```
on mouseUp
   if the mouse is up then
     beep
   end if
   if the tabKey is up then
     play "boing"
     wait 10
   end if
end mouseUp
```

zero through ten

Action: Lets you substitute the words *zero* through *ten* for their numerals in a script.

Example:

```
on mouseUp
   put five + ten into the msg box
end mouseUp
```

Control Structures

These are statements that make a decision or repeat an action with variations until a desired result is obtained. The most common control structures are *if. . .then, if. . .then. . .else,* and *repeat.* Here is a script example of *if. . .then:*

```
on mouseUp
   get field 1
   if it is less than field 2 then
     add 2 to field 1
     subtract 2 from field 2
   end if
end mouseUp
```

The *if. . .then* part of the statement is testing whether a certain condition is true or false—in this case, whether the amount in field 1 is less than the amount in field 2. If the condition is true—if field 1 is less than field 2—the script then executes the next command lines, which add 2 to field 1 and subtract 2 from field 2. If the condition is false—field 1 is not less than field 2—the script skips to the next command on the same level as the *if. . .then* statement, ignoring the indented command. In essence, the script is making a decision to go one way or another based on information it gathers.

The command *add 2 to field 1* inside the *if. . .then* control structure will be indented automatically in the script window. This helps you read layers of control structures that are nested one within the next, like matryushka dolls. Also note that *if. . .then* control structures have to be closed with *end if. If. . .then. . .else* structures do not, but all repeat structures must end with *end repeat.*

Control structures cannot be operated from the message box; you must test them in an actual script.

exit

Format: exit if
exit repeat
exit <current message handler>

Action: Takes you out of an *if. . .then* structure, repeat loop, or message handler. Useful for cutting short a repeat structure if a condition has already been met.

Example:

```
on mouseUp
   put "2 = 2" into the msg box
   repeat 10
     if the value of the msg box is true then
       beep
       exit repeat
     else play "boing"
   end repeat
end mouseUp
```

```
on mouseUp
   put "2 = 3" into the msg box
   repeat 10
     if the value of the msg box is true then
       beep
       exit repeat
     else play "boing"
   end repeat
end mouseUp
```

if. . .then

Format: if <true or false expression> then <command>
end if

Action: Tests for the truth or falsity of an expression and takes action based on the result of the test.

Example:

```
on mouseUp
   if "a spade" is "a spade" then
     beep 3
   end if
end mouseUp
```

if. . .then. . .else

Format: if <true or false expression> then <command>
else <command>

Action: Tests for the truth or falsity of an expression and takes a "then" action based on a true result, or an "else" action based on a false result.

Example:

```
on mouseUp
   if "black" is "white" then
     beep 2
   else play "boing"
end mouseUp
```

next repeat

Format: next repeat
Action: Provides a way to shorten a repeat loop if a condition is met.
Example:

```
on mouseUp
    put 10 into the msg box
    wait 30
    repeat until the mouse is down
      add 10 to the msg box
      if msg box < 100
      then
        next repeat
      else beep 2
      exit repeat
    end repeat
end mouseUp
```

pass

Format: pass <message>
Action: Allows you to pass trapped messages on up the hierarchy. Use pass when you want to trap certain forms of a message but not others; always pass a trapped menu option at the end of a handler.
Example:

```
on doMenu snooper                              --snooper is a variable
    if snooper is "Find . . . ": then
      ask "Search this way . . . "
      find it
    end if
    pass doMenu
end doMenu
```

repeat
repeat until
repeat while
repeat

Format: repeat [for] <number of repeats> [times]
repeat until <true or false expression>
repeat while <true or false expression>
repeat with <variable> = <low number> to <high number>
repeat with <variable> = <high number> down to <low number>

Action: Repeats a command or set of commands for a specified number of times, until certain conditions are met, while another action is going on, or until a boundary is reached.

Examples:

```
on mouseUp
   repeat for 5 times
    beep 2
    wait 30
    end repeat
end mouseUp

on mouseUp
   repeat until the mouse is down
    beep 2
    wait 30
   end repeat
end mouseUp

on mouseDown
   repeat while the mouse is down
    beep 2
    wait 30
   end repeat
end mouseDown

on mouseUp
   repeat with i = 1 to the number of bkgnd buttons
    hide bkgnd button i
    wait 10
    show bkgnd button i
   end repeat
end mouseUp
```

Repeat with structures provide a convenient way to change a number of similar objects at once, including scripts.

Functions

A *HyperTalk function* is a term that asks for and retrieves the current state of a *HyperCard* or Macintosh activity. A function always returns a result in text or numbers, such as the current time and date or the number of characters in a text field. Try these functions in the message box:

- the long date
- the number of cards

- the seconds
- the ticks

Functions are often specified right after a command; for example, *get the long date* or *put the seconds into field "Elapsed Time."* Function terms are usually preceded by *the.*

Functions also require *arguments,* which you can think of as being like parameters. In the statement below,

```
sqrt of 169                                   --square root
```

of 169 is the argument. Arguments can be written in two formats:

the time	**or**	**time ( )**
the random of 1000	**or**	**random (1000)**

with the function preceded by *the* and the argument following *of,* or with the argument in parentheses. (Even if there is no value for the argument, the second format requires parentheses.)

You can use the name of the function to stand in for the value it represents in any script.

the abs

Format: the abs of <number>
Action: Returns a number's absolute value
Examples:

```
the abs of −50
   abs (−1)
   abs (50)

on mouseUp
   get the abs of 100
   put it into the msg box
   wait 2 secs
   add abs (−25) to it
   put it into the msg box
end mouseUp
```

the annuity

Format: the annuity of <periodic rate, number of periods>
Action: Returns the present value of an annuity payment. The

formula is:

$$\text{annuity of rate (r), number (n)} = \frac{1 - (1 + r)(-n)}{r}$$

Multiply the result by the amount of a payment to get the present value of the payments on an annuity.

Examples:

```
the annuity of 0.15,24
   annuity (0.15,24)
```

```
on mouseUp
   get the annuity of 0.25,12
   multiply it by 500                    --the amount of the payment in dollars
   put it into the message box
end mouseUp
```

the atan

Format: the atan of <angle in radians>
Action: Returns the arctangent of the specified angle.
Examples:

```
   the atan of 45
   atan (45)
```

```
on mouseUp
   ask "arctangent of what angle?"
   get the atan of it
   put it into the message box
end mouseUp
```

the average

Format: the average of <number list>
Action: Returns the mean average of numbers in a list. The numbers must be separated by commas. You can also take the average of a container that evaluates to a series of comma-separated numbers.
Examples:

```
   the average of 10, 20, 30, 40, 50
   average (1, 2, 3, 4, 5)
```

```
on mouseUp
   repeat with i = 1 to 10
    get the random of 100
```

```
    put it & " , " & space into word i of the msg box
    wait 10
  end repeat
  get average (msg box)
  put it into the msg box
end mouseUp
```

the charToNum

Format: the charToNum of <character>
Action: Returns the ASCII number of a character. Every keyboard character has an ASCII number; lowercase letters have an ASCII value exactly 32 less than the uppercase version of the same letter. CharToNum reverses the action of numToChar (see below).
Examples:

```
  the charToNum of "A"
  the charToNum of "a"
  the charToNum of "&"

on mouseUp
  repeat with i = 1 to 9
    put the charToNum of i & space into word i of the msg box
    wait 10
  end repeat
end mouseUp
```

the clickH (version 1.2 only)
the clickV (version 1.2 only)

Action: ClickH returns the number of pixels from the left side of the card window to the location of the last mouse click (the same as item 1 of the clickLoc). ClickV returns the number of pixels from the top of the card window to the location of the last mouse click (the same as item 2 of the clickLoc).
Example:

```
on mouseUp
  click at 100,200
  put the clickH                    --puts 100 in the msg box
  wait 1 secs
  put the clickV                    --puts 200 in the msg box
end mouseUp
```

the clickLoc

Action: Returns the coordinates of the previous mouse click. This can be used instead of mouseLoc (see below) if the user has time to move the mouse while the script is running.

Example:

```
on mouseUp
    get the clickLoc
    if item 1 of it < 50 then
      answer "Move to the Right"
    end if
end mouseUp
```

the commandKey

Action: Returns whether the Command key is up or down. Use this to test whether the key is being pressed.
Examples:

```
on mouseUp
    if commandKey is down then
      answer "Your wish is my Command"
    end if
end mouseUp
```

the compound

Format: the compound of <periodic rate, number of periods>
Action: Returns the future value of a periodic payment. The formula is:

compound of rate (r), number (n) = (1 + r)n

Multiply the result by the periodic payment to get the future value of the investment.
Examples:

```
    the compound of 0.15,24
    compound (0.15, 24)
```

```
on mouseUp
    get the compound of 0.15,24
    multiply it by 500                  --the periodic payment in dollars
    put it into the message box
end mouseUp
```

the cos

Format: the cos of <angle in radians>
Action: Returns the cosine of an angle.

Examples:

```
the cos of 60
cos (60)

on mouseUp
   ask "Cosine of what angle?"
   get the cos of it
   put it into the message box
end mouseUp
```

the date
the long date
the abbreviated/abbrev/abbr date

Action: Returns today's date.

- *the date* returns the format 12/1/88
- *the long date* returns the format Monday, December 1, 1988
- *the abbreviated date* returns the format Mon, Dec 1, 1988

Examples:

```
the long date
put the date into field 1
put word 2 of item 2 of the long date into field 2      --puts in the day

on newCard
   put the long date into field "Date of Order"
end newCard
```

the diskspace

Format: the diskspace
Action: Returns the unused space on the current disk in bytes.
Example:

```
the diskspace

on doMenu anyitem
   if anyitem is "Quit HyperCard" then
     if the diskSpace is < 10000 then
       doMenu "Compact Stack"
     end if
   end if
   pass doMenu
end doMenu
```

the exp
the exp1
the exp2

Format: the exp of <number>
the exp1 of <number>
the exp2 of <number>

Action: *Exp* returns the natural (base-e) exponent; *exp1* returns the natural exponent less 1; *exp2* returns the base-2 exponent.

Examples:

```
the exp of 5
exp1 (5)
exp2 (5)
```

```
on mouseUp
   ask "Exponents of what number?"
   put the exp of it & " , " & space into word 1 of the msg box
   put the exp1 of it & " , " & space into word 2 of the msg box
   put the exp2 of it into word 3 of the msg box
end mouseUp
```

the foundChunk (version 1.2 only)
the foundField (version 1.2 only)
the foundLine (version 1.2 only)
the foundText (version 1.2 only)

Action: These four functions return the chunk, field, line expressions, or text within the box, where the most recent find command located its argument. Empty is returned if nothing is found.

Example:

```
on mouseUp
   find whole ""Four score" in background field "Speeches"
   put the foundChunk & "," && the foundField & "," && the foundLine & "," && the
FoundText into msg box
                                 --returns "chars 1 to 10 of bkgnd field 1, bkgnd field 1,
                                 --line 1 of bkgnd field 1, four score"
end mouseUp
```

the length

Format: the length of <container>

Action: Returns the number of characters in a text string in a container.

Examples:

```
the length of field 1
the length of the msg box

on mouseUp
  put "With malice toward none, with charity for all" into the msg box
  get the length of the msg box
  wait 2 secs
  put it into the msg box
end mouseUp
```

the ln
the ln1

Format: the ln of <number>
the ln1 of <number>

Action: The *ln* returns the natural log of a number; *ln1* returns the natural log of 1 plus the number.

Examples:

```
the ln of 5
ln (5)
ln1 (5)

on mouseUp
  ask "Natural logs of what number?"
  put the ln of it & " , " & space into word 1 of the msg box
  put the ln1 of it into word 2 of the msg box
end mouseUp
```

the max

Format: the max of <list of numbers>

Action: Returns the highest number in a list.

Examples:

```
the max of 10, 40, 20, 30, 80, 2, 3, 68
max (10, 40, 20, 30, 80, 2, 3, 68)

on mouseUp
  repeat with i = 1 to 10
    get the random of 100
    put it & " , " & space into word i of the msg box
    wait 10
  end repeat
  get max (msg box)
  put it into the msg box
end mouseUp
```

the min

Format: the min of <list of numbers>
Action: Returns the lowest number in a list.
Examples:

```
    the min of 110, 20, 30, 45, 43, 2, 89
    min (110, 20, 30, 45, 43, 2, 89)

on mouseUp
    repeat with i = 1 to 10
      get the random of 100
      put it & " , " & space into word i of the msg box
      wait 10
    end repeat
    get min (msg box)
    put it into the msg box
end mouseUp
```

the mouse

Action: Returns whether the mouse button is up or down; use this to test for when the mouse button is being pressed.
Examples:

```
    the mouse

on mouseUp
    if the mouse is up then
      put "Please click" into the message box
    end if
end mouseUp
```

the mouseClick

Action: Returns true if the button has been clicked, false if it hasn't. Use the mouseClick to test for whether the user has clicked the mouse button since the beginning of the handler. You can also use clickLoc to locate the most recent click.
Example:

```
    the mouseClick

on mouseUp
    answer "Please click when this box disappears" with "Will" or "Won't"
    wait 2 secs
    if the mouseClick is true then
      answer "Thanks—I needed that"
    else answer "C'mon—I really need it!"
    wait 2 secs
```

```
    if the mouseClick is true then
      answer "Thanks—I needed that"
    end if
end mouseUp
```

the mouseH

Action: Returns the horizontal coordinates of the cursor active spot. Use mouseH to precisely locate the cursor active spot along the *x*-axis of the screen.

Examples:

```
    the mouseH


on mouseUp
    put the mouseH into the msg box
    if the mouseH is less than 10 then
      answer "Move to the right please"
    end if
end mouseUp
```

the mouseLoc

Action: Returns the horizontal and vertical coordinates of the cursor active spot. Use mouseLoc to determine the exact location of the cursor active spot on the screen.

Examples:

```
    the mouseLoc                          --returns coordinates in format (h,v)


on mouseUp
    show message at the mouseLoc
    show tool window at the mouseLoc
end mouseUp
```

the mouseV

Action: Returns the vertical coordinate of the cursor active spot.

Examples:

```
    the mouseV


on mouseUp
    put the mouseV into the msg box
    if the mouseV is less than 10 then
      answer "Move down please"
    end if
end mouseUp
```

the number

Format: the number [of] <components> in <container>
the number of cards buttons fields

Action: Returns the total number of components in a container, or the number of cards, buttons, or fields in the current card or background, and the number of cards or backgrounds in the current stack.

Examples:

```
the number of chars in the message box
the number of cards
the number of bkgnd buttons                --in the current background


on mouseUp
  repeat with i = 1 to the number of bkgnd fields
    put "This is field number" && i into bkgnd field i
  end repeat
end mouseUp
```

the number of cards in <background name, id> (version 1.2 only)

Action: Returns the number of cards with the specified background.

Example:

```
on mouseUp
  put the number of cards of this background into the msg box
  put the number of cards of bkgnd id 2345
end mouseUp
```

the numToChar

Format: the numToChar of <ASCII value>

Action: Returns the character of an ASCII value (any number between 0 and 255); reverses the action of charToNum.

Examples:

```
the numToChar of 65
the numToChar of 97
the numToChar of 38


on mouseUp
  repeat with i = 33 to 47
    put the numToChar of i & space into word i of the msg box
    wait 10
  end repeat
end mouseUp
```

the offset

Format: offset (<expression>, <expression>)
Action: Returns the number of the character that a word begins with, or the position of an individual character in a text string.
Example:

```
on mouseUp
   put "the better angels of our natures" in the msg box
   get the offset ("angels", msg box)
   wait 2 secs
   put it in the msg box
end mouseUp
```

the optionKey

Action: Returns whether the Option key is up or down. Use this to test whether the key is being pressed.
Example:

```
on mouseUp
   if optionKey is down then
     answer "Please release my key"
   end if
end mouseUp
```

the param
the paramcount
the params

Format: the param of <parameter number>
the params
the paramcount
Action: The *param* returns the text of the specified parameter of the current message; the *paramcount* returns the number of parameters in the current message; the *params* returns all the parameters of the current message, including the command word. The param, the params, and the paramcount are useful when you want to retrieve part or all of the parameters of a message for use in another script; this is called *parameter passing.*
Example:

```
on mouseUp
   doMenu "Find . . . "
end mouseUp


on doMenu anyitem
   if anyitem is "Find . . . " then
     get param(1)                          --returns "Find . . . "
```

```
    put it in the msg box
    wait 2 secs
    get the paramcount                     --returns "1"
    put it in the msg box
    wait 2 secs
    get the params                         --returns "doMenu Find . . . "
    put it in the msg box
  end if
  pass doMenu
end mouseUp
```

The second handler gets the param, paramcount, and params of the first handler.

the random

Format: the random of <upper limit>
Action: Returns a random number between 1 and the upper limit (not more than 32,767).
Examples:

```
  the random of 3                          --repeat this a few times
  the random of 1000
  if the random of 6 is 6 then put "It's a match!" into the message box

on mouseUp
  repeat with i = 1 to 20
    put the random of 12 into dice
    put dice & " , " & space into word i of the msg box
    if dice is 2 then
      answer "Snake eyes!"
      exit repeat
    end if
    if dice is 7 then
      answer "You win"
      exit repeat
    end if
  end repeat
  put empty into the msg box
end mouseUp
```

the result

Action: Returns an error message if a Find or Go command has failed.
Example:

```
on mouseUp
  find "phobosuchus"
  put the result in the message box
end mouseUp
```

the round

Format: the round of <number>
Action: Rounds the number to the nearest integer.
Example:

```
on mouseUp
   put the round of 12.48999 into the msg box
   wait 3 secs
   put round (99.50010) into the msg box
end mouseUp
```

the screenRect (version 1.2 only)

Action: Returns the coordinates of the screen containing the card window.
Example:

```
on mouseUp
   put the screenRect in msg box      --returns 0,0, 512,340 for the standard Mac screen
end mouseUp
```

the seconds
the secs

Action: Returns the number of seconds since 12:00 a.m., January 1, 1904.
Example:

```
on mouseUp
   get the secs
   put it into the msg box
   wait 30
   divide it by (24 * 60 * 60)            --number of days since Jan. 1, 1904
   put the trunc of it into the msg box
end mouseUp
```

the selectedChunk (version 1.2 only)
the selectedField (version 1.2 only)
the selectedLine (version 1.2 only)
the selectedText (version 1.2 only)

Action: These new functions return a chunk, field, line, or text expression for the text that's currently selected; they return the empty string if nothing is selected.

Example:

```
on mouseUp
   select line 1 of card field "Gettysburg Address"
   put the selectedChunk & "," && the selectedField & "," && the selectedLine & "," &&
the selectedText into the msg box
                                    --returns "chars 1 to 20 of bkgnd field 1, bkgnd field 1,
                                    --line 1 of bkgnd field 1, four score and seven"
end mouseUp
```

the shiftKey

Action: Returns whether the Shift key is up or down. Use this to test whether the key is being pressed.
Example:

```
on mouseUp
   wait until the shiftKey is down
   answer "Shift into overdrive?"
end mouseUp
```

the sin

Format: the sin of <angle in radians>
Action: Returns the sine of the specified angle.
Example:

```
   the sin of 30
   sin (90)

on mouseUp
   ask "Sine of what angle?"
   get the sin of it
   put it into the msg box
end mouseUp
```

the sound

Action: Returns the name of a sound resource that is playing, and returns "done" when the sound is finished. Use *the sound* to trap for the continued playing of a sound you don't want to interfere with by accessing the disk or proceeding with the script. You won't be able to test this from the message box.
Example:

```
on mouseUp
   beep 10
   put the sound into the msg box
   play "boing"
   wait until the sound is "done"
   beep 2
   put "Done again!" into the msg box
end mouseUp
```

the sqrt

Format: the sqrt of <number>
Action: Returns the square root of the number
Examples:

```
   the sqrt of 1521
   sqrt (225)

on mouseUp
   set the numberFormat to "0.##############################"
   get sqrt(2)
   put it into the msg box
   wait 20
   put it * it into the msg box
end mouseUp
```

the stackSpace

Format: the stackSpace
Action: Returns the size of the current stack in bytes.
Examples:

```
   the stackSpace

on mouseUp
   if the stackSpace is > 780000 then
     doMenu "Compact Stack"
   end if
end mouseUp
```

the tan

Format: the tan of <angle in radians>
Action: Returns the tangent of the angle.
Examples:

```
   the tan of 70
   tan (275)

on mouseUp
   ask "Tangent of what angle?"
   get the tan of it
   put it into the msg box
end mouseUp
```

the target

Action: Returns the id of the object (or, if it was a stack or higher object, the name of the object) that was the recipient of the most recent message. For example, you can use target in a background or card script to trap for a message sent to one of many identical buttons or fields so that each need not have a script itself.

Examples:

```
   the target                                  --from the message box,
                                               --this is always the current card
   put the name of the target into the message box

on mouseUp
   get the target
   set the name of it to "Target"
end mouseUp
```

the ticks

Action: Returns the number of ticks (jiffies, or 1/60 seconds) since you last turned on or reset the Mac. The ticks are not an absolute measure of duration and should not be used for very accurate timing of intervals longer than a few seconds. For most tasks, use the secs instead.

Examples:

```
   the ticks
   put the ticks into field 1
   multiply value of field 1 by the ticks
   wait 10                                     --10 means 10 ticks, not secs

on mouseUp
   put the ticks into the msg box
   wait 10 secs
   put the ticks                               --msg box into the msg box
end mouseUp
```

the time
the short time
the long time

Action: Returns the exact time (if you've properly set the internal Mac clock from the Control Panel). You can select 12- or 24-hour time from the Control Panel.

- *the time* and *the short time* return the format 12:01 PM
- *the long time* returns the format 12:01:30 PM

Examples:

```
   the time
   put the long time into field 1
```

```
on mouseUp
    get the time
    put it into the msg box
    wait 2 secs
    get the long time
    put it into the msg box
    convert it to secs
    put it into the msg box
end mouseUp
```

the tool

Action: Returns the current tool.

Examples:

```
    the tool

on mouseUp
    put the tool into the msg box
    wait 20
    choose button tool
    get the tool
    choose browse tool
    put it into the msg box
end mouseUp
```

the trunc

Format: the trunc of <number>

Action: Returns the nearest whole number before the specified number.

Examples:

```
    the trunc of 2.99
    trunc (10.478)

on mouseUp
    put the secs into the msg box
    wait 20
    get the secs / (365.25 * 24 * 60 * 60)
    put the trunc of it into the msg box      --number of years since January 1, 1904
end mouseUp
```

the value

Format: the value of <container or expression>

Action: Calculates the value of an arithmetic expression and returns the answer.

Example:

```
on mouseUp
  put "5 * (12 + 14) / 2" into the msg box
  put the value of the msg box into the msg box
end mouseUp
```

the version

Format: the version
Action: Returns the number of the version of HyperCard in use.
Example:

```
on mouseUp
  put the version into msg
end mouseUp
```

the version (version 1.2 only)

Format: the version of <stack name or stack expression>
Action: Returns 5 items: the version of HyperCard used to create the stack; the version last used to compact the stack; the oldest version of HyperCard used to modify the stack since it was last compacted; the last version of HyperCard used the modify the stack; and the date in seconds (see the secs) of most recent modification of the stack. Most useful for creating scripts to automatically compact a stack that was created or modified under an early version of HyperCard.
Example:

```
on openStack
  if item 3 of the version of this stack < 1.2 then
    doMenu "Compact Stack"
  end if
end openStack
```

Custom Functions

You can define your own functions using this format:

```
function <function name> [parameters]
  <statement list>
  return <value>
end <function name>
```

Function names must begin with a letter and must not include punctuation marks. Put the custom function definition somewhere high in the hierarchy (the stack or Home script) so any other script can have access to it.

You must call custom functions with the parentheses form, as in

<function name> (<argument>)

Here's a sample custom function that converts any word to pig Latin:

Example:

```
function pigLatin ordway                 --ordway is the parameter
                                         --(you would substitute your own word for
                                         --ordway when you call the function)
   repeat with i = 1 to 5                --5 is the maximum # of consonants
                                         --before a vowel in any English word
     get char i of ordway
     if it is in "aeiouy" then           --if it is a vowel
       get char 1 to (i – 1) of ordway   --do the manipulations
       put it & "ay" after ordway
       delete char 1 to (i – 1) of ordway
       exit repeat                       --no more iterations
     end if
   end repeat
   return ordway                         --send back the value of ordway
end pigLatin
```

Test this custom function with a button script:

```
on mouseUp
   put pigLatin(scram) & " , " && pigLatin(buster) & "!" into the msg box
end mouseUp
```

It will return "amscray, usterbay!" in the message box.

If you redefine an existing function, the new definition will take precedence over the old one.

Operators

An operator is a mathematical function, such as + (plus), * (multiply), and > (greater than). Like functions, operators return a value, such as a sum or the result of a comparison between two numbers. Try these in the message box, hitting Return after each line:

```
   put 3 into a
   put 4 into b
   put 5 into c                           --a, b, anc c are local variables
   a<cir>2 + b <cir> 2 + c <cir> 2        --<cir> is the exponent symbol
```

This should return the word *true*, meaning a <cir> 2 (9) + b <cir> 2 (16) = c <cir> 2 (25).

+ (plus)
– (minus)
* (multiply)
/ (divide)

Action: Returns the result of the arithmetic operation.

Examples:

```
12 + 15
1122 – 456 – 11
33 * 17
33 / 17
```

```
on mouseUp
   put "10 + 20" into the msg box
   wait 10
   get the value of the msg box
   put it / 3 into the msg box
end mouseUp
```

= (equals)
is
< > (is not equal to)
is not

Action: Compares two expressions or containers and returns true or false.

Examples:

```
2 = 2
2 < > 2
```

```
on mouseUp
   if "men" is not "women" and "boys" is not "girls" then
     put "How true" into the msg box
   end if
   wait 30
   if "peace" is "war" and "truth" is "lies" then
     put "How cynical!" into the msg box
   else put "These are definitely false" into the msg box
end mouseUp
```

> (greater than)
< (less than)
> = (greater than or equal to)
< = (less than or equal to)

Action: Compares two expressions or containers and returns true or false.

Examples:

```
3 < 2
3 < = 4


on mouseUp
   put 10 into the msg box
   wait 10
   if the msg box > = 15 then
     subtract 5 from the msg box
   else add 5 to the msg box
end mouseUp
```

^ (exponent)

Format: <number or container> ^ <power>

Action: Returns the number or container raised to a power.

Examples:

```
3 ^ 2                                  --returns 9
12 ^ 3
total ^ 2                              --total is a local variable
field 1 ^ field 2                      --the number in field 1 raised
                                       --to the power of the number in field 2


mouseUp
   put 10 ^ 1 into the msg box         --10
   wait 30
   put 10 ^ 10 into the msg box        --1 billion
   wait 30
   put 10 ^ 10 ^ 10 into the msg box   --returns INF, infinite
end mouseUp
```

& (concatenate)
&& (concatenate with space)

Action: Returns the result of putting together two or more pieces of text, with or without spaces between the text items.

Example:

```
on mouseUp
   put"TRex" & "theropod" into the msg box     --returns "TRextheropod"
   wait 2 secs
   put "TRex," && "theropod" into the msg box  --returns "TRex, theropod"
end mouseUp
```

and

Format: <true or false expression> and <true or false expression>

Action: Returns whether the two expressions taken together are true or false. Both expressions must be true to return true.
Examples:

```
3 > 2 and 2 > 3

on mouseUp
   if "true" is "false" and "black" is "white," then
     beep
   else play "boing"
   wait 2 secs
   if 3 is 3 and "green" is "green," then
     beep 2
   else play "boing"
end mouseUp
```

contains
is in

Format: <text1> contains <text2>
<text1> is in <text2>

Action: *Contains* returns true or false as to whether text1 includes text2; *is in* returns true or false as to whether text2 includes text1.
Examples:

```
"TRex" contains "ex"                    --returns true
"TRex" is in "TRex, theropod"
field 1 is in field 2

on mouseUp
   if "woman" contains "man" then
     beep 1
   end if
   wait 2 secs
   if "man" is in "woman" then
     beep 2
   end if
   wait 2 secs
   if "man" contains "woman" then
     beep 3
   else play "boing"
end mouseUp
```

div (divide and truncate)

Action: Returns the division of one number by another as an integer with no remainder.
Example:

```
on mouseUp
   put 12 div 5 into the msg box            --returns 2
```

```
   put 144 div 11 into the msg box          --returns 13
end mouseUp
```

mod (modulo)

Action: Returns the remainder after one number is divided by another.

Example:

```
on mouseUp
   put 12 mod 5 into the msg box            --returns 2
   wait 2 secs
   put 144 mod 11 into the msg box          --returns 1
end mouseUp
```

not

Format: not <true or false expression>

Action: Returns the converse of whether the expression is true or false.

Examples:

```
   not (2 = 2)                              --returns false
   not ("a spade" is "a spade")

on mouseUp
   if not (3 = 3) is true then
     play "boing"
   else beep 2
   wait 10
   if not ("time" is "money") is true then
     play "boing"
   else beep 2
end mouseUp
```

or

Format: <true or false expression> or <true or false expression>

Action: Returns true if at least one of the expressions is true.

Examples:

```
   if (field 1 is true) or (field 2 is false) then beep

on mouseUp
   if ("seeing" is "believing") or ("green" is "green") is true then
     beep
   else play "boing"
   wait 10
   if (4 = 5) or (5 = 4) is true then
     beep 2
   else play "boing"
end mouseUp
```

--

Format: --<comment>
Action: HyperTalk ignores any text after double hyphens; use this feature often to explain and document any unique or unusual aspects of your scripts. A well-documented script is easier for someone else to understand, and may help you later as well.
Example:

```
go card 5                              --the answer card
```

within (version 1.2 only)

Action: Lets you find out if a point is contained with the rect of an object or the screen. It returns true or false.
Example:

```
on mouseUp
   if the clickLoc is within "100,100,200,200" then
     beep 3
   end if
   if the mouseLoc is not within the rect of button "Mouse Perimeter" then
     ask "Move the mouse inside the button, please"
   end if
end mouseUp
```

Properties

A property is any characteristic of a *HyperCard* object, such as its location. Properties can be global (they can be shared by all objects in *HyperCard*), or very narrow, (for example, the name of a button). There is a HyperTalk term for every object property and every painting property:

```
set style of button "TRex" to transparent
set textFont of field 1 to Chicago
set the pattern to 22                  --patterns are numbered from top left
```

Most properties are used in conjunction with the get or set commands in the following way:

get the <property>
set the <property> to <true | false> | <property number | name>

You can think of the property as being "on" when it is true, and "off" when it is false. It's easy to test most properties from the message box with an appropriate object. Remember that the get command puts the property into the local variable *It*.

- Global properties (those that belong to *HyperCard* itself) include *blindTyping, cursor, dragSpeed, editBkgnd, language, lockMessages, lockRecent, lockScreen, numberFormat, powerKeys,* and *userLevel.*
- Window properties (the message box and Tools and Patterns palettes are windows) include *loc(ation), rect(angle),* and *visible.*
- Painting properties include *brush, centered, filled, grid, lineSize, multiple, multiSpace, pattern, polySides, textAlign, textFont, textHeight, textSize,* and *textStyle.*
- Stack properties include *freeSize, name, script,* and *size.*
- Background properties include *name* and *script.*
- Card properties include *id, name, number,* and *script.*
- Field properties include *id, loc(ation), lockText, name, rect(angle), script, scroll, showLines, style, textAlign, textFont, textHeight, textSize, textStyle, visible,* and *wideMargins.*
- Button properties include *autoHilite, hilite, icon, id, loc(ation), name, rect(angle), script, showName, style, textAlign, textFont, textHeight, textSize, textStyle,* and *visible.*

autoHilite

Format: autoHilite <true | false>
Action: Governs button auto highlighting (except radio buttons and check boxes). True means the autoHilite property is on; false means it is off.
Example:

```
on mouseUp
   get autoHilite of bkgnd button "Home"
   set autoHilite of bkgnd button "Home" to true
   put autoHilite of bkgnd button "Next" into the msg box
end mouseUp
```

autoTab (version 1.2 only)

Format: autoTab <true | false>
Action: Governs whether the autoTab property of fields is on or off. With autoTab on, the user can move from the last line of a field to the next field by hitting the Return key.
Example:

```
on openCard
   repeat with i = the number of bkgnd fields
```

```
      set the autoTab of field i to true          --all bkgnd fields
                                                  --will now autotab
   end repeat
end openCard
```

blindTyping

Format: blindTyping <true | false>
Action: Governs whether you can type commands to the message box when it is hidden.

```
on mouseUp
   set blindTyping to true
   hide the msg box
put "BlindTyping works" & return into the msg box
   wait 20
   show the msg box
end mouseUp
```

brush

Format: brush <1 to 32>
Action: Governs which brush is selected from the Brush Shape dialog box. There are 32 brushes, numbered 1–32, beginning with the top left and working down the columns. The default brush number is 8.
Example:

```
on mouseUp
   choose brush tool
   set brush to 1                          --the large square
   drag from 100,100 to 200,200
   set brush to 13                         --the long vertical line
   drag from 200,200 to 300,300
   set brush to 31
   drag from 300,300 to 100,100
   reset paint
end mouseUp
```

cantDelete (version 1.2 only)

Format: cantDelete <true | false>
Action: Governs whether the user can delete a stack, background, or card.
Example:

```
on openStack
   set cantDelete of this stack to true        --user can't delete stack
end openStack
```

cantModify (version 1.2 only)

Format: cantModify <true | false>
Action: Governs whether the user can modify a stack—in effect, write-protecting the stack. If cantModify is set to true, a padlock icon appears on the right of the menu bar.
Example:

```
on openStack
   set cantModify of this stack to true          --user can't modify stack
end openStack
```

centered

Format: centered <true | false>
Action: Governs Draw Centered in the Options menu.
Examples:

```
on mouseUp
   choose rect tool
   set centered to true
   set dragSpeed to 150
   drag from 256,170 to 300,250
   wait 30
   set centered to false
   drag from 256,170 to 400,250
   reset paint
end mouseUp
```

cursor

Format: cursor <id or name>
Action: Sets which cursor will be displayed. Four cursors are available: *I-beam, crosshairs, Maltese cross,* and the *wristwatch.* You cannot "get" the cursor setting; the cursor will return to its previous setting when the script is finished.
Example:

```
on mouseUp
   set cursor to 1
   wait 30
   set cursor to 2
   wait 30
   set cursor to 3
   wait 30
   set cursor to 4
   wait 30
end mouseUp
```

cursor (version 1.2 only)

Format:
cursor <iBeam plus | cross | watch | none
| busy | arrow | hand>
Action: Governs the cursor icon. The I-beam is the text-insertion cursor (number 1); plus is the crosshairs (2); cross is the Maltese cross (3); watch is the wristwatch (4); none is no visible cursor; busy is the beachball (it turns an eighth turn each time it is set); arrow is the standard cursor arrow; and hand is the browse cursor.
Example:

```
on mouseUp
   set cursor to iBeam
   wait 1 sec
   set cursor to plus
   wait 1 sec
   set cursor to cross
   wait 1 sec
   set cursor to watch
   wait 1 sec
   set cursor to none
   wait 1 sec
   repeat 16 times
     set cursor to busy
   end repeat
   set cursor to arrow
   wait 1 sec
   set cursor to hand
end mouseUp
```

dragSpeed

Format: dragSpeed <number>
Action: Governs the drag speed. The fastest drag speed is 0; otherwise, drag speed is measured in pixels per second, with low numbers being slower than high numbers.
Example:

```
on mouseUp
   choose line tool
   set lineSize to 3
   set dragSpeed to 0
   drag from 0,0 to 512,340
   wait 5
   set dragSpeed to 50
   drag from 0,340 to 512,0
   reset paint
end mouseUp
```

editBkgnd

Format: editBkgnd <true | false>
Action: Governs whether you're editing in the background or card domain.
Example:

```
on mouseUp
   set editBkgnd to true          --puts you into the bkgnd domain
   wait 20
   set editBkgnd to false         --puts you into the card domain
end mouseUp
```

filled

Format: filled <true | false>
Action: Governs the Draw Filled option in the Options menu.
Example:

```
on mouseUp
   choose round rect tool
   set pattern to 6
   set filled to false
   set dragSpeed to 100
   drag from 100,100 to 200,300
   wait 10
   set filled to true
   drag from 100,100 to 200,300
   choose select tool
   drag from 100,100 to 200,300
   doMenu "Clear Picture"         --erases picture
   reset paint
end mouseUp
```

freeSize

Format: freeSize
Action: Tells the free size of a stack in bytes. You can't set the freeSize of a stack.
Example:

```
on mouseUp
   put the freeSize of stack "Home" into the msg box
   if the freeSize of stack "Home" > 2000 then
     doMenu "Compact Stack"
   end if
end mouseUp
```

grid

Format: grid <true | false>
Action: Governs the Grid option in the Options menu.

Example:

```
on mouseUp
    set grid to true
    choose line tool
    set dragSpeed to 150
    drag from 0,159 to 501,164
    set grid to false
    drag from 0,159 to 501,164              --slight difference
```

hilite

Format: hilite <true | false>
Action: Governs highlighting of radio buttons and check boxes.
Example:

```
on mouseUp
    go to last card of stack "Home"
    get hilite of card button "Browsing"            --on User Prefs card
    set hilite of card button "Browsing" to false   --radio button won't fill
                                                    --in when clicked on
end mouseUp
```

icon

Format: icon <number | name>
Action: Governs the icon of a button. An icon can be specified by its name or number as found in the icon selection box.
Example:

```
on mouseUp
    get icon of bkgnd button "Home"
    put it into the msg box
    wait 30
    set icon of bkgnd button "Home" to "Sort"
    wait 30
    set icon of bkgnd button "Home" to 2002
    wait 30
    set icon of bkgnd button "Home" to 0        --no icon
end mouseUp
```

id

Format: id
Action: Tells the id number of the specified object. You can't set the id of an object.
Example:

```
on mouseUp
    get id of button "Home"
    put it into the msg box
    wait 10
```

```
   get id of this card
   put it into the msg box
end mouseUp
```

language

Format: language <language name>
Action: Governs operation of the language translator. Some versions of *HyperCard* have built-in foreign language translators that translate English scripts into the language checked on the User Preferences card. The language property lets you set the language from a script, usually a stack script.
Example:

```
on mouseUp
   set language to German
end mouseUp
```

the left
the righttop
the bottom
the topLeft
the bottomRight/botRight
the width
the height

Format: the left of <button> | <field> | <window>
the top of <button> | <field> | <window>
the right of <button> | <field> | <window>
the bottom of <button> | <field> | <window>
the topLeft of <button> | <field> | <window>
the bottomRight of <button> | <field> | <window>
the width of <button> | <field> | <window>
the height of <button> | <field> | <window>
Action: These new properties of windows, fields, and buttons let you get and set elements of their rects. The left returns item 1 of the rect of the specified object; the top returns item 2 of the rect; the right returns item 3 of the rect; the bottom returns item 4 of the rect; the topLeft returns items 1 and 2 of the rect; the bottomRight returns items 3 and 4 of the rect; the width returns the horizontal dimension of the object in pixels; and the height returns the object's vertical dimension in pixels.
Example:

```
on mouseUp
   show the msg box
```

```
    put the left &",“&& the top &",“&& the right &",“&& the bottom of the msg box into msg
    wait 2 secs
    put the width &",“&& the height of the msg box into msg
    doMenu "New Button"
    set the width of card button "New Button" to 50
    set the left of card button "New Button" to 30
end mouseUp
```

lineSize

Format: lineSize <1 to 8>
Action: Governs the drawing line width in pixels. There are six widths: 1, 2, 3, 4, 6, or 8. The default size is 1.
Example:

```
on mouseUp
    choose line tool
    put lineSize into the msg box
    set lineSize to 4
    set dragSpeed to 0
    drag from 250,250 to 350,250
    set lineSize to 8
    drag from 250,260 to 350,260
    reset paint
end mouseUp
```

loc

Format: loc(ation)
Action: Governs the location of the upper left corner of a window, field, or button.
Examples:

```
on mouseUp
    put the loc of the msg box into the msg box
    show tool window
    set loc of tool window to 400,100
end mouseUp
```

lockMessages

Format: lockMessages <true | false>
Action: Governs which messages will be allowed to pass while a script is running. Set lockMessages to true to prevent *HyperCard* from passing any automatic messages—open stack card, close card, and so on—except for the ones generated by the current handler. LockMessages will always reset itself to false at the end of a script, but you can do this earlier if the script calls for it.
Example:

```
on mouseUp
    set lockMessages to true
```

```
   wait 10 secs
   set lockMessages to false
end mouseUp
```

For the duration of this handler, you'll be unable to do anything with the program—no messages will pass.

lockRecent

Format: lockRecent <true | false>
Action: Governs whether cards will be posted to the Recent card.
Example:

```
on mouseUp
   push card
   set lockRecent to true
   go to first card of "Address"
   go to "Phone"
   go to first card of "Area Codes"
   doMenu "Recent"
   wait 3 secs
   set lockRecent to false
   go to first card of "Address"
   go to "Phone"
   go to first card of "Area Codes"
   doMenu "Recent"
   pop card
end mouseUp
```

lockScreen

Format: lockScreen <true | false>
Action: Governs what screens will be shown while a script is running. Set lockScreen to true to keep a desired screen visible, even though the script is going to and from other cards. LockScreen will always reset itself to false at the end of a script, but you can do this earlier if the script calls for it.
Example:

```
on mouseUp
   set lockscreen to true
   push card
   go to card id 3011 of stack "Home"          --User Preferences
   get card field "User name"
   pop card
   put it into the msg box
end mouseUp
```

lockText

Format: lockText <true | false>
Action: Governs the locking of text in a field.
Example:

```
on mouseUp
    go to card 3011 of stack “Home”
    set lockText of card field “User Name” to true  --locks the text in the field
    put “more text” into word 3 of card field “User Name” --can't do it
    play “boing”
    wait 2 secs
    set lockText of card field “User Name” to false
    put “more text” into word 3 of card field “User Name”
    beep
end mouseUp
```

multiple

Format: multiple <true | false>
Action: Governs *Draw Multiple* in the Options menu.
Example:

```
on mouseUp
    choose oval tool
    set lineSize to 2
    set multiple to true
    set centered to true
    set dragSpeed to 100                    --a slow drag lets multiples form
    drag from 100,10 to 300,300
    drag from 300,300 to 0,0
    drag from 50,50 to 250,250
    drag from 450,50 to 350,300
    reset paint
end mouseUp
```

multiSpace

Format: multiSpace <1 to 9>
Action: Sets the spacing between multiples. The numbers 1–9 refer to the number of pixels separating multiple images made with the Draw Multiple feature.
Example:

```
on mouseUp
    choose rect tool
    set multiple to true
    set centered to true
    set multiSpace to 9
    set dragSpeed to 200                    --a slow drag lets multiples form
    drag from 256,170 to 350,270
    set multiSpace to 1
    set dragSpeed to 100
```

```
    drag from 256,170 to 350,270
    reset paint
end mouseUp
```

name

Format: [short | long] name of <object>
Action: Governs the name of any object. There are several name formats that are returned by invoking the name property.

The default name format for a card field named "Total" on a card named "May Expenses" in a stack with the pathname "Financial Stacks: Expenses 88" is

card field "Total"

The short name returns

Total

The long name returns

card field "Total" of card "May Expenses" of stack "Financial Stacks:

Expenses 88"

Example:

```
on mouseUp
    get the name of this background
    put it into the msg box
    wait 2 secs
    get the name of this stack
    put it into the msg box
    wait 2 secs
    get the long name of this stack
    put it into the msg box
    wait 2 secs
    set the name of card button "Home" to "House"
end mouseUp
```

numberFormat

Format: numberFormat <format>
Action: Governs the way numbers are displayed. Typical number formats are:

"0.00"	Dollars and cents
"0."	Whole numbers only
"0.########"	Fractional precision to eight places, with no trailing zeros

You can have any number of crosshatches for any desired degree of precision.

Example:

```
on mouseUp
   set numberFormat to "0.00<inch>
   put 3.98765 * 2.54321 into the msg box
   wait 30
   set numberFormat to "0.###############"
   put 3.98765 * 2.54321 into the msg box
end mouseUp
```

pattern

Format: pattern <1 to 40>

Action: Governs what pattern is currently active

Each pattern in the Pattern palette has a number, beginning with 1 at the upper left and working down the columns.

Example:

```
on mouseUp
   choose rect tool
   set lineSize to 4
   set pattern to 37                      --the trellis
   drag from 0,0 to 512,340
   set pattern to 1                       --white
   drag from 0,0 to 512,340 with optionKey
   reset paint
end mouseUp
```

polySides

Format: polySides <any number over 2>

Action: Governs the number of sides of the regular polygon tool. This lets you set more kinds of regular polygons than are available from the Polygon Sides dialog box.

Example:

```
on mouseUp
   choose regular polygon tool
   set multiple to true
   set multiSpace to 4
   set lineSize to 1
   set polySides to 9                     --a nonagon
   set dragSpeed to 50
   drag from 256,170 to 256,200
   wait 2 secs
   set polySides to 100                   --a near-circle
   drag from 256,170 to 256,312
   reset paint
end mouseUp
```

powerKeys

Format: powerKeys <true | false>
Action: Governs whether the power keys are active or inactive. This is usually set from the User Preferences card.
Example:

```
on mouseUp
   if field "User Age" > 12 then
     set powerKeys to false              --if you don't want the user to have
                                         --access to the power keys
   else set powerKeys to true
end mouseUp
```

rect

Format: rect(angle)
Action: Gives upper left and lower right coordinates of a window, field, or button. The rect property cannot be set.
Example:

```
on mouseUp
   show tool window
   show the msg box
   show the pattern window
   put the rect of tool window into the msg box
   wait 30
.  put the rect of pattern window into the msg box
   wait 30
.  put the rect of the msg box into the msg box
end mouseUp
```

script

Format: script of <object>
Action: Lets you manage a script from another script. You can start, stop, and modify any script from another script by getting and setting the target script.
Example:

```
on mouseUp
   get the script of this card                       --puts the script into It
   put "push this card" & return into line 2 of it   --changes a line in the script
   put it into bkgnd field 1
   set the script of button "Sort" to newScript      --replaces the script with a new script in
                                                     --the container newScript
end mouseUp
```

scroll

Format: scroll <pixels>

Action: Governs the scrolling of a scrolling field in pixels from the top of the field. Lets you scroll the text in a scrolling field automatically or save the scroll position so the text will go back to that scroll position later.

Examples:

```
on mouseUp
   set scroll of bkgnd field 1 to 2 * textHeight of bkgnd field 1          --down two lines
end mouseUp

on mouseUp
   repeat with i = 1 to the number of lines in bkgnd field 1
     set scroll of bkgnd field 1 to i * textHeight of bkgnd field 1
     wait 5
   end repeat
end mouseUp
```

This script automatically scrolls a scrolling field as you read. Adjust the scrolling speed using different values for *wait.* To scroll pixel by pixel (a very smooth but very slow scroll), use this:

```
on mouseUp
   repeat with i = 1 to the number of lines in bkgnd field 1 * ¬[soft return]
   textHeight of bkgnd field 1
     set scroll of bkgnd field 1 to i
   end repeat
end mouseUp
```

This will work a lot faster on a Mac II or an accelerated Plus or SE.

showLines

Format: showLines <true | false>
Action: Governs whether a field shows lines.
Examples:

```
on mouseUp
   set showLines of bkgnd field 1 to true          --shows lines in field
   wait 10
   set showLines of bkgnd field 1 to false
end mouseUp
```

showName

Format: showName <true | false>
Action: Governs the showName button feature.

Example:

```
on mouseUp
    get the showName of button "Home"
    put it into the msg box
    set it to true                        --name shown
    wait 2 secs
    set it to false                       --name not shown
end mouseUp
```

showPict (version 1.2 only)

Format: showPict <true | false>
Action: Governs whether the picture of a specified card or background is visible. If showPict is true, the picture is visible; is showPict is false, the picture is hidden.
Example:

```
on mouseUp
    set showPict of this card to true
    set showPict of this background to false
    get the showPict of next card
    put it into msg box
```

size

Format: size
Action: Tells size of stack in bytes; you cannot set the stack size.
Example:

```
on mouseUp
    put size of stack "Home" into the msg box
end mouseUp
```

style

Format: style <style type>
Action: Governs style of buttons and fields. Field styles include *opaque, rect(angle), scrolling, shadow,* and *transparent.* Button styles include *checkBox, opaque, radioButton, rect(angle), roundRect, shadow,* and *transparent.*
Examples:

```
on mouseUp
    set style of bkgnd button "Home" to checkBox
    wait 20
    set style of bkgnd button "Home" to shadow
    wait 20
    set style of bkgnd button "Home" to transparent
    wait 20
```

```
    set style of bkgnd button "Home" to roundRect
    wait 20
    set style of bkgnd field 1 to rect
    wait 20
    set style of bkgnd field 1 to shadow
    wait 20
    set style of bkgnd field 1 to scrolling
    wait 20
    set style of bkgnd field 1 to transparent
end mouseUp
```

textAlign

Format: textAlign <left | right | center>
Action: Governs alignment of text in a button, a field, or in graphic text.
Example:

```
on mouseUp
    set textAlign of bkgnd field 1 to right
    wait 10
    set textAlign of bkgnd field 1 to left
end mouseUp
```

textFont

Format: textFont <font name>
Action: Governs font of text in a button, in a field, or in graphic text.
Example:

```
on mouseUp
    put"This is a test of textFont" into card field 1
    set textFont of card field 1 to Chicago
    wait 20
    set textFont of card field 1 to New York
    wait 20
    set textFont of card field 1 to Venice
end mouseUp
```

textHeight

Format: textHeight <leading>
Action: Governs points between lines of text (leading) in a button, in a field, or in graphic text.
Example:

```
on mouseUp
    put"This is a test of textHeight" into line 1 of card field 1
    put"This is a test of textHeight" into line 2 of card field 1
```

```
    set textFont of card field 1 to Chicago
    set textHeight of card field 1 to 12
    wait 20
    set textHeight of card field 1 to 16
    wait 20
    set textHeight of card field 1 to 20
end mouseUp
```

textSize

Format: textSize <font size>
Action: Governs point size of text in a button, in a field, or in graphic text.
Example:

```
on mouseUp
    put"This is a test of textSize" into line 1 of card field 1
    set textFont of card field 1 to New York
    set textSize of card field 1 to 12
    wait 20
    set textSize of card field 1 to 16
    wait 20
    set textSize of card field 1 to 24
end mouseUp
```

textStyle

Format: textStyle <style type[, style type] >
Action: Governs text style of text in a button, a field, or in graphic text. Available styles are *plain, bold, italic, underline, outline, shadow, condense,* and *extend*. You can combine these styles however you like (except with plain, the default setting).
Example:

```
on mouseUp
    put"This is a test of textStyle" into line 1 of card field 1
    set textFont of card field 1 to New York
    repeat for 10 times
      set textStyle of card field 1 to bold
      wait 10
      set textStyle of card field 1 to bold, underline
      wait 10
      set textStyle of card field 1 to bold, underline, shadow, italic
      wait 10
      set textStyle of card field 1 to plain
      wait 10
    end repeat
end mouseUp
```

userLevel

Format: userLevel <1 2 3 4 5>
Action: Governs user level; *browsing* is level 1, *typing* is 2, *painting* is 3, *authoring* is 4, and *scripting* is 5.
Example:

```
on mouseUp
   get user level
   if it < 5 then
     answer "Okay to script?" with "No" or "OK"
       if it is "no" then
         answer "It can wait"
       else set user level to 5
     else answer "Scripting is OK"
   end if
end mouseUp
```

userModify (version 1.2 only)

Format: userModify <true | false>
Action: Global property that allows the user to type into fields and use paint tools in a write-protected stack. User changes are temporary when userModify is set to true.
Example:

```
on mouseUp
   set the userModify of this stack to true
end mouseUp
```

visible

Format: visible <true | false>
Action: Lets you set the visibility of a button, a field, or a window. The hide and show commands let you do the same thing as setting the visible of an object.
Example:

```
on mouseUp
   repeat with i = 1 to the number of bkgnd buttons
     set the visible of bkgnd button i to false
     wait 30
     set the visible of bkgnd button i to true
   end repeat                                    --buttons will blink on and off in succession
end mouseUp
```

wideMargins

Format: wideMargins <true | false>
Action: Governs margins of a field

Example:

```
on mouseUp
    put "This is a test of wideMargins" into line 1 of card field 1
    set textFont of card field "Test" to New York
    set wideMargins of card field 1 to true        --widens margins of field
    wait 20
    set wideMargins of card field 1 to false       --narrows margins
end mouseUp
```

System Messages

Scripts are triggered by *system messages*, messages sent by *HyperCard* about the mouse, keyboard, and other actions within the program. A *trap* for a system message—*on mouseUp,* for example—opens every script. *MouseUp,* the message that the mouse button has been released, initiates the majority of button scripts and is probably the system message most familiar to you. There are, however, many others. For example, *mouseEnter, mouseWithin,* and *mouseLeave* detect the position of the pointer in relation to the boundaries of buttons and fields. Keystrokes are detected with system messages such as *returnKey* and *arrowKey.* You can even detect events like the creation of new objects or the choice of a menu option—*on newCard,* for example. Every handler must end with an *end* message—*end mouseUp,* for example.

System message can also be sent from within a script. For this, use the send command:

```
on mouseUp
    send mouseUp to bkgnd button "Home"       --will activate the "Home" button
end mouseUp
```

arrowKey

Format: arrowKey <direction>
Action: Traps for or sends message of the keypress of an arrow (cursor) key.
Example:

```
on arrowKey right                             --a card script
    go to card "Asia"
end arrowKey right
```

The arrowKey message can be used to substitute for the standard use of the arrow keys, which is navigating from card to card. With arrowKey, you can assign any other function to keys.

For example, in a stack of maps, arrowUp might move the browser to a card that shows a region north of the map on the current card.

close

Format: close<object type>
Action: Traps for and sends message of the closing of objects.
Example:

```
on closeStack                                --a stack script
   show the msg box
   put "Goodbye" into the msg box
   wait 2 secs
end closeStack
```

delete

Format: delete<object type>
Action: Traps for or sends message of the deletion of a button, field, card, background, or stack.
Example:

```
on deleteButton                              --a card script
   put "Goodbye button" into the msg box
end deleteButton
```

doMenu

Format: doMenu item
Action: Traps for the selection of a menu option.
Example:

```
on doMenu anyitem
   if anyitem is "Quit HyperCard" then
     ask "Are You Sure?" with "No" or "OK"
     if it is "OK" then
       quit HyperCard
     else exit doMenu
   end if
   pass doMenu
end doMenu
```

Be sure to include "pass doMenu" (see the pass command), so that doMenu won't trap any additional menu choices.

enterInField (version 1.2 only)

Format: enterInField

Action: Intercepts the Enter key when it's typed into the currently selected field.
Example:

```
on enterInField
   put the value of me into the msg box
end enterInField
```

enterKey

Format: enterKey
Action: Traps for or sends message of the keypress of the Enter key.
Example:

```
on enterKey
   put card field 1 into the msg box
end enterKey
```

Hitting the enter key puts the contents of field 1 into the message box.

idle

Format: idle
Action: Traps for or sends an idle message.
Example:

```
                                    --first put "100" into the message box
on idle                             --a card or bkgnd script
   subtract 1 from the msg box
   wait 1 secs
   pass idle
end idle
```

This script subtracts 1 from the value in the message box every second, as long as the script continues to receive an idle message. *Idle,* like doMenu, should be passed before the end of the handler.

mouseDown

Format: mouseDown
Action: Traps for or sends message of the downpress of the mouse button.
Example:

```
on mouseDown
   go home
end mouseDown
```

mouseEnter

Format: mouseEnter
Action: Traps for or sends message of the entry of the pointer into a defined area, like the boundary of a button or field.
Example:

```
on mouseEnter
   go to next card
end mouseEnter
```

This script traps for the entry of the pointer into the area of the object to which the script is attached—for example, a field. The script is triggered as the pointer crosses the object boundary.

mouseLeave

Format: mouseLeave
Action: Traps for or sends message of the exit of the pointer from a defined area, like the boundary of a button or field.
Example:

```
on mouseLeave
   go to prev card
end mouseLeave
```

This script traps for the exit of the pointer from the area of the object to which the script is attached—for example, a field. The script is triggered as the pointer crosses the object boundary.

mouseStillDown

Format: mouseStillDown
Action: Traps for or sends message of the continuing downpress of the mouse button.
Example:

```
on mouseStillDown
   play "boing"
   wait 20
end mouseStillDown
```

This script detects the continued downpress of the mouse button and plays the sound "boing" at 20-click intervals.

mouseUp

Format: mouseUp
Action: Traps for or sends message of the release of the mouse button.

Example:

```
on mouseUp
   send mouseUp to bkgnd button "Home"
end mouseUp
```

This button script is triggered by a mouseUp message and sends another mouseUp message to a button "Home."

mouseWithin

Format: mouseWithin
Action: Traps for or sends message that the position of the pointer is within a defined area, like the boundary of a button or field.
Example:

```
on mouseWithin
   wait 2 secs
   put "This area is now off-limits to humans" into msg box
end mouseWithin
```

This button script traps for the continued existence of the pointer within the area of an object, such as a field. The script is triggered as long as the pointer remains within the button boundary.

new

Format: new<object type>
Action: Traps for or sends messages on the creation of new objects.
Example:

```
on newCard                                    --a bkgnd script
   put "Don't forget to add links to this card!" into the message box
end newCard
```

open

Format: open
Action: Traps for or sends messages upon the opening of an object (usually a field, card, or stack).
Example:

```
on openStack
   put "Hey good buddy!" into the message box
end openStack
```

This stack script puts a greeting into the message box when you open the stack.

quit

Format: quit [HyperCard]
Action: Traps for quitting the program.
Example:

```
on quit
   put "Goodbye to all that" into the msg box
   wait 3 secs
end quit
```

resume

Format: resume [HyperCard]
Action: Traps for reentering *HyperCard* from another application that was opened from within *HyperCard*. After a resume message, you'll be returned to the exact place from which you exited *HyperCard*.
Example:

```
on resume
   show msg box
   put "Welcome back" into the msg box
   wait 3 secs
   hide msg box
   pass resume
end resume
```

Normally, resume scripts would be placed at the Home stack level of the hierarchy. Pass the resume message so that another handler (there are several in the Home stack script) can trap for it.

returnInField (version 1.2 only)

Format: returnInField
Action: Intercepts the Return key when it's typed into the currently selected field. If the returnInField message is not intercepted by a handler, autoTab of the current field is true, and the I-beam is in the last line of the field, *HyperCard* moves the I-beam to the next field.
Example:

```
on returnInField
   put the value of me into the msg box
end returnInField
```

returnKey

Format: returnKey
Action: Traps for the keypress of the Return key.
Example:

```
on returnKey
   put "Return of the Native" into the msg box
end returnKey
```

This card script puts text into the message box when the return key is pressed.

startUp

Format: startUp [HyperCard]
Action: Traps for the startup message when you enter *HyperCard*.
Example:

```
on startUp                                    --a home script
   show the msg box
   put "Let's get going" into the msg box
   pass startUp
end startup
```

This handler could be added to the end of the actual startUp script in the Home stack. Take a look at the Home stack for more on what startUp scripts must do.

suspend

Format: suspend [HyperCard]
Action: Traps for the suspend *HyperCard* message when another application is opened from within *HyperCard*.
Example:

```
on suspend                                    --a home script
   put "Au revoir" into the message box
   wait 3 secs
end suspend
```

This works much like the quit script above; it puts a goodbye message into the message box as you exit *HyperCard*. In most situations, it isn't necessary to have a message handler for the suspend message. The Home stack, for example, has handlers only for the *startUp* and *resume system* messages. However, under forthcoming versions of *HyperCard* operating under *MultiFinder*, you may be able to use the suspend message to trigger a script that carries on some *HyperCard* action behind the scenes while another program is in the foreground.

tabKey

Format: tabKey
Action: Traps for or sends message of the keypress of the Tab key.
Example:

```
on tabKey                                --a field script
   doMenu "New Card"
end tabKey
```

This field script could automatically create a new card when the tab key is pressed at the end of data entry on the current card.

Appendix B

HyperTalk Quick-Reference Index

Appendix C

Keyboard Shortcuts and Mouse Moves

HyperCard offers many keyboard shortcuts for commands and menu options. In addition, you can often drag or click the mouse to enhance the action of a keystroke. Shortcuts for commands, navigation, graphics, and scripting are listed below.

Command and Navigation Keys

Command	Key
Back through cards	Down Arrow
Background on/off	Command-B
Bring Closer	Command-+ (plus)
Browse tool	Command-Tab
Cancel current action	Command-. (period)
Copy	Command-C
Cut	Command-X
Delete selected object or text	Command-Backspace
Find (text)	Command-F
First card	Command-1 or Command–Left Arrow
Forward through retraced cards	Up Arrow
Help stack	Command-**?**
Home card	Command-H
Last card	Command-4 or Command–Right Arrow
Message bar on/off	Command-M
Message box	Command-M
New card	Command-N
Next card	Command-3 or Right Arrow
Next field on card	Tab
Open stack	Command-O
Previous card	Command-2 or Left Arrow
Previous field on card	Shift-Tab
Print card	Command-P
Quit *HyperCard*	Command-Q
Recent	Command-R
Return to stored card	Command–Up Arrow
Send farther	Command-– (minus)
Show all buttons	Command-Option
Show all fields	Command–Shift-Option
Store card location	Command–Down Arrow
Undo	Command-Z

Graphics and Text Formatting Keys

Note: Power Keys work only if a paint tool is selected.

Command	Key
Black pattern in Patterns palette	B
Center (toggle on/off)	C
Darken	D
Clear selection	Backspace
FatBits (toggle on/off)	Option-F, Command-click with Pencil on
FatBits scrolling	Option-drag
Fill	F
Flip horizontal	H
Flip vertical	V
Font, next available	Command–Shift->
Font, previous available	Command–Shift-<
Graphic Text	Command-S
Grid (toggle on/off)	G
Hide/show menu bar	Command–Space bar
Invert	I
Keep	Command-K
Less space between text lines	Command–Option-<
Lighten	L
Line widths	1,2,3,4,6, or 8
More space between text lines	Command–Option->
Multiple (toggle on/off)	M
Opaque	O
Paste minicard from clipboard	Command–Shift-V
Patterns palette (toggle on/off)	Tab
Pickup	P
Revert	R
Select	S
Select all	A
Show card picture (paint tool on)	Option-D
Show opaque areas (paint tool on)	Option-O
Spacing between multiples	Option–1 through 8
Text size, larger	Command->
Text size, smaller	Command-<
Text Style dialog box	Command-T
Tools palette (toggle on/off)	Option-Tab
Trace edges	E
Transparent	T
White pattern in Patterns palette	W
Rotate left	[
Rotate right	]
Undo last action (paint tool on)	˜(tilde)
Undo	Command-Z

Dragging the General and Painting Tools

Tool	Drag w/ Command key	Drag w/ Option key	Drag w/ Shift key
Brush	Erase	--	Paint horiz. or vert. only
Button	Make new button	Copy button	Move button horiz. or vert. only
Curve	--	Patterned border	--
Eraser	Erase white	--	Erase horiz. or vert. only
Field	Make new field	Copy fieldMove field horiz. or vert. only	
Lasso	Lasso all	Copy selection	Move selection horiz. or vert. only
Line	--	Draw with pattern	Draw 15-degree angles
Oval	--	Patterned border	Draw circle
Pencil	Toggle in/out of FatBits	--	Draw horiz. or vert. only
Polygon	--	Draw with pattern	Draw 15-degree angles
Rectangle	--	Patterned border	Draw square
Regular Poly.	--	Patterned border	Rotate by 15 degrees
Rounded Rect.	--	Patterned border	Draw rounded square
Selection	Select close to shape	Copy selection	Move selection horiz. or vert. only
Spray	Erasing spray	--	Spray horiz. or vert. only

Double-Clicking the Paint Tools

Tool	Result of Double-Clicking
Brush	Displays *Brush Shapes* box
Bucket	Turns *Pattern* palette on/off
Curve	Turns *Draw Filled* on/off
Eraser	Clears picture
Lasso	Lassos all
Line	Displays *Line Size* box
Oval	Turns *Draw Filled* on/off
Graphic Text	Displays *Text Style* box
Pattern	Displays *Pattern Edit* box

Tool	Result of Double-Clicking
Pencil	Turns *FatBits* on/off
Polygon	Turns *Draw Filled* on/off
Regular Polygon	Displays *Polygon Sides* box
Rectangle	Turns *Draw Filled* on/off
Round Rectangle	Turns *Draw Filled* on/off
Selection	Selects all

Script Editing and Formatting Keys

Command	Key
Copy	Command-C
Cut	Command-X
End command line	Return
Find	Command-F
Find again (in scripts only)	Command-G
Find selection (in scripts only)	Command-H
Paste	Command-V
Print	Command-P
Save script	Enter
See script directly	Shift-select object Info box from Objects menu; Shift–double-click on button or field
Select	Command-S
Select all	Command-A
Set proper indention	Tab
Soft return	Option-Return
Stop action of script	Command-. (period)
Stop printing	Command-. (period)
Undo	Command-Z

Version 1.2 Additions

Command	Key
Choose button tool	Command–Tab-Tab
Choose field tool	Command–Tab-Tab-Tab
Find whole	Shift–Command-F
Increase line spacing in selected field	Command-Shift–Option->
Decrease line spacing in selected field	Command-Shift–Option-<
See script of any button or field	Shift–Command–Option–click on field or button (with browse tool)
See script of any field	Command–Option–click on field (with field tool)
See script of any button	Command–Option–click on button(with button tool)
See script of current card	Command–Option-C

Command	**Key**
See script of current background	Command–Option-B
See script of current stack	Command–Option-S
Exit script editor	Command–Option–click or press any key

Appendix D
HyperCard Resources

Publications, commercial programs, and public domain stacks have been proliferating ever since *HyperCard*'s introduction. Collected here are a few of the more important resources. This is not meant to be a comprehensive list—there are hundreds of public domain stacks out there, of which only a fraction are listed below—but merely a selection of interesting and useful materials to get you started in your own explorations.

Books and commercial products are available from the publishers or at bookstores and computer stores. Public domain and shareware stacks can be found on the major online services, such as Compuserve and GEnie; through the stackware supply houses; in the collections of Mac user groups; or directly from the authors. If the stack is a shareware product, please pay the requested royalty.

Books and Articles on Hypermedia

"As We May Think"
Vannevar Bush
Atlantic Monthly (July 1945)

Farsighted article by FDR's science advisor that set the idea of hypermedia in motion.

Literary Machines ***$15.00***
Ted Nelson
Box 128
Swarthmore, PA 19081

Thought-provoking tract by visionary inventor of the "hypertext" concept; available directly from the author.

"Memex Revisited"
Vannevar Bush
In *Science Is Not Enough*
William Morrow & Company, Inc. (1967)

Follow-up that looks at the memex idea from a more modern perspective.

Odyssey: From Pepsi to Apple
John Sculley
Harper & Row (1967)
Memoirs of Apple's CEO; includes lengthy description of the knowledge navigator and its relation to HyperCard.

Books, Publications, and Tutorials on *HyperCard*

The Complete HyperCard Handbook ***$29.95***
Danny Goodman
Bantam Books
666 Fifth Ave.
New York, NY 10103
Groundbreaking book on the subject; doesn't cover recent developments.

COMPUTE!'s Quick and Easy Guide to HyperCard ***$12.95***
Steven Anzovin
COMPUTE! Books
240 West Wendover Ave., Ste. 200
Greensboro, NC 27408
(919) 275-9809
An easy-to-use overview of HyperCard *and HyperTalk.*

HyperCard Power: Techniques and Scripts ***$17.85***
Carol Kaehler
Addison-Wesley
Rt. 128
Reading, MA 01867
How-to by an original member of the HyperCard *development team.*

HyperCard Script Language Guide ***$19.95***
Apple Programmer's and Developer's Association
290 SW 43rd St.
Renton, WA 98055
HyperTalk documentation and hints for stack design, including a disk with XCMDs, XFCNs, and drivers for videodisk players. You must be a member of APDA to order APDA products; membership fee is $20.

HyperJournal
4505 75th
Urbandale, IA 50322
(515) 253-9612
A newsletter.

HyperLink Magazine ***$4.95*** (single issue)
Publishers Guild, Inc.
P.O. Box 7723
Eugene, OR 97401
(503) 484-5157
Slick magazine devoted to HyperCard

Hypernews ***$6.95*** (single issue) ***$60.00*** (one-year subscription)
TRU
31849 Pacific Hwy. South, Ste. 115L
Federal Way, WA 98003
Monthly on-disk newsletter covering all aspects of HyperCard.

HyperTalk Programming ***$24.95***
Dan Shafer
Hayden Books (A Division of Howard W. Sams & Co.)
P.O. Box 7092
Indianapolis, IN 46206
Also available from Apple Programmer's and Developer's Association. Advanced HyperTalk programming, including language extensions in C and Pascal.

HyperTalk Scripting ***$16.95***
Jeff Stoddard
Walking Shadow Press
Apple Programmer's and Developer's Association
290 SW 43rd St.
Renton, WA 98055
Tutorials, sample scripts, and a HyperTalk reference section.

HyperTalk Scripting Reference Guide ***$9.95***
HyperSource
2619 S. 302nd St.
Federal Way, WA 98003
(206) 946-2011
Introduction to HyperTalk and scripting.

HyperTalk and the External Commands ***$11.95***
Hyperpress Publishing
Foster City, CA 94404
A desktop reference guide to HyperTalk.

HyperTutor ***$49.95***
Teligraphics
936 Sir Francis Drake Blvd., Ste. R
Kentfield, CA 94904
(415) 454-7519
Stack-based tutorial on HyperTalk commands.

HyperUser ***free***
COVE Associates
P.O. Box 1602
Edgartown, MA 02539
(617)-627-8974
A newsletter.

The Open Stack ***free***
Walking Shadow Press
P.O. Box 2092
Saratoga, CA 95071
Monthly newsletter.

Using HyperCard ***$39.95***
Creating Cards and Stacks ***$49.95***
Basic Scripting ***$49.95***
Advanced Scripting ***$49.95***
Personal Training Systems (PTS)
P.O. Box 54240
San Jose, CA 95154
(408) 559-8635
Four audio training packages on various aspects of the program. Each package includes an audio tape, a training disk, and a summary card.

Commercial *HyperCard* Applications

The Big Apple Stack
Kabisa Computer Creations
914 President St.
Brooklyn, NY 11215

All you need to know about Gotham, with Manhattan maps and tips for the explorer.

Business Class ***$49.95***
Activision
P.O. Box 7287
Mountain View, CA 94039
(415) 960-0410

Database for world travelers.

City to City ***$49.95***
Activision
P.O. Box 7287
Mountain View, CA 94039
(415) 960-0410
Travel information on U.S. cities.

Computer-Based Training Disks ***$135.00***
First Reference
516 Fifth Avenue, #706
New York, NY 10036
(212) 730-8211

Stacks and manual containing routines and ideas for creating HyperCard*-based training materials.*

ClickArt Disks ***$49.95–$129.95***
T/Maker Co.
1973 Landings Dr.
Mountain View, CA 94043
(415) 962-0195

Collections of clip art.

The Curator ***$139.95***
Solutions
Montpelier, VT

Graphics cataloguing program.

The DTP Advisor
HyperSoft
P.O. Box 566
San Francisco, CA 94101
(415) 431-2466
Desktop publishing stack and document tracker.

Focal Point ***$99.95***
Activision
P.O. Box 7287
Mountain View, CA 94039
(415) 960-0410
Personal planner and organizer for business people.

HyperANIM
Aegis Development
2115 Pico Blvd.
Santa Monica, CA 90405
(213) 392-9972
Eight-bit color animation tool for HyperCard.

HyperAnimation
Bright Star Technologies
1003 111th Ave. N.E.
Bellevue, WA 98004
(206) 451-3697
A talking head for HyperCard; *says whatever you type in.*

HyperBook Maker ***$59.95***
IdeaForm
P.O. Box 1540
612 West Kirkwood
Fairfield, IA 52536
(515) 472-7256
Print your stacks in various notebook formats.

Hyper Business Tools
HyperSource
2619 S. 302nd St.
Federal Way, WA 98003
(206) 946-2011
Business applications, forms, and readymade tools.

HyperDA ***$69.00***
Symmetry
761 E. University Dr.
Mesa, AZ 85203
(800) 624-2485; in Arizona (602) 844-2199

Desk accessory that gives you access from another application to information stored in HyperCard; *works with 512K Macs.*

HyperSpell ***$79.95***
Hyperpress Publishing
Foster City, CA 94404

100,000-word spelling checker for stacks.

Icon Library ***$49.95***
Hyperpress Publishing
Foster City, CA 94404

Icon editor, art library, and button customizer.

MacRecorder
Farallon Computing
2150 Kittredge St.
Berkeley, CA 94704
(415)-849-4632

Sound digitizer hardware plus sound utility stackware.

King James Bible ***$120.00***(set)
Alpha & Omega
P.O. Box 81056
South Burnaby, B.C.
Canada V5H 4K2
(604) 732-7171

HyperCard *edition of the all-time best seller.*

MacSMARTS
Cognition Technology
55 Wheeler St.
Cambridge, MA. 02138
(800)492-0246

Expert system with a HyperCard *front-end.*

MacWEEK News Stack
525 Brannan St.
San Francisco, CA 94107
(415)882-7370
Text of Mac news weekly on a stack.

Open Stack ***$5.00***
Mike Westphal & Hunt Stoddard
Apple Library Users Group
10381 Bandley Dr.
Cupertino, CA 95014
Offers acquisition, cataloguing, circulation, and labeling functions for small libraries.

PhoneNET
Farallon Computing
2150 Kittredge St.
Berkeley, CA 94704
(415)-849-4632
Local area network management system.
Plant Encyclopedia

Macsolutions
241 12th St.
Del Mar, CA 92014
(619) 481-0479
Stackware for universities, nurseries, and landscape architects.

Reports! ***$99.95***
Nine to Five Software
P.O. Box 915
Greenwood, IN 46142
(317) 887-2154
A complete report generator and printing utility.

Script Expert ***$79.95***
Dan Shafer
Hyperpress Publishing
Foster City, CA 94404
Readymade scripts you can use in your own stacks.

Stackpacks ***$99.95*** (each)
Educomp
742 Genevieve, Ste. D-6
Solana Beach, CA 92075
(800) 843-9497; in California (800) 654-5181
Collections of utility stacks.

The Typefaces of DT Publishing ***$24.95***
Publishing Resources
Boulder, CO
(303) 442-1100
Documents nearly all PostScript *fonts; also offered is a $29.95 book on DTP; book and stack together are $39.95.*

VideoDisk Drivers
Voyager Company
2139 Manning Ave.
Los Angeles, CA 90025
(213) 475-3524
HyperCard *interfaces for videodisk programs from the National Gallery, NASA, and others.*

VideoWorks II Clip Animation Driver for HyperCard
MacroMind
1028 West Wolfram St.
Chicago, IL 60657
(312) 871-0987
Insert animations made with VideoWorks II *into your stacks.*

Selected Public Domain and Shareware Stacks

Application Utilities

VersaCAD Help
VersaCAD
7372 Prince Dr.,
Huntington Beach, CA 92647
Online aid for VersaCAD users.

Desktop Utilities

Calculator
Ricardo Batista
1532 Hornblend #3
Pacific Beach, CA 92109

Engineering calculator.

Checkwriter
Robert J. Alexander
13856 Bora Bora Way, # 303-C
Marina del Rey, CA 90292

Well thought-out HyperCard *checkbook.*

HomeDesk
Russell A. Lyon
CompuServe (71735.632)

Alternative HyperCard *environment for those who like roll-top desks.*

HyperWrite 1.1
Andre Hinds
Fanques
Box 3271
Tulsa, OK 74101

Word processing and printing utility.

Shareware Accountant (shareware)
Francis S. Patrick
Software Development Tools
721 E. Brookside Ln.
Somerville, NJ 08876

Keep your books with HyperCard.

Spreadsheet Construction Set (shareware)
Al Kanode
Kanode Associates
4709 E. Sandra Terr.
Phoenix, AZ 85032

Make your own simple spreadsheets.

XRefText (shareware) ***$7.50***
Frank Patrick
721 E. Brookside Ln.
Somerville, NJ 08876
Index card implementation of hypertext concepts.

Databases

The AIDS Stack (shareware)
Michael Tidmus
Up-to-date AIDS/HIV infomation and statistics.

MacVendors
B. Menell
Pisces Software
616 Rancheria, Ste. #C
Chico, CA 95926
List of Mac hardware and software developers.

Timetable of Science and Innovation (demo) ***$50.00***
XIPHIAS
13464 Washington Blvd.
Marina del Rey, CA 90292
Timeline of tech and scientific innovation—part of a proposed encyclopedia on disk.

Desktop Publishing

Relational Equations in Desktop Publishing
Andrew Burns
843⅘ South Carson Ave.
Los Angeles, CA 90036
Equations for sizing type, lines, and special characters.

Education/Kids

Circuits
Robert M. Delaney
Physics Department, St. Louis University
221 N. Grand Blvd.
St. Louis, MO 63103
Experiment with electrical circuits.

FlashCards (shareware) ***$10.00***
John Sudderth
3797 Crosby Dr.
Birmingham, AL 35223
Teach your child to read with talking flashcards.

HyperX
Ron Evans
Millenium Software
1970 S. Coast Hwy.
Laguna Beach, CA 92651
Learn the basics of AI.

Inigo Gets Out
Amanda Goodenough
Charming adventures of a kitten; appropriate for any age.

Laura's Letters
Bill Atkinson
Alphabet and spelling stack with Bill saying the letters and numbers.

Neural Net Construction Stack
Larry Halff
4918 N. 33rd Rd.
Arlington, VA 22207
Design your own brain simulation.

Periodic Table
Pisces Publishing
616 Rancheria, Ste. C
Chico, CA 95926
The Periodic Table, with vital statistics on the elements.

Games

Tilt 1.1 (shareware) ***$10***
Neil Schapiro and Mike Gilbert
MCU
P.O. Box 520
Bethpage, NY 11714
Jousting simulation; good graphics.

HyperCard Utilities

Color XCMD
Bill and Steve Tuttle
Imaginetic Neovision

Add background and foreground colors to HyperCard *on a Mac II.*

DeProtect
Ned Horvath, Allan Foster

Removes a password from a protected stack and sets user level to scripting. Try it if you've forgotten your password—but it's not guaranteed to work.

File Importer (shareware) ***$10.00***
Stephen Michel
1027 Pomona
Albany, CA 94706

Reads tab-delimited files from other applications into HyperCard.

Full-Page Paint
David K. Simerly

Lets you print two cards as one 8½ × 11 inch picture.

HyperBase
Henry Lowe
58 Waverly St.
Belmont, MA 02178

Use HyperCard *like the Finder, complete with program icons.*

Hyper PostScript
Ray Sanders
GEnie: RAYSANDERS

Send your stacks in PostScript *to a laser printer.*

HyperZap 1.3
Doug Levy
macPUBLIC

Unprotects stacks and resets user level to scripting.

Import PICT
Andy Herztfeld

Imports PICT resources into HyperCard.

Menus for HyperCard
Michael Long
Nine to Five Software
P.O. Box 915
Greenwood, IN 46142
(317) 887-2154

Add pull-down menus to your stacks.

Resource Copier 1.2
James L. Paul

Move resources without ResEdit.

Script Report 1.2 (shareware) ***$10.00***
Eric Alderman
48 Shattuck Square, Ste. 13
Berkeley, CA

Essential utility for printing out all scripts in a stack.

Scrolling Fields
Irv Kanode
Kanode Associates
4709 E. Sandra Terrace
Phoenix, AZ 85032

How to link the contents of scrolling fields.

Stack Builder
Debbie Iwatate
GEnie: KIWATATE

Automatic stack creation utility.

Stack Starter
Robertson Reed Smith
586 Lagunita Dr. #48
Stanford, CA 94035

A must-have; crammed with amazing HyperCard *gadgets and goodies.*

Sound

HyperMacinTalk 1.0
Dennis C. DeMars

All about speech synthesis with HyperCard *and* MacinTalk.

Keyboard Stack
Ed Kietlinski
Micro Maniaxs
P.O. Box 1597
Rutherford, NJ 07070
Keyboard (white keys only) with a variety of digitized sounds.

Sound Stacks
Sample scripts for synching sound and visuals—not for novices.

Sound Convert 1.01
Kelly E. Major
GEnie: KMAJOR
Useful utility for converting SoundCap *and* SoundWave *audio files to snd resources.*

Sound Converter 2
Peter Fierlinger
Another utility to convert SoundCap *audio files to snd resources.*

Sound Studio Stack
Steven Drazga
450 Byberry Rd. #1
Philadelphia, PA 19116
Keep your sounds in one handy jukebox environment.

Visions

Apple 1987 Annual Report HyperCard Supplement
Apple Computer
20525 Mariani Ave.
Cupertino, CA 95014
(408) 996-1010
Free stackware supplement to Apple's annual corporate report; not strictly public domain, but a good indication of where HyperCard *may be going.*

HyperSpace
Thom Cate
GEnie: THOMCATE
Voyage through space and time.

NeuroTour #1
Jim Ludtke
Take a look inside your head.

Traffic 4K
Desktop Graphics
85 S. Washington, #306
Seattle, WA 98104

Hypercomic space opera.

What They're Saying About HyperCard
Prehistoric Stackware Ltd.
Hasslefree, TX

Unprofound ruminations on the HyperCard *phenomena.*

Stackware Suppliers

Acme Dot Company
P.O. Box 5923
Titusville, FL 32783

Advantage Computing
24285 Sunnymead Blvd. #212
Moreno Valley, CA 92388
(800) 356-4666; in California (800) 346-9105

Berkeley Macintosh User Group (BMUG)
1442-A Walnut St. #62
Berkeley, CA 94709

Sells stacks for $3.00/disk; a Hyper-Catalog is available that lists all stacks distributed.

Budgetbytes
2231 SW Wanamaker Rd., Suite 102
P.O. Box 2248, Topeka, KS 66601
(800) 356-3551

Offers collections of stacks on disk.

Educomp
742 Genevieve, Suite D-6
Solana Beach, CA 92075
(800) 843-9497; in California (800) 654-5181

Comprehensive catalogue of PD and shareware stacks.

HyperHouse
6521 Pardall Rd.
Goleta, CA 93117
(805) 968-4632
Distributes and markets stacks and shareware.

International Software Library
511-104 Encinitas Blvd.
Encinitas, CA 92024
(800) 992-1992; in California (800) 992-1993

MaxStax+
P.O. Box 2719
Oakland, CA 94602

SportsWare
940 Hoxett St.
Gilroy, CA 95020
(408) 8420190
Baseball stats and other sport-related stackware.

The Stack Exchange
Heizer Software
1941 Oak Park Rd. #30
Pleasant Hill, CA 94523
(415) 943-7667

Any large Macintosh user group will be able to supply PD and shareware stacks on disk, usually at lower prices than the commercial stack suppliers. You can also download most PD stacks from bulletin boards and information services, but this may be more costly in phone-connect time than buying a disk, especially for a large stack.

If you're a stack author who's considering distributing your stack through a stack supply house, make sure you retain the copyright on your product, and get a decent royalty with regular income statements.

Conclusion

This book hardly begins to touch the possibilities *HyperCard* offers. There are worlds of stacks to explore, and you'll learn more from using them than from reading any book. Also, there are increasing numbers of commercial products adding to *HyperCard*'s already considerable powers. Apple and Bill Atkinson are committed to improving *HyperCard* so that it will eventually occupy an important position in new operating systems for the Macintosh. And, of course, you'll find many uses for current versions of the program—from managing your business to educating your children to creating your own new worlds.

Index